MUSTANGS
and
COW HORSES

Mustangs and Cow Horses

Edited by

J. Frank Dobie,
Mody C. Boatright, Harry H. Ransom

Publications of The Texas Folklore Society Number XVI

University of North Texas Press
Denton, Texas

Copyright © 1940 by The Texas Folklore Society
Southern Methodist University Press
Fourth Printing 1982

Printed in the United States of America

Permissions:
University of North Texas Press
P. O. Box 311336
Denton, Texas 76203
(940) 565-2142 FAX (940) 565-4590

Library of Congress Cataloging in Publication Data

Dobie, James Frank, 1888–1964, ed.
Mustangs and cow horses. Edited by J. Frank Dobie, Mody
C. Boatright [and] Harry H. Ransom. [2d ed.] Dallas,
Southern Methodist University Press [1965, 1940]
Xi, 429 p. illus., map. 24 cm (Texas Folklore Society
Publication no. 16)
Bibliographical footnotes
1. Horses—Legends and stories. 2. Horses—The West. 3.
Cowboys. I. Boatright, Mody Coggin, 1896–1970 jt ed. II.
Ransom, Harry Huntt, 1908–1976 jt. Ed. III-IV

GR1 • T4 no. 16 1965 636 • 168   65-3030
ISBN 1-57441-098-9

Contents

v

Illustrations

Drawings by GUTZON BORGLUM, 339, 362; HAROLD BUGBEE, end papers, 154; GEORGE CATLIN, 87, 147; JAMES GREATOREX, 229; WILL JAMES, 158, 292, 418; TOM LEA, 199; W. R. LEIGH, 374; CHARLES M. RUSSELL, 237, 268, 313, 330, 385, 395; ROSS SANTEE, 56, 351; FRANK A. STANUSH, 45, 63, 403; E. W. THISTLE-THWAITE, 316; JOHN W. THOMASON, 416; JACK VAN RYDER, 397.

Illustrations from Bartlett's Personal Narrative (1854), 97; Parker's Trip to Texas (1835), 37; Sweet and Knox, On a Mexican Mustang (1892), 193, 304; Webber's Wild Life and Wild Hunters (1856), 176; Youatt's The Horse, (1852), 122.

Introduction

"IN TEXAS the history of the horse is equally as important as that of its owner," wrote the foreign-born author of a novel called *The Daughter of Texas,* issued in 1886. "A man is no better than his horse," a saying went, and another: "A man on foot is no man at all."

This book started out to be a brief miscellany of horse lore, with emphasis on traditional elements. It has grown to be the most extensive and informative compilation on mustangs and mustangers ever printed. In addition, it brings together a wide and selected assortment of material on the range horse in general. Yet it is not an anthology—a collection of choice literary treatments of the subject. The purpose and plan of the book have not been anthological. For example, Will James, Ross Santee, William R. Leigh, T. A. Dodge, and other authorities on the western horse are not here represented. Several American anthologies have been published in which the western horse is—to a limited extent—depicted: *Songs of Horses,* arranged by Robert Frothingham; *Hosses,* stories selected by Charles Wright Gray; *Gallant Horses,* "great horse stories of our day," compiled recently by Frances E. Clark.

The object of this book is not to represent writers but to represent horses—mustangs and ranch horses. In carrying out this object, the editors have found an abundance of fresh first-hand chronicles and have been aided by various contemporary writers who go to horses and horse people, rather than to books, for their material. Included are at least two stories, "Old Gran'pa" and "Corazón," published years ago, that future anthology makers may be expected to substitute for some of their stick-horses, and if they do not select Frank Bryan's Canebrake they will miss an opportunity.

If our book teaches anything beyond range horse ways and the ways of range men with horses, it is that a vast richness of chronicle pertaining to the Southwest lies underneath the current of publisher-advertised, critic-accredited, and populace-promoted books. The superb narrative of *Black Kettle*, for example, is taken from a poorly printed, perishable, provincially circulated pamphlet. The meaty accounts of mustanging in Southwest Texas by G. C. Robinson and J. W. Moses—accounts informed with a vitality and directness seldom realized by research scholars and professional writers—have lain buried in newspapers. The old mustanger, Frank Collinson, writes for a pulp-paper magazine beyond the realm recognized by either history or literature.

The one thing needful to good writing, to literature, is vitality, and that kind of grasp on the subject that a bulldog has when he picks up a fice in his jaws and shakes him. This vitality and grasp will be found in all sorts of chronicles that lusty livers of the Southwest have set down, generally more vigorously than coherently, and that await discoverers and translators.

Several of the illustrations have been selected for their historical interest as well as for their pertinence, illuminating past conceptions of wild and masterful horses as well as the present text. The editors thank the following artists for original drawings: Harold Bugbee, of Clarendon, Texas; Tom Lea, of El Paso; Ed Borein, of Santa Barbara, California; Will James, of Montana; and Gutzon Borglum, of Mount Rushmore, South Dakota. For the use of illustrations from their works, thanks are due Will James, W. R. Leigh, Ross Santee, Frank A. Stanush, E. W. Thistlethwaite, John W. Thomason, Griswold Tyng, and Jack Van Ryder. For assistance or for permission to reprint illustrations, the Society is indebted to the estate of Charles M. Russell; the Naylor Company, of San Antonio, publishers of *Epic-Century Magazine;* Miss Winnie Allen of the University of Texas Archives; the publishers of *Hoofs and Horns;* the Milton Bradley Company, publishers of *Patches;* Charles Scribner's Sons, publishers of Thomason's *Gone to Texas* and Will James's *Big Enough* and *Cowboys North and South;* the Huntington Press, publishers of W. R. Leigh's *The Western Pony;* John McCarty, editor of the *Amarillo Globe-News;* the Appleton-Century Company, publishers of Ross Santee's *Men and Horses;* Farrar and Rhinehart, publishers of Ross Santee's *The Pooch;* and Wallace D. Coburn, author of *Rhymes from a Round-up Camp.*

Marcelle Lively Hamer, Treasurer of the Texas Folk-Lore Society, has chosen the typographical design of the book.

A Sign in Red River County 1840

Mustang Texas

STEPHEN F. AUSTIN'S MAP OF TEXAS, 1829

Mustangs and Mustanging in Southwest Texas

By G. C. Robinson[*]

I. The Earliest Mustangs

THE very word *mustang* is of the long ago. Like the animal it denotes, the use of the word spread northward from Texas. In the time of Washington Irving and much later, the term commonly used on the plains north of the Spanish country was *wild horse*. The word *mustang* comes from the Spanish *mesteño*, which comes from *mesta*—a group of stockraisers. Horses that escaped from a range controlled by a *mesta* and ran wild were called *mesteños*, the suffix *eño* meaning "pertaining to" or "belonging to." The man who chased the *mesteños* was called a *mesteñero*, or "mustanger."

Although descended from Arabian stock, which was brought to America more than four centuries ago, the mustang had virtually become a native wild animal of Texas long before Stephen F. Austin brought the first English-speaking settlers to tame the land. Even among the roving Indians the coming of the first horses into their ranges was only a vague tradition. These Indians, especially the Comanches and Lipans, had at the opening of the last century been horsemen for generations beyond their own count.

It is remarkable that the mustangs should have multiplied

*Reprinted, with some revisions, from *The Dallas Morning News*, Sunday, September 9, 1928.

3

so fast in the wild. This was because the country was adapted to the horse. In other words, it was a natural horse country, and the horses thrived on the native grasses. The mustangs spread voluntarily to the northward, or were driven there by the Comanches. The Kiowas, Osages, Sioux, and other Indians of the western prairies had horses from a remote period in the past.

The Comanches were probably the first to use the horse, since they were exclusively horsemen and were the owners of large numbers of horses when the people from the United States first came in contact with them. They were noted horsemen long ago. As far back as the beginning of the nineteenth century travelers who came into Texas wrote of the thousands of wild horses on the prairies. In 1804 a Spanish judge came from Reynosa to inspect a land bordering on the Nueces River not far from what is now the southern boundary of Live Oak County. In his report of the inspection he said that mustangs were so numerous that the settlers could not raise horses on the range because they would go away with the wild herds. He also reported that the only improvements of any character on the land were some old mustang pens in bad condition.

The Mexicans enacted laws regulating the chasing of mustangs and wild cattle. One of these was enacted by the State of Coahuila and Texas in 1827. It held that only licensed persons could chase these wild animals; provided how branded animals captured in the chase must be disposed of, and levied a charge of two reals for each mustang captured, two pesos for each mule, and four reals for each head of horned cattle. The season for the chase was from the first day of October to the last day of February. The Legislature of Texas enacted similar laws in 1852, 1854, and 1856. These laws applied to the territory west of the San Antonio River and were repealed in 1858.

Various old mustang pens were to be found in Southern Texas when the first Americans settled here. Some of these had a name and a history. The ruins of others had been forgotten even by legend—just a few old posts outlining the pen, large trees and underbrush within, and possibly a few loose pieces of wood indicating where the wings of the pen had once been. Some ruins in the hills south of Ramirena Creek in Live Oak County were of this character. A few old Mexicans used to say that the pen had been used by one Palacios, but they could not remember when it was in use, and everything about it was hearsay. At or near watering places these old pens were frequent, but some could be found far away from any permanent water.

II. WAYS OF CATCHING MUSTANGS

The mustangs were chased and caught in many ways, but the professional *mesteñero* went out to take a whole drove, and nothing less. Usually, he constructed his pen in a clump of trees or brush. It was shaped circular so that the trapped mustangs could not rush into a corner and thereby break the fence. A ditch was dug where the fence was to be; then posts were placed upright in the ditch and the dirt was thoroughly tamped around the posts. Then the posts were well lashed together at the top with strong rawhide thongs. This made a fence that was somewhat elastic, but hard to break. Next in order were the wings, which went out from either side of the gate, forming an immense V, with the gate at the apex. The wing fences were made of brush and treetops; the longer wing was half a mile or more in length, the other about half as long. The gate was made to be closed with bars—strong poles. Usually the pen was strategically situated with reference to the surrounding hills, hollows and timber, when such could be found. The idea was to build the pens so that the mustangs would not see the wings until they were between them. Sometimes the gateposts and other evidences of man's handiwork were carefully concealed with green brush.

When everything was ready for the chase, a rider was stationed near the end of either wing. The other horsemen, well mounted, located a suitable bunch of mustangs and gave chase. The herd was circled in the direction of the longer wing and the horsemen there turned the fleeing animals down the wing toward the gate. At this juncture the rider from the short wing pointed in and kept the mustangs against the wing. All hands crowded forward as fast as they could, yelling to hasten the flight of the mustangs. As soon as the herd was in the pen a man dismounted and hastily put up a bar or two, over which he threw a blanket. A man on the shorter wing would be close to the herd and could get to the gate promptly. Should the mustangs turn and make a rush for him, no power on earth could stop them. But once the bar was up with the blanket spread over it, they would not come near.

Then came the real work—roping out the mustangs. This was done by throwing a rope from the outside, and when the horse was caught he was dragged out through the gate or through an opening in the fence made by removing some posts. Frequently the mustang fought its captors until it was thrown and tied.

Once the animals were caught, various methods were used to enable the captors to drive them away. They might be necked to gentle horses or burros. Sometimes heavy wooden clogs were fastened around the front leg just above the hoof. Some were "side-lined." This was done by tying one end of a short rope around a front leg and the other end around a hind leg. Thus handicapped, the mustangs could be driven away with gentle horses. Whatever the means used, the wild horses were badly bruised and otherwise injured before they could be handled and driven away.

However, after they had been driven for two or three days from their accustomed range, it was not so hard to manage and control them as one might think. And usually they recuperated from their injuries quickly. The *mesteñero* now sought a buyer for his captives. Two dollars and a half a head was a fair price, usually. Sometimes he could not realize that much. While money was hard to get, time was not much of an item.

Sometimes a pen was built near a watering place with one wing reaching to the water and the other leading out so that the mustangs might be chased into the pen readily when they came to drink. If the mustangs had been chased, they watered at night. Thus it was easy for the riders to conceal themselves near by, but all of them must be on the lee side of the mustangs. Like other wild animals, they had a keen scent and once they "sniffed the tainted gale," they gave a loud snort, wheeled, and were gone before reaching the position where the riders could force them into the pen. This method could be used only in a time of drought when the mustangs were compelled to go to water at certain watering places, far apart.

Another method of capturing mustangs, which could not be dignified by the term chase, was called "walking mustangs down." This was done by a lone man on horseback who started following the band of mustangs. Of course, at the start, the mustangs ran away. But the man followed on, not discouraged by the flight of the mustangs. The fear of the man caused the mustangs to repeat the flight, but the "walker" never attempted to chase them. Gradually they permitted the rider to approach closer, and finally paid no heed to him, and he stayed with them night and day. He usually had a confederate who stayed out of sight and out of scent of the mustangs. The follower could slip away at night and thus procure food and water. Necessarily, the mustangs went to water, but the rider might need it before the mustangs did, and it was difficult to carry a supply. After some days the rider could ride about the herd without disturbing them, even among them. In effect, the wild herd had permitted him to "take up" with them. He must not even change horses during this time, nor permit any other rider to come near the herd, since the mustangs, upon the approach of a stranger, would at once flee. By degrees the rider began to drift the mustangs about, and finally he could drive them slowly. His plan was to drift the mustangs toward a mustang pen. His confederate, in the meantime, kept himself advised of the locality of the herd. When the rider had maneuvered the herd into or near the wings of the pen, the confederate came into position, probably accompanied by others. The mustangs at once took fright, but it was too late. The riders rushed them into the pen somewhat in the manner described in the chase.

Many persons, even those who have taken mustangs in the chase, might doubt that a man would be allowed to take up with such wild and distrustful creatures. It was, in early days, done many times. It may be that the Americans learned the method from the Mexicans; possibly they learned it from the Indians. I have heard that a man on foot could, if he were skillful, take up with mustangs.

This acceptance of man may be accounted for by the fact that the mustang differed from the other animals of the wild in that his ancestors, for a period much more remote than history, had been close associates of man. The feeling of companionship returned, and the mustangs felt a sense of security in the presence of this lone rider. Certainly the very wildest of the wild horses can be gentled more easily, and will become much gentler than any of the true wild animals. Some have claimed that the "walker" kept the mustangs from sleeping until their senses were so dulled that they no longer experienced fear. This manner of accounting for the success of the method of capturing the mustang will hardly appeal to those who have ridden horses long distances without change or rest. Many a mustang that had been walked down later carried a rider as long as he could sit on the animal's back and then, immediately upon being freed, began to graze, apparently unconcerned about sleep and rest. It required some eight or ten days to capture the mustangs by "walking," if all went well.

Another method of catching the mustang was best practiced by but two men. Taking advantage of the wind, they waylaid the mustangs at a waterhole. If in an isolated place, the mustangs might water in the daytime; otherwise the mustangers had to choose a moonlight night. One man concealed himself near the water and the other watched near the trail a mile or more back. This watcher let the mustangs pass unmolested on their way to water; then he concealed himself as near the trail as possible. The man at the waterhole waited until the mustangs had drunk their fill. He then rushed from his covert and hotly pursued the fleeing mustangs back along the trail, urging his mount to the limit of its speed. The mustangs, full of water, would be somewhat blown when they reached the covert of the man on the trail, and the best animals would be in the lead. Having selected a desired animal, the concealed rider made a dash from his hiding place. The racing mustang must needs change its course at this sudden apparition, and thus lost speed. This gave the rider an opportunity to get within roping distance, and with good luck he took what all those who chased mustangs prized most—the pick of the herd. Should he fail in this, he still had an opportunity for a try at others which were behind. Amidst the confusion created by this rider, the man from the waterhole likely overtook the herd and roped a good colt, or possibly something better.

This method of capture required good riders, good ropers, and swift mounts. With all these requisites, some measure of success was assured. In a chase of this kind the riders usually rode their mounts bareback, tying the free end of the reata around the mount's neck. Of course, it was tied in a "horse knot" so that when the pull came the rope would not tighten and cut the horse's wind off. When the roper cast his loop over the mustang's head, there was no escape unless the rope broke, and it was less likely to break when tied to the horse's flexible neck instead of to the unyielding saddle horn.

Sometimes the mustanger gave the wild horses a hard run of say nine or ten miles and circled them into a herd of gentle horses held for the purpose. Being well winded and mixed with the gentle animals, the mustangs might be held by riders on fresh mounts and driven into a pen.

The chase of chases, the real chase, was to take after a mustang wherever he could be found and run him until the mustanger got within roping distance. Such a run was usually long and hard. In all long chases, bottom was the first requisite of the mount. Many a good one has been ruined trying to run down a mustang hardly worth the capture. Some saddle horses that could with difficulty catch a swift steer inside three or four hundred yards could hold out for long distances and be first "in at the roping." Many horses of the mustang breed possessed this bottom and yet could not be classed as swift. Early spring was the most favorable time for long distance chases, for at that time the mustangs were at their weakest and in poor condition to endure long runs.

III. QUALITIES OF THE MUSTANG

But the best mustangs, like the biggest fish, usually got away, regardless of how they were chased. Mustang lore has many stories of these. One of them, told by early white settlers, was of a white pacing stallion that ranged on the prairies between the San Antonio and Nueces Rivers. This noted animal was chased many times. Even race horses were brought here for no other purpose than to run after this one animal. But all of these chases had the same result. The stallion would rack away and leave his pursuers, never breaking his pace. And the last that they would see of him, as he disappeared in the distance, would be his long white mane flowing in the breeze and his long tail waving an *adios*. But after all his bunch had been captured, this horse was taken by guile. During a drouth some men fenced in a lake, leaving a gate open apparently leading to the water, but in reality it merely opened into a pen, designed to trap wild cattle and horses. This stallion, in an evil hour, went into this trap in the night-time when a watcher was hard by, and the watcher closed the gate. The stallion was taken east by his captors, and this is the end of the story. Some people said that this horse was no real mustang, but that he was a colt of a white mare that was lost out of the horses of some soldiers from possibly Kentucky or Tennessee, when they passed through the country on their way to join General Taylor's army during the Mexican War; that this colt was raised with the mustangs. But he had all the spirit of a mustang, regardless of his blood. There are many stories of white mustang stallions, on the average of one for each locality where mustangs were chased. The only difference in this one's story is that it ended in his capture.

Many of the mustangs were good horses, and the mustangs of the old times were superior to the horses of the same breed now to be found in Mexico and Texas. Shortly after the Civil War a fine stallion was captured in the southern part of Live Oak County. This was done by "walking" the bunch down, and the captors sold the stallion out of the pen for fifty dollars, which in that day and time, was a fabulous price for a real mustang, and would compare with ten times that amount now.

The average mustang horse was fourteen to fifteen hands in height. Rarely was one as high as sixteen hands. With few exceptions they were good saddle horses, and many of them were well gaited. As a rule they were poor work horses, and had a very strong aversion to being harnessed. Quite a number of them were natural pacers, and paced footloose. These pacers were of two kinds: the "side-at-a-time" pacers, and the "quick-step" pacers. The first moved the hind foot and front on the same side at the same time, and were not highly prized as saddle horses. But the quick-step pacers were very highly prized as saddlers. They paced, but the hind-leg and fore-leg did not move in unison. Usually they were showy horses and carried themselves well. Many of them could run well, and a good one had no superior as a saddle horse for fast traveling.

No horse ever traveled a gait that some mustang could not go. Mustang gaits were as varied as their colors, and their colors were too varied to be described except generally. Many of the shades of color can be described only by using the Mexican name. Take for instance, the *duns*, or *bayos*—bayo in Spain means "bay"; in the Mexican language it means "dun." There were many shades of these; the *bayo cabos negros*, or dun with black mane and tail; *bayo naranjado*, or orange-colored dun; *bayo azafranado*, or saffron-colored dun. There were many other shades distinguished, but space forbids details of these. The bay horse was a *colorado*. The sorrel was an *alazan*. A very red sorrel was a *rosillo*. Then there were *prietos*, or blacks; *tordillos*, or grays. The *dorado* was a golden bay; the *palomino* was dove-colored and was a beauty when in good condition and showed the iris like the dove. There were a few of the blacks that had an appearance like the iris. On these there were places where the hair lay in spots in different directions, and shining spots appeared on the animal; and when it changed position the location of the shining spots would change.

The *hueros*, or albinos, and the *pintos*, or paints, may yet be seen in almost any circus. The albino is absolutely worthless except for a show, but some of the *pintos* were fine horses.

It is a fact that generally animals of certain colors amongst these mustangs possessed certain qualities. For instance, the dun with black mane and tail was usually very hardy and easily kept in condition; likewise the blood bays and the blacks. The blacks, especially those with heavy and wavy mane and tail, were likely to be tricky and dangerous, unless carefully handled in breaking. So the description of the special characteristics might be prolonged into a treatise on these horses. But from what has been said, it may be inferred that there were once different strains of these horses, before they were mingled together; and that the different colors were once different strains bred to a more or less uniform color.

The great majority of the mustangs were very hardy, possessing good bottom and endurance. Quite a number of them made race horses, and could run a quarter. Many could run short distances, and get away in a hurry. All this belongs to the story of the cow-pony.

Probably the steeds of this breed were ridden by the Spanish conquistadores under Cortez. It is improbable that these horses deteriorated in the wild. They ranged far and wide over a country covered with an abundance of nutritious grasses. They were frequently compelled to travel long distances between grass and water, especially in times of drought.

Usually they were bred from the strongest and most powerful stallions. These gathered together good-sized bunches of mares. Defective and crippled animals could not keep up with the herd, and they fell prey to wild animals. An instinct of the mustang prompted the stallion to drive the yearling fillies from the herd each year, which in a large measure prevented inbreeding. The yearlings would be found scattered over the range, with teeth marks on them, showing how they resisted the action of the inexorable sire when he drove them away. The young stallions remained with the herd until they were old enough to gather up bunches of mares for themselves.

When the American settlers first settled in the country, the mustangs were a nuisance, since their gentle horses would frequently take up with a wild bunch. The mustang stallions gave them the most trouble. The lone stallions and those which had only a few mares would drive off gentle mares whenever opportunity offered. The ranchman resorted to

"CREASING" MUSTANGS IN TEXAS.—Sketched by A. R. Waud.

the rifle to get rid of these pests. Sighting one of these stallions on his range, he would approach it unobserved, dismount and unsaddle his horse and drive his mount ahead of him to a point where the mustang could see the horse. The stallion would run up within gun-shot and stop with his head high in the air, and the concealed rifleman would shoot him. Frequently the magnificent appearance of the mustang made him hesitate, but an inspection of the dead animal would generally reveal an old stallion, bearing the scars of many battles. This one had once been the leader of a large herd, but had met one mightier than he, and after a fierce battle had been driven away from his cherished bunch. Yet when his wounds had healed, he had started out with a proud step and a high head to gather up a new drove on a new range.

Sometimes the stallion was "creased" and captured. This was done by shooting him through the upper part of the vertebrae of the neck. The stallion fell and remained helpless for a few moments while the rifleman secured him with a rope. Creasing required a steady hand and a true aim, and was generally attended with success. Nevertheless, it was a barbarous practice, and this method of capture was not often practiced. But a great number of stallions were shot, and even mustang mares. These mares sometimes took up with gentle horses and when the ranchman attempted to drive his horses to the pen the wild ones would run away, and usually some of the gentle ones would follow. Thus the wild ones would spoil the gentle ones.

Frequently there were wild mules with the mustangs. On the open range horses were bred and branded in vast numbers. The stock horses were kept in *manadas*, consisting of a number of mares, a stallion, *potros*, and fillies, and these were about the same in organization as a band of mustangs. Frequently they were almost as wild as the mustangs, and hard to pen.

The branded horses and the captured horses were driven away in large droves and sold. These were somewhat similar to the trail herds of cattle, though, as a rule, the herds were not so large as the herds of cattle. These droves of horses were called *caballadas,* corrupted into "cavayard" by Americans.

Herds of horses are much more easily driven than cattle, and travel faster. Yet large droves of horses are hard to handle. A stampede of a large drove of wild horses is a frightful thing. The cattle stampede is a tame affair in comparison. For instance, a small drove, not more than 120 head, were being driven through San Antonio in the latter '80s. Becoming frightened, they ran into a blind alley at the end of which was a house. The door being open, the horses charged through the house, four or five of them being killed. Of course, many others were injured. The extent of the wreckage of the house may be left to the imagination.

IV. DID THE MUSTANG ORIGINATE PITCHING?

It may be that the mustang was the original pitching horse. When one speaks of a mustang, it implies a bad horse now. History does not help us to trace the pitching horse. Xenophon wrote a lengthy treatise on the horse several centuries before the Christian era. Although he is well known as the general who led the retreat of the 10,000 Greeks, of which he gives an account in his *Anabasis,* few persons have read his treatise on the horse. He goes into the details of rearing, gentling, riding and judging of horses. Evidently he was an authority on horses in his day, and much of what he writes is instructive. He wrote at a time when the horse was ridden bare-backed, and was used principally as a war horse, either ridden or driven hitched to a chariot. Since this writer goes into such detail in describing the qualities of the horse, both good and bad, one may assume that if pitching horses were known at that time, he would have at least mentioned them. Very likely he would have told how to stay on one during the performance. Yet he mentions nothing of a pitching horse.

And we have the later story of how Alexander first rode his great war horse, Bucephalus, after all the other *jinetes* had failed. And a careful reading of this story disproves the idea that Bucephalus pitched off these would-be riders.

Now the panther was the mustang's worst enemy; and while it preferred a nice fat colt, yet it did not hesitate to attack a grown animal. Concealed in the branches of a tree over a mustang trail, it would spring upon the horse's back. Then if it could cling on long enough, it could disembowel the horse by clawing it with the hind claws in the region of the flank. But sometimes the mustang would pitch the panther off before receiving the death wound. Nevertheless, the mustang bore the marks of the panther ever afterward. Occasionally a captured mustang had panther marks to show that once it had thrown a panther. A real good *jinete* might be excused if he hesitated to mount one of these panther-marked mustangs.

Now, if it could be shown, as some assert, that the mustang invented pitching, some evolutionist might explain that the mustang pitches because the ones which threw the panthers survived and transmitted this quality to their progeny. Hence, the inherent repugnance of the mustang to having anything whatsoever perched upon its back, for the mustang does have a strong disposition to shed whatever gets on its back. Possibly someone well versed in horse lore may cite us authority to show that the mustang is not guilty of having invented pitching. A big wild calf can and will do the same thing; it is sure to do it the first time any venturesome boy tries to be a buster and ride it. And heavy odds can safely be posted on the calf as the winner. In fact, all ruminants have the instinct to pitch off any animal or man. The mule, and even the lowly burro, will do this with surprising efficiency.

V. The Last of the Wild Manadas

As the country was settled, the mustangs took to the brush, like the deer and the coyote, and like these they stayed longer in the midst of civilization than many of the other animals of the wild. As an instance of this there remained in Live Oak County a number of droves of mustangs as late as 1880. And in one locality there was a large bunch as late as 1902, notwithstanding the fact that these had ranged in a fenced pasture since 1881. There is recorded evidence as to these, which was preserved by an appeal from a conviction for horse theft. This may be read in almost any lawyer's office in the case of Mapes vs. State (14 Court of Appeals, page 129). The Fant pasture there mentioned was enclosed in 1881 and had an area of about 130,000 acres, partly in McMullen County. When it was first fenced, there were a number of persons who owned land within the enclosure. These afterward sold to Fant or to G. W. West, who purchased Fant's lands in 1882. But the mustangs stayed on just the same, protected by the brushy portions. A number of parties chased them, and occasionally a few were captured. And probably some branded animals joined the wild ones.

Neville Dobie, one of the witnesses in the Mapes case, gave

them one or more chases. This was some years after the events described in the Mapes case. And about 1902 Dr. Simmons, who had acquired about 50,000 acres of the old Fant pasture, found that he had quite a bunch of mustangs on hand. He first had a Negro, Atlee Weston, to attempt to capture them. Atlee was drowned in the Nueces River. The doctor then made a written contract with Jim Pugh, the effect of which was that Pugh could have the mustangs if he would get them out of the pasture, and Pugh agreed to try to take them. Pugh knew a few tricks that helped a lot. Taking some white twine he built some "wire" fences out of this, tying it to trees and bushes in the brushy part and putting up small poles or sticks for posts in the open places. He built some wings for the pens, and fenced off some watering places with his twine. These mustangs had had experience with barbed wire, and would not run against a wire fence, nor any imitation of it. To make a long story short, Pugh, with the assistance of a number of men, captured the greater portion of the mustangs, and scattered the remainder. The few that were not caught were probably snared or shot, afterward.

Anyway, in Southwest Texas there are no mustangs now. There is nothing but the story of what "has been." Even these last of their race, like their ancestors, had escaped from many a chase. But they had degenerated and were hardly worth the taking.

The mustang chases, too, are of the past. And these were the peer of any chase that was ever run. The horn and hound could never keep the pace set by the mustang. It was tame sport compared with the chase of *mesteñero* led by the mustang. But we have no song of the mustang chase; no song about the fleeing herd; no song of the noble steed that fell in the chase, pushed beyond endurance by the rider; nothing of the exalting thrill of the rider when he took the pick of the band. It deserves both song and story, for it was indeed a noble sport.

A Mustanger of 1850

By J. W. Moses*

I

IT WILL be just thirty-eight years ago next month if the writer lives to see that time (for, in common with many old Texans, he is suffering greatly now from the effects of early exposure) that he started from Paso Santa Margarita crossing of the Nueces River, just opposite to San Patricio, with a party of some fourteen or fifteen mustangers, of which he was the *comandante,* or captain, with the intention of making some big runs, and not returning to the settlement until at least 100 head of the wild horses and mares of the prairie had been made captives.

A safe return, so we anticipated, would likely mean a satisfactory settlement of outstanding accounts as well as a pleasant reunion of friends—for these trips were always attended with more or less danger. Apart from casualties of the chase, the falls and probabilities of getting hurt, sometimes crippled, and the danger of sunstroke and exposure to all kinds of weather, there were the roving bands of Comanches and other Indians, who not only had an inordinate love for horse flesh but a decided penchant for scalps, which they never failed to take when they could do so without running much

*Four articles reprinted from the *San Antonio Express* of April 1, April 8, April 15, and July 29 (Sundays), 1888. All these articles, as well as many others by the author during the year 1888, are dated from San Diego, Texas, and are signed "Sesom"—the pen name taken by Judge J. W. Moses, his own name spelled backward.—J. F. D.

risk of their own lives. The captain of a party of mustangers had to get out a permit, or license, for which he had to pay a tax; a small one, very true, but he got in return absolutely nothing in the way of protection or anything else, and if despoiled of his property, or if he or any of his party were murdered by the savages, that was the end of the matter.

We had hardly gone a league upon our journey when the sky, which had been serene, clouded over, and in an incredibly short time a heavy spring storm was upon us. The bottom dropped out, and the water just poured down on us until about 4:00 or 5:00 o'clock in the afternoon, when the sun came out. As it looked like it would be a tempestuous night, I gave order for all to halt at a point called La Puerta de la Agua Dulce, that we might dry our wet clothing, blankets, etc., and prepare for another heavy downfall of water. Very little water was coming down the Agua Dulce, indicating that the rainfall above—at least, immediately above—had been light. We stopped in one of the clumps of wide-spreading oaks, covered with clusters of Spanish moss, which we counted on to help protect us against the pelting rain.

James Miller, a son of Samuel Miller, who kept the ferry at Paso Santa Margarita, and who was one of my men, proposed that we should bunk together and, by making a sort of *toro,* as the Mexicans call it, try to keep dry. We picked out the best rising ground we could find under a bushy-topped oak—without regard to the danger from lightning—and, gathering a large quantity of moss, made our couch from two and one-half to three feet high. Then, to keep the provisions dry, we piled our sugar, coffee, and flour bags upon the highest side, where we intended to place our heads. Our Mexican *frezadas,* or blankets, were good and impervious to the rain, and we expected to have a tolerably comfortable night, let it rain as it would. We had hardly gone to bed before the rain began to come down steadily and heavily.

I had fallen into a sound sleep, when about midnight I heard a great rumpus occasioned by Sam May, the only other American of my party, who had fallen from a perch which he had constructed in the fork of an oak tree, and in his sleep had rolled off, not on ground, but in about three feet of water. The effort that I made to get up and see what was the matter caused the yielding moss to sink, and Jim Miller and myself found ourselves floundering in water also. The rain must have been very heavy up the creek, for the Agua Dulce was on a rampage, and rising rapidly. We had to stir our stumps to get out to the high ground. It was as black as Hades, and the horses that had not pulled up their picket pins were almost in swimming water and had to be gotten out without delay. We could hardly see our hands before us, except when the lightning flash guided us, and there were several very narrow escapes from being swept away by the fast increasing flood.

It was nearly morning when we had gathered all that we could on a knoll near our night camp, and the dawn broke upon as demolished and forlorn a set of mustangers as the world ever saw. Our only serious loss was in the provisions; they were utterly destroyed, wrecked beyond redemption— sugar, flour, coffee, salt, and everything soaked.

The sun rose bright and clear and gave us a chance to dry our things, but with the exception of the coffee and a little rice, there was not much that could be saved. The Agua Dulce, too, was impassable, a roaring river, and in some places more than a league wide; it looked as though a second edition of the deluge had come down in a single night; there was a perfect waste of waters all around us.

There was nothing left to be done but to return to Paso Santa Margarita and get up another outfit. This I did right away, and after a day or two we went to higher and drier ground to run. We found the mustangs in large droves on the rolling prairies and near the foothills and prepared to make a run to a pen at the foot of a long declivity, which ever afterwards went by the name of El Hediondo, for in our eagerness to make a large haul to recompense us for lost time and extra expenses, we overdid the thing entirely. We made such a large drove that when we got them fairly going for the pen the rush that they made was uncontrollable, and the *cortador,* or man whose duty it was to cut off the *caballada* when the pen was full, was unable to do so. The pen was on a downward slope and the mustangs poured into it with such a rush that the *cortador* was in great danger of being run over and trampled to death by the wild and headlong charge. He did manage to save himself, with a few slight bruises, but the rush into the pen was so furious that it was filled to repletion.

The animals in their wild stampede actually ran over one another so that the bottom of the corral, or pen, was covered with crippled and dying animals, while over those the stream still rushed, the horses crushing and bruising themselves against the pickets until the pen could stand the pressure no more, but gave way, and then thundering over their dying and dead companions, the maddened survivors vanished in a cloud of dust. The mustangers, seeing the evident destruction of the corral and the loss of the *caballada,* prepared themselves and roped as many as they could, but upon the whole the adventure proved a failure of the worst kind. The stench which arose from the dead carcasses of a hundred or more mares, horses and colts rendered the atmosphere in the vicinity of the pen unendurable, obliging us to move away, and it was a very long time before "the steam of sweet mortality" ceased to hover around the ruins of the pens correctly called Hediondo, or "Stinking."

About a week afterwards we managed to make a very successful penning at La Amargosa, and saved something over a hundred head of good mares from that run. After we had taken them out of the pen and had them under control so that we could drive them slowly from one place to another, we moved our camp back to the Agua Dulce, on account of the range being better there and water more abundant.

Two or three days later, returning from a chase, we were joined by Captain John J. Dix (of late years surveyor in Duval, Nueces and adjacent counties). He was leading a very fine mustang that he had recently lassoed. The horse did not lead well, and the one that the captain was riding was a little fiery; the mustang was tied fast to the horn of the saddle, and, just as we were going into camp on a narrow trail, lined on either side by prickly pears, the mustang set back with all his strength while the steed the captain was riding surged ahead. The saddle girth broke, and off went Captain Dix, saddle and all, backward into a dense clump of prickly pear. The mustang, scaring worse at the fall, dragged him through the cactus leaves and thorns. Two or three men caught the rope and released Captain Dix. There were, more or less, a thousand prickly pear thorns in his back from his neck to his heels. For the remander of the afternoon, there was full occupation for every pair of pincers in the crowd and for all who could get near enough to use them. The captain, though, said he would feel a great deal better when they got done hunting.

II

A short time after the great fair, gotten up by Colonel H. L. Kinney[1] and other old-timers in Corpus Christi, I went out with a small party of mustangers to chase, lasso or pen wild horses on the prairies between the Nueces and the Rio Grande, wherever we could find them. My party being small, about ten or twelve men, poorly armed, and there being many signs of Indians around, I thought it prudent to join in with another party of mustangers under Don Clemente Zapata, a son of old General Zapata, one of the best Indian fighters and one of the most intrepid men Mexico ever boasted of. Clemente, even though then a young man, inherited the valor of his ancestor, though he lacked his experience; yet he had seen some Indian warfare, and was cool and collected in time of danger.

The Comanches were in our vicinity and had attacked one or two ranches; so we took all the precautions that we could. Our two companies united consisted of twenty-five men, of whom say half were tolerably well armed; the others were miserably equipped, either for attack or defense. We were, however, on the alert, and thought ourselves tolerably safe; yet we were destined to be taken by surprise by the wily savages when we least expected it. We had found the mustangs in large numbers near the pens called Los Patricios, and located our camp—or *real*, as it is called—at a water hole in a very thick clump of timber, a most fortunate move, as it turned out.

The next morning we prepared to make our drive to the pen. We had posted our men—that is, placed them at their stands, and sent the *aventadores*, or starters of the *caballada*,

---

[1]Kinney's Ranch was the foundation for the town—now city—of Corpus Christi.

to circle the mares and head them towards the corral. They found a large drove already in motion, galloping in the very direction they wanted to drive them. The dust they made kept our men from seeing that quite a large force of Comanches, forty or fifty, were running just behind the mustangs. By the time they discovered the Indians, if not before, they were themselves seen. In no time two vaqueros— for these advance riders were Mexicans—had been run down and killed. One vaquero (being well mounted and very quick, luckily for us) escaped and came back on a full run giving the alarm, crying "Los Indios! Los Indios!" at the top of his voice.

Now as the men were stationed out in a V, or triangular form, the runner could only give the warning to one line of pickets, but Don Clemente, who was at the farthest post on the other line, had dismounted from his horse, Sangrelinda, and climbed a mesquite tree to observe how the *caballada* was coming. Thus he was able to discover the Indians in time to save himself and the most of the men on his line. They all came running into the *real*, or camp, pell-mell, with the savages close behind. Three more of the mustangers were unlucky enough to be cut off, however; two of whom were shot and lanced to death, and the third was badly wounded.

We had lost four men killed at the very outset. The rest of us got to our camp and made preparations to fight desperately, knowing that it was for life. The Indians charged almost up to our *real*, and captured all of our loose horses, but by showing a determined front and firing a few well directed shots, we made them keep at a respectful distance. They continued, however, to charge up as close as they dared, shooting their arrows in perfect showers into our camp, wounding two of our men, and killing one and wounding three of our horses. We were obliged to reserve our fire as much as possible, only discharging three or four rifles and as many pistols when they came too close; for, though greatly protected by the timber that we had around us, we had no ammunition to spare, and did not know how long the savages might continue to attack or whether there might be another party of them still behind. The Indians after charging would range out in front, and use vile epithets and gestures, daring us to go out and fight them. If we had been rangers, or even if we had all been well armed, we would probably have taken the dare, but for some twenty men, not more than half-armed, it would have been sheer madness.

One or two amusing circumstances occurred at which I could but laugh. I had an iron-grey mustang, caught the day before, which to gentle I had tied to a small tree, eighty or ninety yards from our camp, and to keep him from running round the tree had hung a red blanket on another branch close by. As the Comanches made one of their swoops down towards us, I noticed one of them, mounted on a large sorrel horse, dash to where my mustang was tied. I rested my rifle against a hackberry and thought: "Now, when you stop to get the rope that horse is tied with, I'll try titles with you, my buck." It was not, however, the horse, but the red blanket that he wanted. As he grasped the blanket, he partly straightened himself on his horse. At that moment I fired. I shouted, "I've hit you" (*Ya te di*), in Spanish. The Indian whirled half round, and, shaking his lance, cried, "*Es mentira*" (It's a lie). I believe I did hit him, for I did not see him amongst those who charged any more. After trying to dislodge us nearly all day, just before sundown the Comanches rode off, leaving us a pretty badly demoralized party of mustangers, four of our men killed and three pretty badly wounded, with scarcely half enough horses left to mount. I am confident that we wounded some of them, and I think we killed some of their horses.

The next day we hunted up and buried our dead, and found the man they had seriously wounded in the race concealed in a thicket and nearly in the last agonies; but he got well finally. Some of our men had experienced quite enough and returned home, but we managed to keep the best armed with us, and the next day joined Don Cecilio Balerio, who had about twenty men with him. Our numbers being thus increased to some thirty odd, and nearly all of us being well armed, we decided to have a good run after the wild horses before we returned to the settlements.

A few days after joining Don Cecilio, we moved up to near Lara, above the Preseñas, where I met with an adventure with a Mexican lion, or panther. I had gone out from the camp early in the morning to look after my horses. Passing a small bunch of chaparral, I suddenly came face to face with *"el señor león."* We were both taken by surprise. I pulled out my pistol in a hurry, but as the panther did not advance, I thought it would be best to reserve my fire, for I knew if I only slightly wounded him he would spring upon me in a second, and I was too far away from the *real* to expect any one to hear me if I called; so, holding my pistol on the cock, I retreated backward until the bushes and the uneven ground concealed me from his sight; then I made for the camp on the double quick. Two of the young men, Andrés Ximenes and José María Villareal, had just saddled up their horses to take a look around when I told them of *el león.* They said they would go and try to rope him.

I told them that I thought it would be very dangerous, as he was a large animal, but as they were bent on trying it,

Don Cecelio and I and one or two others saddled as fast as we could, and, taking our carbines, followed them. When we came up with them, they had found the panther, and as he was making for the timber of the Preseñas, José María roped him. The panther sprang at the horse, and came very near catching him before Andrés Ximenes could make his mustang get up close enough to throw his lasso on also, for horses have a natural dread of these animals and the scent will often run them nearly wild with fear. That was the great danger in this instance, for the horse that José María was on was almost unmanageable through fright, and would plunge and run to the length of the rope to the great risk of throwing both himself and his rider.

At last Andrés got a chance to throw his lasso, and caught the panther round the neck and one front leg, so they then had him stretched out between them, and commenced dragging him towards camp; but the panther fought savagely, pulling back and snapping and clawing at the ropes. He came very near pulling down one of the horses two or three times, but at last they got the lassos round a tree and pulled the panther up to it, and we dispatched him with balls. It was a very exciting sport, but dangerous, and one that even Andrés or José María did not want to try again. They said that lassoing a wild bull was child's play in comparison to lassoing *un león. Caramba!*

When running mustangs we would often get out of provisions, and would have to pick out some of our best men to rope wild cattle or *javalis* (as the Mexican wild hogs are called). These latter were very abundant in the country at that time, and are, in fact, plentiful yet. Though hard to lasso until one gets the knack of it, they are easy enough to rope when the manner of doing so is learned; and though it is true of *javalis* that when one is wounded and squeals, the drove will stay around and fight fiercely, yet we have never regarded them as a very dangerous animal. I have seen Mexicans often ride into a herd of them and kill two or three with their machetes and even with the butt of a loaded quirt. In fact, I have done as much myself. The meat of the javelinas, though not to say very excellent, is not unsavory, and that of a young sow, seasoned with the sauce of hunger, goes mighty well.

III

I think it was about the year 1854 or 1855 that I had captured a very fine sorrel stallion, a fast pacer with a very long, beautiful mane, which reached nearly to his knees when his neck was arched and his head erect, and which gave him a magnificent appearance. I had him in camp breaking him to the saddle with great care, having designed him as a present to a special friend, when Dr. Lucket, afterward a colonel in the Confederacy, came by on a trip to the Rio Grande and expressed so strong a desire to possess the proud steed that I could not resist him, especially as his solicitations were backed by a very liberal bid in *dinero*. I had heard, too, of a bright dun horse with a perfectly white mane and tail as long or longer than the sorrel's, and I resolved to lasso him if possible.

Accompanied by Romaldo Longoria, who had a very fast horse, and who was almost a sure shot with the reata, and taking with us another man to care for the extra horses and keep camp, we started down the country towards the coast, keeping near the Grullas, where we had been told that the *bays naranjado*—orange colored dun, with white mane and tail—was seen frequently. Romaldo was more interested in a piebald or paint mule, a remarkably fine animal, which had been lost by one of the Chapas from a ranch and for the capture of which a good round reward was offered. It had been seen in the same herd. After cruising about for a couple of days and roping a couple of half-broken and branded horses from out of a herd we found near Palo Alto, we were fortunate in spying the *manada* in which the dun stallion ran, and also the *mula pinta*. The horse was indeed a magnificent looking animal, of a rich orange color, with a snow-white mane reaching below his knees, and so heavy that it bent his neck over to one side while grazing. He stood about fourteen hands high, broad breast closely coupled, small head with a white stripe down the face, limbs clean and muscular, and a tail that actually dragged on the ground.

I was considerably excited, but took Don Romaldo's advice and we kept from disturbing the *manada,* which was grazing toward the water, so as to let them drink—for it is a well-known fact that horses cannot run near as fast just after they have filled themselves with water. In the meantime we fixed our camp, or *real,* and taking our fastest horses only and divesting ourselves of all extra weight, slipped up as close as we could to the mustangs, taking advantage of the wind. As soon as they came out from the waterhole we started for them, Don Romaldo trying to cut out the paint mule, and I after the dun stallion. Gavilan (Hawk) I named him—for he did seem to fly, but I knew my old Selim was good bottom, and that I would overhaul the wild stallion in a league or so. Fortunately for me, however, he bore up the country through some scrubby brush, toward what is called Monte Redondo. I pressed him as hard as I could, but he got the advantage in the brush and when we got through it the soil was light and full of gopher holes and I was compelled to hold a pretty tight rein to keep my horse from falling.

Finally I ranged up alongside of the *gavilan*, and was tearing forward to throw the reata, when old Selim plunged into a gopher hole with both fore feet, and for a considerable time I remained unconscious where I fell. When I recovered my senses, the sun was going down. It was early in the afternoon when I commenced the chase, and I must have been lying there for more than a couple of hours. I was perfectly dazed for a while, and when I attempted to get up I found that I could not stand on my right leg. My horse had fallen on it or struck it. The knee was fearfully swollen. I had hold of the rope, and had, in fact, fallen with it under me, so old Selim was there. It was with great difficulty that I could get into my saddle, and I was so confused and addled from the fall that I did not know where camp was. I concluded to give my horse his head and trust to his instinct to take me where his companions were staked. After going for a very long time in what appeared to me to be the wrong course, we came to the place where we had started the mustangs.

I recognized the watering place, and being nearly distracted with pain from my swollen knee and from thirst, I crawled off my horse and drank of the muddy water and bathed my knee in it for some time. I then managed to drag myself on again and found my way into camp. Don Romaldo and the *mozo* had been alarmed, and were about to start out to hunt for me, though they had no expectations of finding me before morning. Don Romaldo had been lucky and had roped the mule; I had to nurse my leg for some days, and though I did secure Gavilan a short time after, it was by purchasing him from a mustanger who had caught him. I had the pleasure of gentling and riding him, but, though a beautiful animal, he was never a fast horse under the saddle.

Mustangs in those days were so plentiful that the price for one very seldom ran up above $5.00; yet for extra fine or fast ones, after having been broken to harness or to ride, a much higher price was often paid. I owned a dark bay called El Dormido, from his quiet, sleepy look, when not excited; when once started in the chase, there were very few horses that could keep up with him, and not one that could outlast him. Fifty dollars was more than once refused by me for Dormido, and he went into his last long sleep in my possession.

The wild herds were then so plentiful that no one would have believed that they could ever have been caught out, killed out or in any way so completely done away with and destroyed as they have been. In Texas, of the hundreds of thousands of wild mustangs, only the "tale" remains. There are a great many old Texans yet living who can well remember the time when the prairies fairly trembled with their tread, and when in driving gentle *caballadas* through their range the greatest precautions had to be taken to keep the wild steeds from stampeding them. They could often be seen within a few miles of the small towns.

There used to be a story told of Colonel Kinney (I do not vouch for the truth of it) that one day, boasting over his wine to some northern visitors of his vast amount of land and countless herds of livestock, he took them for an afternoon ride towards his Oso ranch, and coming by where a large drove of mustangs were grazing, he pointed them out as a small portion of his horse property, remarking that they were rather wild and scary but that when he wanted any of them all that he had to do was to send a *caporal* with a few *vaqueros* and have them penned. This drove, he said, was only one of many droves running upon his domain. That part of it was true enough, for the colonel claimed nearly all of the territory between Corpus Christi and the Rio Grande, or at least as far as Sal Colorado, or Little Colorado as it is sometimes called—a stream which has to be crossed going from Corpus Christi to Brownsville.

Not long after the mustang chase which ended so disastrously with me, I had another experience which came very near putting an end to my running after sylvan animals. We had gone up on to Lagarto Creek, near where the village of that name now is located, in Live Oak County, to lasso wild cattle. The country there is thickety and somewhat hilly, and while pursuing a young bull, a very fat animal, which was about to get away from me in the thick brush, I had no other chance to catch him but to rope him as he was passing through a small clearing, one side of which was lined with very thick *granjeno* bushes and the other two sides with mesquite and prickly pear. I threw the lasso over his head just as he was entering this small clearing. My horse being very hard-mouthed, I could not hold up until he had run past the bull, when I found myself in a natural pen and the bull in the gap.

I did not have very much time to reflect on the situation, for the *toro* came charging, giving me barely time to throw myself on the opposite side of my horse, when he struck the animal. Fortunately, one horn went into the saddle where the fork of the foretree holds the side-boards, and the other near where the cantle comes on. The jar threw me up into a bunch of *uñagatos* (catclaws), a very badly scratched and worse scared man. By good luck for both myself and horse, the bull, as he backed off, got loose from the lasso, and, shaking his head defiantly, plunged into the thicket without renewing the attack. I was very glad to have him part company without more ado, but when I came to find that neither I nor my horse had been much damaged I began to feel a great deal of anger at *el toro*, and determined not to let him get off so easily. I fixed up my saddle as quickly and as well as I could and took his trail. When I came up with him, he seemed nothing loath to renew the fight; so I coquetted with him until I got him into a little more open country. Then drawing my machete, I rode rapidly by him and in three or four charges hamstrung him in both hind legs. After that I dispatched him at leisure, and got one of my men and packhorse to take the meat and hide to camp.

Thus it may be seen that chasing the wild horses and cattle was not always as funny as it might seem; that it really was attended frequently with considerable toil and danger.

"Frontispiece," Parker's *Trip to Texas*, 1835

IV

Sometimes as many as 10,000 mustangs joined in one grand stampede. These immense herds, however, were never found quietly grazing together. Not more than one two-hundredth of that number was ordinarily taken care of by one vigorous stallion. Many droves were forced to join in a run by pursuers —wolves, panthers or men. Each drove was controlled by its leader, and after a run was over it was an interesting and amusing sight to see them gather their different bunches of mares, young horses and colts, separating and cutting them out of the general herd, each stallion selecting his own with jealous care.

Often, however, one leader would endeavor to appropriate some good looking filly, or fillies, not his own, and then there would be a battle royal between him and the legitimate patriarch, who would contest the claim bravely and stubbornly, the younger stallions occasionally, though not very often, taking part in the fight. Two veterans have been known to contend fiercely with tooth and hoof until one or the other was killed; and even after the *manadas* (or bunches) of each had been separated from one another, the leaders would neigh defiantly and often run out a hundred yards or more to renew the contest. When all was finally settled, each commander would marshal his forces and maneuver them like trained calvary, driving them from a half-mile to a mile apart, carefully rounding up and guarding his drove as long as the other was in sight. Then, but not before, the leader would relax and begin grazing himself.

The mustangs of America generally, and of this country particularly, are hardy, active animals, capable of great endurance and easily domesticated when properly handled.

I have often heard surprise or wonder expressed at the fact that the wild horses caught upon the *llanos,* or prairies, were generally better animals than the Mexican stock from which they sprang. The Mexicans paid little or no attention to improving their stock; they made their best and likeliest colts into geldings for saddle or harness, and left their most inferior stallions. In their free and wild condition the most vigorous and courageous horses were the sires. Besides, they had the wide and extensive prairies covered with luxurious grass upon which to feed, and were not restrained to the scanty range on which their tame brethren were herded or allowed to run, nor were they caught up and stunted in their growth by being forced to labor in harness or under a rider before having matured.

A *corral de aventura,* or pen to catch mustangs, was built of mesquite posts, when they could be procured, or any timber that could be easily found in the vicinity. It was nearly spiral shaped, so that when the animals were run in at the gap and, following around the fence, came to the entrance again, they were by the inward curve of the pickets directed to about the middle of the pen, and so, in place of trying to rush out of the gap or entrance, continued to mill. The area of the corral was from fifty to sixty or more feet in diameter. The posts of which the fence was composed (stout pickets set firmly in the ground and from five to five and one-half feet high) inclined a little inward, and were as strong as could be procured, so as to resist the heavy pressure often cast against them. The fence was braced from the outside, and about two-thirds of the distance up from the ground stout poles were lashed by rawhide horizontally to the pickets to further strengthen them.

About one-third of the way from the gap where the horses

were to be run in another gap was made to take them out. This latter was well secured with stout bars. Then the wings were added to the pen. These were made somewhat in the shape of an acute angle, or rather a V, one straight line of fence starting from the right side of the entrance and the other from the left, widening as it increased in distance from the pen until it was seven or eight hundred yards long and nearly as wide. These wings were built of brushwood and were not very strong or high, the object being simply to guide the horses when running for the gap of the corral.

About thirty or forty yards from the entrance to the corral, under a blind made of green bushes (either growing naturally or constructed for the purpose), was posted one of the mustangers, called the *encerrador* (one who shuts the gate). After enough mustangs to fill the corral had passed him, he entered a gap prepared for the purpose near his stand, and ran into the entrance or gap of the pen to keep the mustangs that had been driven in from running out again. He carried with him a white blanket, sheet, or some white garment, which he would wave before the frightened animals. A little further off on the opposite wing would be stationed another man, who was called the *cortador* (cutter). His business was to assist the *encerrador* by also running into the wing and cutting off the mustangs when too many of them were crowding into the gap, and help to close the entrance and secure the pen. From two hundred to two hundred and fifty or three hundred yards from these were stationed other men along each wing, the ones farthest out being called the *recibidores* (or receivers). These closed in on the *caballada* as they were run up by the advance riders.

These last were the men who went round the mustangs where they found them grazing. They drove them as easily as possible in the direction of the receivers, who were at each end of the wings, and who in turn would take them along the wings, until the gradual narrowing in would bring the herd close together, when if there was no bad management or contretemps to make them turn, break through the wings and pass the men on post, they would be rushed into the pen, and a catch, great or small, would be secured. Right there and then the fun would be over, and the laborious and dangerous work of taking the stock, mares and horses, out at the side gap would begin.

There would be no rest or let-up in this fatiguing business, for man or horse, until the mustangs were roped one by one, dragged out and side-lined by tying one fore leg to the hind leg on the same side, allowing about twelve inches space to step. This side-lining was done with rawhide well soaked, the straps being cut about two inches wide and the hair side being next to the pastern of the animal.

When all the mustangs caught in a run were so disposed of, they then had to be surrounded by the mustangers and very carefully taught to step hobbled, and were driven to water and grazed, until by degrees the straps could be taken off, one or two at a time, and they had become gentle enough to drive foot-loose. Then they were ready for market, the maximum price being about five dollars a head.

The *corrales de espiar* (or watch pens), so-called because they were built close to the upper, or sometimes lower, end of a water hole, with the obect of catching mustangs when they went into the watering places at night, were just about the same as those I have described, only they were generally smaller, and the wings were not so long as at these corrals. The mustangers usually lay in wait, and when a small drove came to drink, they would let them get inside the wings and then scare them up into the pen at only a short distance. A man would be well hidden near the gap to secure it when they had been run in. The droves caught in this way were generally much smaller than those caught in the regular corrals, and yet a great many were caught in this way, particularly during long spells of dry weather, when the animals had to go to certain waterholes to drink; but when water was abundant, they were not much used.

No kind of corral, or pen, was considered finished until it had been dedicated to some saint and a cross put up at the entrance. I used to tell the Mexicans that if they would pay as much attention to making good, strong wings and lengthy ones as they did to carving out a cross, they would make more successful runs than they did. Another feature of mustang penning was the *lazo de las animas,* or the lasso for the departed spirits. This consisted in appropriating out of every catch of less than one hundred what was called a "mediolazo," or one animal, which was sold, the money accruing therefrom being given to the priest for mass for the repose of the souls of deceased mustangers. If one hundred or more were caught in the run, a whole *lazo,* consisting of two animals, were disposed of in the same way. It was the duty of the captain of the mustang party to see that this was not neglected; yet sometimes I think the padre's perquisites were forgotten, but when "Lo, the poor Indian," was in the country, or danger from him anticipated, the money for *las animas* was religiously paid over.

I remember a surprise which was given to a small party of Comanches by a half dozen mustangers which I will venture to say the Indians themselves never forgot. Just twenty-five years ago this very month, it being a very hot and dry time, the small party I allude to had built one of the

corrales de espiar, or night pens, and were camped close to it
a little higher up on the Amargosa Creek, well hidden, waiting anxiously for a small bunch of mustangs to come to
drink, when José María Roblero, who was on watch near the
pen, came slipping up and said: "There are nine or ten Indians
coming down to the water, and they have scared off the
mustangs." The party, being well armed, determined to give
the poor Lo's a lesson, and, creeping down very carefully to
the other side of the watering place, which was very shallow
and thick with undergrowth, waited until the Indians rode
down to water. When old Tio Fuentes discharged his old
blunderbuss almost in the face of the Indian on the extreme
right, the shot killed him instantly and was followed by yells
and a charge from the rest of the party. The Indians were
struck with panic and rushed up the ravine right into the
pen, hotly pursued by the mustangers, shooting and yelling
like demons. I think the Indians must have supposed a mighty
host was after them, for when they found themselves in the
corral they abandoned their horses, and clambering over the
pickets, fled for their lives, bearing their dead comrade, a
thing they never do except when they are panic-stricken.
The mustangers gained a glorious victory, and ten good
horses, bridles, saddles and other Indian fixings beside great
fame by their night exploit.

Chasing the mustangs to rope them was an exciting and
a really prettier sport; but the pursuer had to be careful to
cut out and separate the animal he wanted to capture from
the herd; otherwise the chances were ninety-nine in one
hundred that he would get others foul of his rope and not
only lose his lasso but run the risk of being run over and
badly hurt.

Nicking the Mustang

By O. W. NOLEN

To CAPTURE and possess the mustang that was the wildest, the most beautiful and the fleetest animal on the prairies was the supreme ambition of many a Texan in the days when every man used a horse, most men prized fine horses, and wild horses were to be obtained by whoever had the skill and patience to capture them. The time and patience required by the widely practiced and generally effective method of walking the mustangs down made many men take a chance on a quick but risky alternative—the practice of *nicking*, called also *creasing*.

To nick a mustang the hunter aimed a rifle to send a ball—in later days a bullet—just through the top of the animal's neck, at the root of the mane, a little in front of the shoulder. Here a nerve center—connected with the spinal cord and the brain—may be so shocked as to stun or temporarily paralyze the horse, causing it to drop to the ground senseless for a minute or two, in which brief time it could be securely roped and tied down. The chief disadvantage of this method was that if the aim at the moment of the shot was not accurate the whole attempt was an instantaneous failure, for if the shot did not strike the exact spot for which it was intended the animal either fled because the bullet missed its mark, or dropped dead with a broken neck.

At Dilley, Frio County, Texas, lives S. H. Ellis. He used to accompany his father when the elder Ellis, a noted mustanger,

44

would attempt to capture the animals by nicking them with a shot from his large bore rifle. Young Ellis was about fifteen or sixteen years old, and his part in the work was to have a rope ready and to rush up and tie the mustang down the instant it was felled by a bullet from his father's gun. Ellis tells one experience of his in the following words:

"My father and I had been seeing a beautiful blue mustang for a long time as it ranged over the country with a large herd. It was our constant ambition to capture it some day and have it for our own, but it was so wild and elusive that we never could get within a mile of it.

"We haunted every waterhole for miles around in hopes of getting a chance to nick it, but it was so wary we never could get a chance. Sometimes it would be in the middle of a herd where we could not get a shot at it; sometimes it would sense our presence and suddenly turn and run madly away before we could raise a gun. Day after day we spent hours in vain lying in wait at different waterholes, occasionally getting a fleeting glimpse at the beautiful horse, often not seeing it at all.

FRANK ANTHONY STANUSH IN *Epic-Century*

"One afternoon while we hid near a waterhole our hearts nearly jumped up into our throats as we caught sight of the animal warily and gingerly approaching. I instinctively began fingering and clutching at the rope I held, and I could see my father's face tense with emotion and expectancy as he held his gun in readiness. In a few moments the mustang reached the waterhole, and after several preliminary sniffs he lowered his head and eagerly began to drink. My father raised his rifle, took tense, steady aim and suddenly pulled the trigger.

"At the instant the loud boom of the gun broke the stillness the mustang dropped in its tracks and I jumped up and ran forward to tie it down before it could recover its senses. Before I could reach the fallen animal my father called out in heart-broken dismay:

" 'Don't, son. It ain't no use. It's dead!'

"Unbelieving, I ran on until I reached the mustang and as I stood over it my father joined me. He said: "Its neck is broken. It started to raise its head just as I pulled the trigger.'

"Dumb with agonizing disappointment and regret, I stood looking down upon the dead mustang, a moment before the wildest and most graceful and beautiful I had ever seen. What would have been one of our proudest and most prized possessions now lay there lifeless. Its alertness in raising its own neck, just a fraction, had, while saving it from capture, brought an end to life."

From Mustangs to Mules

By Thomas A. Dwyer[*]

I

I WELL remember when I first came to Texas, in 1847, seeing thousands and tens of thousands of wild horses, called "mustangs," running in immense herds all over the western country, as far as the eye or telescope could sweep the horizon. The whole country seemed to be *running!* And I have had my gentle led pack-mules "cut off" from my party whilst traveling, by mustangs circling and circling around us, and gradually closing in, until by a rush, they cut off my led animals and darted away with them. Even wearied and slow-gaited pack-mules seemed as if "the speed of thought were in their limbs" on such occasions, in their struggle for liberty, and I have lost them, and my commissary on their backs, more than once.

Time and again in traveling, I have had to send out my best mounted men to gallop off and act as *videttes* and *flankers* in scaring away the immense masses of mustangs (charging around and threatening to rush over us) by yelling and firing at them; when they would wheel and go thundering away, as Byron grandly describes the hundred thousand wild Ukraine horses in *Mazeppa!*

---

[*]From *A Brief Description of Western Texas, together with a Report of the Third Annual Fair of the Agricultural, Stockraising and Industrial Association, Held at San Antonio*, San Antonio, Texas, 1872, 42-52.

At that time many Mexicans, whose families resided at Corpus Christi, Goliad, and San Antonio, and also at the towns along the lower Rio Grande from Laredo down, on one side, the eastern side of the river, supported themselves chiefly by "running," that is, catching wild cattle, and by *mustanging,* or hunting wild horses. The supplies of wild cattle and horses then seemed so abundant as to be inexhaustible. The horned cattle were never found in droves, but the horses almost universally ran together in large herds. In the course of a few years, say by 1857, very few herds of mustangs were to be met, and almost no wild cattle, so persistently had they been hunted down, and caught or killed. The grown cattle were hunted for their hides, which were then sold at half a dollar apiece by Mexicans—or the young cattle were caught to be gentled, and sold at a dollar a head.

Mexicans from the towns above named, and from the settlements, formed themselves into regularly organized companies, with a *capitán* at their head, who directed all their movements, as concert of plan and action insured success. The companies of horse-hunters sometimes numbered as many as from one to two hundred men. Each man had one or more gentle running horses, generally kept in the best condition he could afford, as upon his horse's fleetness and staying qualities depended much of the success in running mustangs.

After having agreed upon a point of meeting, the mustangers provided themselves with a few necessaries, such as some coffee, if they could afford it (the greatest of luxuries in the field); *dulce* (small cones of hard, brown Mexican sugar); a bag of *pinole* (parched corn ground on a *metate*); a little shelled corn or wheaten flour for *tortillas* (or griddle cakes); some *lariats,* or ropes made of rawhide, carefully twisted and greased, so as to be very pliable and strong; some tin cups, butcher knives, blankets (Mexican hand-made, generally of brilliant colors, good to shed rain but not warm), and arms and ammunition. In those days Indians were very numerous as well as dangerous, and had not been beaten back hundreds of miles. They were particularly fond of paying delicate attention to mustangers, and had an amiable disposition to relieve them of their animals and scalps. It was a great matter with the mustangers to go in strong parties and to be well and bravely led.

The greatest mustanger in the whole country was a Laredo Mexican named Roque, who had been many years *un cautivo* (a captive) amongst the Comanche Indians. He was not only a dexterous horseman, roper and shot, using almost invariably a bow and arrow whilst his companions used firearms, but also a remarkably brave and able leader, full of daring tempered by judgment. Roque had, at my request, to show me what he could do with his Indian bow, shot through and through one side of a flour-barrel, and nearly through the other side! He could shoot with wonderful precision and rapidly, seemingly taking no aim, but nevertheless striking the mark with great accuracy, the hand, as it were, acting in consentaneous volition with the eye. Roque's brother, Romano, was also a famous *capitán* amongst the mustangers, but he was by no means the equal of Roque, though he came next to him as a leader of men. The acuteness and skill of these men in "striking a trail," or in "following a trail," was marvelous. It appeared to be almost an animal instinct. Others claiming skill as woodsmen and hunters could find a scarcely perceptible trail, and follow over all kinds of difficult ground and concealments resorted to by wild Indians—

during the day time; but Roque and Romano could strike a
trail and follow it, by deceptive moonlight and starlight.

With such simple and slight field equipments as I have
mentioned, parties of mustangers were wont to go forth and
remain in the field for months, winter as well as summer.
Sometimes they erected little shelters for themselves, generally limited to a few branches of trees, with probably a
strip of old blanket overhead and to the north—the side of
"the northers" in winter. They had fresh meat in the greatest
abundance, to be had on all sides merely for the killing, as
the country was in those years literally running over with
wild cattle, and deer, and antelopes, and wild hogs, and
turkeys, and other game such as hares, prairie fowl, quail, and
endless varieties of ducks, geese and swans.

The quantity of deer lying around loose all over the
country, anybody's property that chose to kill them, may be
inferred from one fact within my certain knowledge. In
1857, ten years after I first arrived in Texas, a Mexican made
a contract with me to furnish a considerable number of deer
skins in return for some supplies he stood in need of. In six
months time he had killed between 600 and 700 deer with his
own rifle, in a distance of less than twenty miles, on the road
leading from Corpus Christi to Laredo, between the places
known as Palo Alto and Laguna Trinidad.

Sometimes the mustangers made strong pens of mesquite,
or other durable timber, cut into posts and set on end, some
two and a half feet into the ground, and rising some six to
eight feet above, each post standing as closely as possible next
another. They were held more firmly in place by long poles
lashed by rawhide horizontally, in a continuous line, all
around the pen, about two-thirds of the height above the

ground. The enclosure had the form of a horseshoe, but was a little more oval. From each side, at right angles, projected a long line of posts. Each of these wings, or walls, extending sometimes as far as half a mile, was intended to stop the mustangs in their flight, and to turn them, with the assistance of the mustangers, when they chased them at full speed in the direction of the pen. Then the running parties, from different sides, skillfully converged, taking care to close in gradually with concerted action, so as to catch the whole herd they had in chase in the *cul de sac* of the pen.

In preparing for the run, the mustangers frequently divested themselves of their hats and short jackets and shirts, and either fastened the girths of their horses very tightly and shortened their stirrups so as to give themselves a good grip with the knees, or else they rode bareback, with their long *lassos*, rawhide *lariats*, ready to be whirled in circles above their heads to catch any particular animal they might cut off from the running herd. To see these mustangers in full chase was to behold one of the most exciting scenes presented by the wild sports and occupations of Texas frontier life. In general, the Mexicans of the frontier ride superbly. The powerful but cruel Spanish bit which they use gives them the most perfect control over their horses, and they can turn them suddenly, at full gallop, in any direction, as if upon a pivot, or stop them in full career instantly, as if they were shot dead, without being moved in their seats!

I have witnessed these mustang chases innumerable times, and reveled in their nomadic excitement. "In life's early morn, when my spirit was young," I do not wonder that I voluntarily took to frontier life for many years, with all its dangers and roughness, tired as I was of city life and its

nerveless and routine occupations and pleasures. Eleven years
at law in London and Dublin, *with few briefs,* and just forty
guineas in fees (equal to $200 of our American money) in
four years' practice at the Irish bar had given me a big
disgust, not only of law but even of civilization at its over-
crowded centers, fenced in by all kinds of restrictions, conventionalities, and infinitesimal etiquette and artificiality and
"red tape."

The mustangers sometimes caught several hundred horses
in their pens at one drive. As soon as the animals were so
entrapped, the open part of the pen, guarded carefully by
mounted mustangers, was closed with posts already prepared,
so as to form a perfect and continuous enclosure, impossible
for any animal, short of Homer's Trojan horse, to break
through or escape from. The numbers caught were frequently so great and consequently their value was so trivial
that they were often sold for a dollar or a dollar and a half
a head. Some animals, picked out for beauty or "good points,"
brought five dollars.

Paint or spotted horses were quite numerous amongst the
mustangs. The greater number of wild horses were under-
sized, say under thirteen and a half hands high, showing
generally good points in the forequarters, and rather poor
in the hindquarters. But some of the animals were above
fifteen hands high, and displayed not only fair size, but good
blood, as fine American horses and mares had from time to
time escaped from their owners and joined the mustangs and
bred amongst them. Where such had been the case, a vast
improvement in height, weight, power, and symmetry was
observed immediately. This visible result induced me, as well
as others, to breed fine American blooded stallions and jacks
to Mexican mares.

II

Of course, I was also influenced by the great difference in the price of brood-mares, as I found it would cost me about ten times as much to commence with a hundred American mares, common stock, as to commence with the same number of Mexican mares. In the first case it would cost for one hundred common American mares at $100.00 each, $10,000.00. In the second case, one hundred Mexican mares at $10.00 each, $1,000.00. It was not by any means certain that common American mares would show anything like the vast improvement in the progeny that I saw in the *half-breeds, i.e.,* half American and half Mexican, resulting from putting fine stallions to Mexican mares. Evidently the Mexican stock came originally from the south of Spain, where there is a good deal of Arab blood, degenerated if you will, from breeding in and in, etc., but still showing some fine points such as small heads, full, bold and lustrous eyes, wide nostrils, small ears, delicate withers, well-set shoulders, and flat bones from the knees and hocks down, which signs of good blood are wholly wanting in common American and common European horses.

I commenced about 1859 by purchasing two hundred head of mares in Mexico, and paid $8.00 apiece for them, as the days of mustanging and very cheap wild horses were over in Texas when I turned my attention to raising horses and mules. As the animals were in very poor condition when I purchased them, I decided to have them herded and pastured for several months in Mexico, expecting that they would be, by that time, in much better condition for being driven into Texas. Accordingly, I selected a place where I thought they would do well; but unfortunately the whole of that section of Mexico suffered that year from a most severe drought, and horses died there in great numbers, from scanty supplies of herbage and water. Mine amongst the rest were attacked by "blind-staggers," and diseases of the loins and kidneys; so that to save the remaining portion, at the end of the year I had them driven into Texas, though they were in a miserable condition for travel.

I lost exactly one hundred mares out of the original number of two hundred I had purchased a year previous! I also lost about three-fourths of my sucking mule and horse colts, which had, as is usual in Mexico, been "thrown in," *i.e.,* not charged for when I bought the mares. Only eighteen mule colts, twenty-five horse colts and fillies, and one hundred mares remained. This was certainly discouraging! Yet in two and a half years afterwards, I sold those eighteen mule colts in San Antonio for fully fifty per cent more than the remaining one hundred mares had originally cost me! Those colts had not meantime stood me a dollar for corn, hay, or handling. I sold them, *unbroken,* for nearly $1,200.00 to Mr. P. Martin, through a friend who took them to San Antonio for sale.

As soon as my stock arrived in Texas and were placed where mesquite grass and good water were abundant, the animals commenced to improve; in five years following I lost only two mares! That shows the importance of good grass and water. The two animals I lost died of disease; one of blind staggers, the other of loin disease.

I established my ranch (or stock farm) at a place called the Diesmero, about eighteen miles from Corpus Christi, on the west bank of the Nueces River. I rented the place for a year, as it was not for sale. At the end of the year I moved up the country some twelve miles farther, on the same side of the river, to a place containing some sixteen to seventeen hundred acres of ground, which I purchased because it had *the three requisites of a good ranch*—abundant mesquite grass, plenty of water, and a good deal of timber, affording shelter in winter during "northers."

I built a nice house and outhouses on my ranch, and erected *corrals,* or pens, for my horse-stock, and also for a stock of horned cattle which I raised and took care of at the same time. The same Mexican *vaqueros,* or herdsmen, who tended my horses took care of my cattle. The only additional expense necessarily incurred was that I had to buy a lot of gentle horses for herding purposes, more than I should have otherwise required.

I bought on the Rio Grande thirty head, at $15.00 apiece, and put a very gentle and *lazy old white mare* with them, a bell fastened around her neck so that its tinkle always indicated where she and the gentle horses, called the *remuda,* were. The horses get to love an old bell-mare and one another's company very much, and so keep together. The bell-mare has not only to be gentle but lazy, to suit the purposes of a *remuda,* which must never wander off far from certain places, else it cannot easily be found or driven up to the corral to provide a remount. The bell-mare also should be white, as that color is easily recognized at a distance.

Having, as already stated, one hundred mares, I divided them off into four *manadas,* or herds, of twenty-five mares each, with a herding horse for each *manada.* The herding horse, if required only to keep the mares together, is "fixed" by the Mexicans in a certain manner, which requires a good deal of skill. The horse so *fixed* is called by them *un garañón dispuesto.* The stallions, on the contrary, that are intended at once to herd and to breed from are not operated on in any manner. With two of my *manadas* I put two Mexican *fixed* stallions, and a jack with each of the other two. *I took care to get jacks accustomed to wild mares.* Many ranchmen make a serious mistake in buying expensive jacks that are driven off easily by the kicks and bites of wild mares; as a result, few, if any, mule colts are raised. Apart from the height, girth, and general formation of the jack, there are two points very essential for a sure foal-getter. The jack's head ought to be *large,* and his *under-jaw heavy.* If the jack is running with a *manada,* the state of his chest will show his keenness or sluggishness. If keen to cover, then his chest will be one mass of lumps or sores; if sluggish, then he will have no marks from the kicks of the mares. Jack's attentions to the mares are shamefully resented. He suffers much.

If Balaam's ass were again on earth, he might moralize with "Childe Harold," and exclaim:

> "Alas! our young affections run to waste—
> Or water but the desert."

As the jacks will not herd mares, "fixed" horses have to be used for that purpose, to keep the *manadas* together. At first there will be severe fighting between the jack and the herding horse; but Jack invariably conquers; and after a short time

ROSS SANTEE IN *Men and Horses*

remains the undisputed master of both horse and mares. With two *manadas* I put fine young American stallions, and kept a *vaquero* to watch each *manada*, and assist the stallion in "herding" until he became accustomed to it. To restrain the mares from running off, I took recourse to the Mexican plan of "toeing" them, which consisted of cutting off a small piece from one of the foreleg hoofs, close up to the quick, so as to render it very tender, and liable to bleed a little on being much used. The mares may have to be "toed" twice before they learn to keep together, and obey the herding stallion. It is cruel, but it is certainly effective, and saves a great deal of hunting after animals, and running them down.

I fed *jacks* and *American stallions* corn twice a day when grass was good and abundant, and three times when it was indifferent or rather scanty. With this object in view, and also for the purpose of doctoring them for any kick, bite, or other hurt, I had my *manadas* driven up and penned (each *manada* in a separate pen, to keep the stallions from fighting) twice a day, at noon, when the *vaqueros* dined, and at night, when they came home to sleep. During the day in "northers" I left the *manadas* in the shelter of timber, and only had them penned at night. The pens afforded good shelter from the northers. After the *manadas* had become perfectly accustomed to being herded, and kept together, and also more habituated to their grazing grounds, I seldom had them driven up and penned, unless to examine and doctor them if necessary. I would send out the corn to the jacks and American stallions in nose-bags. By this means I kept up the spirit and stamina—a most important matter—of my sires. The results were most satisfactory. I had not a single mare that failed to breed; and, besides, their progeny, whether mule or horse colts, were of good size and spirit; whilst several acquaintances, engaged in the same business but managing differently, had (comparatively) bad success. I lay particular stress on the benefits resulting from *feeding corn* regularly to American jacks and stallions.

My first crop of mules foaled and raised in Texas I exchanged for cotton with Mr. Green Gay of the Aransas, where that river crosses the high road between San Patricio and Goliad; and that cotton netted me about $5,000.00 in Matamoras, Mexico, during "our late family unpleasantness."

I was so unsuccessful in *breaking* my horse colts by the Mexican mode, which is very rough and severe, as pursued in Northern Mexico and Southern Texas, that I let most of them run unbroken until I sold my entire stock, when I had been four years on my ranch and one at the Diesmero.

Mexicans are good hands for hunting up horse and mule stock, and for herding them, and have a number of simple and efficacious remedies for "doctoring"; but they are too severe and rough in breaking or gentling them for the saddle; and they usually know nothing about breaking animals to harness. Many of my colts were severely injured by their mode of handling, and I am satisfied that our American methods of handling and gentling are far superior to Mexican methods. The Mexicans starve, scare, and beat the *potros* (young geldings) almost to death, to reduce their strength and diminish their spirit, till they can offer but feeble resistance, instead of preserving their strength, and making their spirit docile, by good treatment and gentle handling.

My average crop of mules, from two jacks at first, each running with twenty-five mares, and afterwards from three jacks and four, as I gradually increased the number of my *manadas*, by the addition of their fillies, amounted to twenty mules from every twenty-five mares. Late in the season I always took the jacks away from their *manadas* and replaced them at night, when they were penned, by stallions, taking care to tie up the Mexican "fixed" herding stallions, lest they might injure the fine-blooded American stallions. By this management, I secured a fine colt or filly in lieu of a mule, when any mare failed to breed to the jack.

It is a Mexican custom to rub a little sweet oil over the jack's loins in spring, just before turning him out with his *manada*; but the Mexicans seem very careful not to apply much oil. I allowed mine to be treated so, and saw no reason to change the practice in five years, though I did not understand its philosophy.

The horse colts and fillies from my mares, by fine-blooded American stallions, showed a vast improvement on Mexican stock, not only in size, but in symmetry and power. The second crop would have shown still further improvement, judging from other stock, and the third, I have no doubt, would have produced splendid animals; but I had to "break up," on account of our war, and sell out before I could raise a second or third cross. As it was, I did very well indeed, as I had about five hundred head of horse and mule stock when I sold out; and I traded them off for cotton, and a train of wagons and ox teams, with Colonel Henry Jones of Corsicana, Navarro County. I got fully $20,000.00 net proceeds out of that operation—and I think I did remarkably well, though I have no doubt that it would have paid me well to have held on to the stock, under any circumstances. However, the threatening aspect of matters preceding the break-up of our Confederacy induced me, much against my inclinations, to dispose of my stock, as there would be no security for it amongst general disorder.

I shall close my "personal experiences" as a raiser of horse and mule stock by a well-known quotation from Horace, which I deem very appropriate, and which I hope the compositor won't alter (to suit his Anglo-Saxon preference) as he has done with my previous bit of Latinity from the same author:

> "Si quid novisti rectius istis
> Candidus imperti: si non [nil] his utere mecum."

There is no necessity that I should "rise to explain." We are all *classical* in Western Texas, and outsiders can consult translations.

The Mustanger Who Turned Mustang

By FLORENCE FENLEY*

IT WASN'T an easy matter to catch a mustang in the sixties, nor in the seventies and eighties, while Southwest Texas was their playground. There were thousands and thousands of horses; they ranged from the plains to the coast, and they ran with easy grace over the entire territory which had long been their kingdom. At that time, there was nothing on four feet that trod the hills or valleys that was superior to horses. They were supreme. They ran for the sheer pleasure of running, and man couldn't *run* them down.

Nevertheless, they were caught. And it is of a unique method that I write, in which Bob Lemons, a famous brush *vaquero,* figured. Bob is one of the few remaining brush hands who rode and roped wild horses and cattle before Texas knew a fence. At the age of ninety-two, he lives today near Carrizo Springs, an example of hardihood and tough fibre because of his life in the open. The brushy bottoms of Zavala, Dimmit and Frio Counties were home to him. He knew the country as only the range riders knew it who worked after the cunning brush cattle that were as wild as the mustangs. Bob, with his strain of African blood—mixed, I dare say, with the Indian—was the spirit of endurance and patience. Days and days passed, finding him on the horse range; days of dewy, spring greenness and blossoming flow-

*Reprinted by permission of publisher and author from *The Cattleman,* September, 1940, Fort Worth, Texas.

ers; days when hot, dry winds scorched the earth's breast, and heavy sworls of gray dust spiraled across the valleys leaving a residue of silt on the drying vegetation; days of Indian summer when hawks whistled and leaves rustled with the murmur of approaching northers. But it was home to Bob—this land where coyotes and javelinas trotted, and panthers screamed at night; where rattlesnakes, centipedes, tarantulas and sand fleas made life interesting! Water holes, then, were often far apart when dry seasons stopped the flow of creeks and rivers, leaving only pools here and there. But Bob knew where the pools were as well as the mustangs, and he knew which bands watered at them. He knew, too, that mustangs always came back to their range and if a person stayed with them long enough, they could be captured.

As he rode his horse and gazed on the magnificent bands that seemed to run with the wind, he thought on the best method of capturing them for saddle animals. When he "turned mustang," he instinctively selected the best plan of capture. If he were a mustang with them, he'd soon win their confidence.

"I've ketched a good many mustangs," he said, "and I've seen as many as two hundred runnin' when bunches got throwed together. Of course, when night come, they'd split up, and each stallion would get his own band together.

"You didn't want to get one of them big bunches in a pen, because they'd kill one another too bad. They'd just run right over anything that got in their way. You had to keep 'em circlin' after you got 'em in the pen. If you didn't know how to circle 'em with blankets and such, you'd get 'em killed. But of course, you want to know how I started out after 'em!

"You see, I was born in 1848 and we come out to Frio County in 1854. I belonged to John English, and he and Levi

English had brought here to Carrizo a bunch of cattle in 1863. That was the same year John was killed. No town of Carrizo then—just the first settlers, who were Charley and Blue Vivian and John Burleson. We pitched camp right where the courthouse stands today.

"When I was set free, I was about seventeen years old. The slaves didn't have names, only those of their masters; so I had to stand around and hunt me a name. Old man Duncan Lemons come along and I told 'im my trouble; so he took me to Eagle Pass and *bogused* my name. So that's how I got the name Lemons. I stayed with old man Duncan till he died, and he taught me everything I knowed about stock. I guess I caught about 103 mustangs for 'im.

"I wouldn't want nothing much to hinder me when I went out after a band of horses. I learned to keep the same outfit all the way through, too. After I got 'em to where they'd let me stay with 'em, I couldn't change horses, or saddle or hat. Not even a canteen, because they'd know it as soon as I come to 'em and they got the wind of me. When they

ROY ANTHONY STANUSH IN *Epic-Century*

begun to get used to me, I never let 'em get too clost to my
horse, and when I'd leave 'em for a little while and come
back to 'em, I let 'em keep the wind of me so they'd know
it was me.

"When I'd spot the bunch I wanted, I went toward 'em
in a walk. They'd watch me a little while and come toward
me to try to figure me out. Then when they made sure it
was a man on a horse, they'd break and run. They'd run
clean out of sight, but I never put my horse out of a walk
and I knew they'd circle back to their range no matter how
far they run. I'd keep that up for days and they'd run from
me every time they saw me, but as time went on they
wouldn't run so far. Pretty soon I could ride up in a short
distance of 'em. It wasn't long before they wouldn't run
from me, and then I got 'em to where they trusted me,
because ever' time they'd scare, I'd scare and run as hard as
they did. Sometimes I'd scare first and away we'd go, with
me in the lead and them follerin' me. I'd soon have a whole
bunch runnin' with me everywhere I went.

"We had spies out from the ranch to watch which way I
had 'em headed and they'd put grub out for me at certain
places. They'd put it in a morral (fiber bag) and hang the
morral on a limb. If I'm goin' north, they'd keep grub for
me ahead, and if I'm goin' south, they'd do the same. When
I'd first leave the mustangs to go get something to eat, we
used to try changin' hats or coats when I'd meet one of the
fellows from the ranch, but when I rode back to the horses
and they got wind of me, you bet they'd run, and it was all
to do over again. You couldn't even change a morral but
what they knowed it. We always had it understood where
they was to leave grub next day, and when the mustangs got
to follerin' me, they'd go with me to the place. I was workin'

'em around toward the pens we were goin' to put 'em in.

"A horse has a heap o' sense. When I'd first get after 'em, they'd sure watch me, even after they got used to me. I'd follow 'em to water when I seen they needed water bad, and let 'em keep the wind on me. I'd ride right into the water with 'em and as soon as they'd see it was me, they'd run out, but they'd come right back.

"On the day we got ready to pen 'em, I'd work 'em around in the neighborhood of the corrals the boys had ready. There'd be wings built out from the gate a ways. When everything was ready and I had 'em just right, I'd scare, and away I'd go with them after me. On that day, I'd run right into the pen and I had to keep ridin' after I got in there, too, till they'd open a gate for me to let me out. Once a Meskin had the gate in charge and when he seen me comin', he got excited and went to slip the bars out of the gate but pushed 'em in, instead, and nearly got me killed. I told Mr. Lemons I didn't want to work with that fellow again.

"We'd circle the horses after we got 'em in the pen, till they finally stopped. Some of 'em was awful mean and hard to handle, but they're a heap easier to tame than you'd think, after all. A lot of times when you'd spot a bunch of horses, you'd think they were mustangs, but you'd find out you had horses that had just gone wild.

"It wasn't uncommon for horses to get taken off by Indians and then go wild if they got away. I followed a bunch clean down to Oakville in Live Oak County once and they carried me right to the owner. I worked 'em about a week, and I wanted 'em to go north, but no, they wanted to go south; so I went with 'em. We got to the place where they come from and they went right to the very ranch house. The owner was sure glad to see 'em and paid me for the return of 'em.

There were nine head of young horses and five head of old mares. They sure were wild. Somebody had stole 'em and carried 'em off and they got loose. We ketched a good deal of horses like that. The most I ever ketched was twelve head. That is, I saved twelve head out of the bunch and killed five.

"Shucks, I could ride as good now as I ever could, if I could see. That bunch of cattle you hear comin' in now belongs to me. Erskin Rhodes is bringin' 'em in. He takes care of my stuff for me and moved me down here on his place where he could look after me better. My place joins him on the west. I ride sometimes yet, but Erskin says I'm getting too old and might get hurt since I can't see. I've spent most of my life on a horse and wouldn't know what to do if I couldn't get on one any more."

Mustangs of the Staked Plains

—W. R. Leigh

Fifty Thousand Mustangs

By Frank Collinson*

I. The Mustang at Home on the Range

IN 1872 I was working on the noted horse ranch of Judge George Noonan west of the Medina River, in the San Antonio territory. Noonan had at that time from three to four thousand head of the best bred range horses I have ever seen in Texas. Our work was to gather them, keep the colts branded up, and break broncos. The country was all open and full of wild horses of the Spanish breed. Every time we went on a horse hunt we'd run into the mustangs.

I saw many that showed Andalusian origin. One band that ran between Quihi Prairie and the Hondo were all palominos —cream-colored with white manes and tails. There must have been nearly a hundred in this band. There were also a great many of the genuine Andalusian duns—what we still call claybank dun—black-striped legs, a black streak down the back, black mane and tail, which was generally heavy. There was also the mouse-colored dun; Mexicans call this color *grulla*. They also have black stripes on the legs and back, and almost all of this color are excellent horses. There are still a good many of these colors in Old Mexico today.

Mustang hunters in that part of Texas, at that time, built corrals, usually in some brushy hollow, with wings made out

---

*A part of the material in this chronicle appeared in *Ranch Romances*, Second March issue, 1936, and First November issue, 1936. Thanks for permission to reprint are due the editor of *Ranch Romances*.

of brush sometimes a mile long, at the extremities spreading a half mile or so apart. The gateway was built, if possible, near a tree. The gate was hung to this tree and when the horses ran in, a man hidden behind this gate slammed it shut. A heavy pole fell into a socket and fastened with a pin over it. There were often two pens in the shape of the figure 8, so that the horses would run into the second pen. If there were only one, they often ran around and got back to the gate before it was securely shut.

The corral fence had to be heavy and of good height to hold these horses. They would make desperate efforts to get out. After they had quieted down for a day or maybe two, the hunters would go in and rope and tie some to trees in the corral; some they tied to logs, and others they hobbled. Sometimes a stallion would fight; he was promptly killed.

In a few days the animals were starved for grass and water. The hunters would let them out a few at a time to water and graze with a bunch of gentle horses that had been brought up, and would then send them back to the pen again. In a week or two they could be driven. What with starvation and rough handling they generally gave up. Of course, some got away, but not many, once corralled.

It was fast, hard riding in this brush country; nearly all the ridges were covered with oak timber, mesquite edging out into the prairies. I knew one young man who was killed riding through this oak timber trying to head a bunch of horses off. He must have expected his horse to stay on one side of a tree; but just as he got to it, the horse dodged the other way. The rider tried to swing over that way, but his head struck the tree and was knocked open.

It was not until I got out on *El Llano Estacado*—the Staked Plain—that I saw mustangs in their natural habitat, an immense open country, five hundred miles north and south, two hundred east and west, with the finest buffalo grass that ever grew and every few miles a fresh-water lake. These lakes were often a hundred yards across and nearly a mile in length. During the rainy season they filled with water and some lasted the year around, but all were apt to go dry, and then the hunters had to water at the few lakes of lasting water like Spring Lake, Black Lake and Bull Lake. Also, nearly all the long draws of the rivers that head into the plains, from Red River on the north to the Concho on the south, and some big creeks that empty into the Canadian and Cimarron rivers, always had water in them.

If ever there was a horse paradise, it was the Staked Plain of Texas, and here the mustangs were in all their glory—tens of thousands of them. I have heard the number put as high as fifty thousand, and I believe that was a low estimate. These horses were well grown, larger than the mustangs in South Texas, fourteen to fifteen hands high. Some of the stallions were over fifteen hands and weighed 1,000 to 1,100 pounds. These were not merely the descendants of horses lost by early Spaniards, for the Indians had been stealing good horses in East Texas and from emigrant trains going to California. Some "American" stallions thus captured had got loose and mixed with the mustangs.

I knew a cowman in Colorado who bought stallions every year in Kentucky. Some of these got away; so by the time I got on to the plains in the seventies the plains were alive with the biggest and the best bred mustangs I ever saw, and the fastest. Some that were caught and taken East were the foundation for some of the fastest horses on the Eastern race tracks.

Mustangs were generally in bunches of thirty to fifty with

one master stallion. This stallion had to fight constantly to hold his harem. There was always a young stallion ready for a fight, and at the least show of age or weakness the older one had to battle. I do not believe there is any animal that fights harder for supremacy than a mustang. It is generally a battle to the death when two stallions meet to fight for a herd of mares. It is almost impossible to describe it.

They generally meet walking on their hind legs, mouths open, strike with their forefeet and clinch with the most powerful jaws and teeth, making cuts inches deep. Since they throw their whole weight against each other, the weaker goes to the ground. The upper horse strikes with his feet and bites and tears hide and flesh off in strips. If the weaker horse manages to gain his feet, he rushes off, glad to escape with his life. He is generally pursued for a mile or more by the con-quering stallion, which bites and tears hide and flesh at every jump.

The master stallion ran all the young stallions out of his herd when they were two years old—younger, if one got too attentive to the mares. I have seen fifeen or more young stal-lions in a bunch, with no mares. They would hang around in sight of the mares and one would slip in and cut a mare out and run her off. If successful in getting away and keeping her, he might try another and in that way start a herd. Some of the master stallions would run off the fillies from their herds, and in that way some young stallion would start a herd. I have seen range stallions take the life of an inbred colt.

When I was on the Noonan ranch, I drove up a stallion with about fifty mares and their young offspring. This stal-lion was said to be a Thoroughbred, a fine horse. Just as I got to the corrals at the home ranch, this stallion ran at a pretty colt about two weeks old, caught it across the back and killed it as a dog would a rat. I called to Will Noonan, who was the ranch foreman, and told him what had happened. He said, "The mare of that colt is one of Sultan's fillies. He did the same thing last year." We cut her out, put her with another *manada* that was under close herd, but she got away and went back to old Sultan, her sire. I left before she had another colt, but guess he killed it like the two previous ones.

When mustangs were running like buffalo, they huddled into one big herd. I have seen two thousand, I believe, in one big run near Spring Lake. When they did stop, then the fights began if one stallion tried to get a mare out of another bunch after they separated it. It is a wrong idea to think the stallion leads the mares. He is always behind looking out for what might be in back and whipping up any that are lagging.

II. MUSTANGING IN CARTS AND OTHERWISE

The mustang hunters got busy right after the buffalo hunt was over. Some of the buffalo hunters turned to catching mustangs. The first hunts were all on horseback. They had to have several good horses, well grained. The best time was toward spring when the mustangs were not so strong and green grass was coming. The hunter would locate his camp on some water, not where the bunch of mustangs were watering, but conveniently near. When all was ready, one man would start the herd off at a fast run. They might run twenty miles or more before turning, but they would invariably turn and circle back to their range. They might go fifty or sixty miles before they got back near to where they started. This man never tried to crowd them, just kept them in sight. It might be the next day before the other men in camp got a sight of him. Then another man and horse would take up the chase. They might go just as far in another direction that time before turning back, when another man would take up the run, and so on. In a week or so they would be getting tired and the hunter could get around them, but never let them stop if he could help it. They would finally slow down to a walk.

One bunch I helped run got tame enough to be driven. We headed them for an extra strong pen on Canyon Blanco that had been built to handle wild cattle in. When the horses got to the pen, they walked around it two days before they could be penned. The stallion, a big pinto, would not go near it. It was fifteen miles to the head of the canyon. We stationed a man every now and then, riding the best horses, towards the point where this stallion would go out if not roped before getting that far.

About a mile below this corral was a Ranger camp. These men were well mounted and spoiling for a run. Wilkerson and a Ranger went to this place and had not long to wait. Although the stallion had been run fifteen miles by good grain-fed horses, he was well in the lead. It was a broad, open way out, but the Ranger was right on him, threw at him once, and missed. That was his last chance; he never got near the horse again. I rather believe, from Wilkerson's account, that this man never tried to catch him.

A very good friend of mine got badly hurt running a bunch on Black Water Draw. Some of his horses had got mixed up with these mustangs, so he went out to try to cut them out. He did not show up that night; they found his horse and saddle the next day; the day following they found him, still alive but unconscious. They got him to camp but he was badly hurt. His horse had stepped in a hole and fallen with him. He went East to a hospital, got some better, went back to the plains, gradually grew worse and one morning, when alone, blew his head off; he'd rather be dead than in that condition.

I have heard a lot of talk about creasing mustangs—that is, shooting them through the muscle of the neck, which will paralyze them for a short time. No doubt this has been done by men at times, but to talk of going out to catch horses this way is pure bunk. I have tried it a great many times and have broken their necks scores of times and never caught a horse that way and never knew anyone else who did.

George Causey, who was a buffalo hunter for twelve years and who later settled on the Black Water Draw on the plains, in the very heart of the mustang range, was one of the best hunters and rifle shots I ever saw. He had the reputation of killing thirty or forty thousand buffalo. I have seen him kill with a rifle a prairie chicken flying straight away from him. When asked if he had ever creased a mustang, he said, "No, but I have killed hundreds trying to. I generally break their necks." And that has always been my experience. Causey was a far better shot than I ever was, and if he could not turn the trick, it was surely an accident if anyone else could.

One day I was out hunting some of our saddle horses with one of our cow-punchers. We saw a bunch of mustangs going in to water at a lake on the east edge of the plains. I said, "We had better take a look at those horses, ours might be with them." I had a very good Sharp's hammerless saddle gun with me—forty caliber, set trigger—about the best saddle gun I ever owned. So we rode up to this lake; got off our horses and looked over the rise at the horses watering. None of ours was with them.

I said to my companion, "I will try to crease that stallion. Get on your horse, and if I knock him down run and get your rope on him." I got my gun and slipped up to where I could see the horse standing. He was a sure enough good-looking stallion, standing broadside to me, about a hundred yards off. I could not have had a better chance to crease him. I lay down, took all the time I needed, had a good rest to shoot from. At the crack of the gun he fell. This man, his rope all ready, ran up to where the horse was lying. He called back, "You got him all right." I had broken his neck, and that is about the way I always creased them.

American mustang hunters finally got to running mustangs in a cart, which was called a mail cart, with a tongue instead of shafts, well balanced on two wheels, with a light bed spring seat. They hitched two horses to this and could take a keg of water along and a small supply of feed for both driver and horses. Two horses to this kind of cart could make just as good time or better than a horse carrying a man. This kind of running was good only in open country, but it was very effective there.

The seventies and eighties were the great days for the mustang hunters. By far the larger part of the plains mustangs were killed as the plains were fenced up. A good many were killed running over wire fences; they were cut and bled to death or died from the cuts. When the Capital Syndicate fenced up their three million acres, secured from the State of Texas in payment for the capitol building at Austin, there must have been ten thousand mustangs on the range. A great number were run out into New Mexico as the fences were built, and eventually the remainder were either killed or caught. Most of the wild horses caught on the north plains were driven to Kansas, sold there, and shipped east.

I knew one ranch on the head of Red River that ran a big bunch off the Cap Rock of the plains. They were a great nuisance to ranchers. Horses would get in with them, would forever be on the run, and would keep the cattle on the move. But like the buffalo, they had to go; their time was up when the cattle took the range.

III. MEXICAN MESTEÑEROS

On the plains, though this was not true of the lower border country, the Mexican mustangers, unlike the Americans, generally cared little for the grown stock, preferring colts. The younger they were, the better they liked them, for the little fellow could be more easily fed and domesticated.

The spring—April, May and June—the time of foaling and also the time when range stock is weak—was their favorite season. I knew two professionals, Pedro and Soledad Trujillo, well. They were brothers and had small ranches above old Fort Sumner, on the Pecos River in New Mexico, where they farmed, raising corn mostly. In April they would load up their whole outfit—women, children, dogs and all they had that was movable; all the cattle they had, mostly milch cows, and a big string of burros. Then they would pull for the plains.

They generally went to Los Portales, a very fine spring of good fresh water. They camped there for a week or so, about seventy miles east of Fort Sumner, going south for mustangs.

The principal part of the outfit was a few very good, fast, roping horses. These horses were taken care of like race horses; grained and groomed for weeks before the hunt. The ropers were light riders; always rode barebacked, with never anything but a surcingle, and not always that. The lariat they roped with was tied to a well-padded rope around the horse's neck, close up to the head, so that it served to hold the colt, or anything else they roped, and also to hold the horse when the rider jumped off to tie his catch.

When all was ready and they had located a *manada* with colts, they waited until the horses came in to water. Then part of the outfit would try to get around so as to start the herd toward where the ropers were hiding, if they could— or to get the herd between them. The ropers gradually closed in from both sides; the young colts could not hold their speed long. The ropers always tried to rope the strongest colts first if possible. When a rider had made a catch he jumped off his horse. The colt was generally about choked down, if not down; so it did not take much to throw him. Then, with a tie rope, the Mexican tied the colt quickly any way he could —a leg to the neck, both feet, or a forefoot and hind foot— anyway, so that the animal could not travel. Then the hunter slipped the loop off, hustled to his horse, and followed the fleeing bunch for another throw. This whole job did not take more than a few seconds when the rider was once near enough to make a catch. A good, fast man and horse could get two or three colts on one run—he was sure to, if the colts were only a day or two old.

The men behind picked up the colts and started to camp with them. Here's where the milch cows and burros came in; also the women, as they helped to feed the colts cows' milk or put them on a burro, if they had any giving milk.

Some years they would get one hundred colts, but fifty or sixty was a good catch. Some died, but most of them lived and made good horses. These outfits came from all along the Pecos from Las Vegas, New Mexico, to Saragosa, Texas. Some of the roping horses cost a lot of money. Trujillo went to Chihuahua and bought well bred Arabians, paying as much as a thousand pesos for something choice. Pedro told me he gave one hundred cattle for one, but cattle were cheap in those days—four and five dollars per head. From the best accounts obtainable there were a thousand colts caught every year from the Cimarron to what is now called Boykin Lake in Roosevelt County, New Mexico.

IV. MAN-FIGHTING STALLIONS

Sometimes, after a bunch of mustangs got tired enough for riders to get near them, the stallion would attack a man, but the mustangers had to put up with him, for if they killed him, then the mares, with no stallion to control them, would scatter.

I knew two buffalo hunters, Havie and Wilkinson, who caught several hundred mustangs. On one occasion the stallion in the bunch was very vicious. Every time either of these men got anywhere near, this stallion would charge him, ears laid back and mouth open. They shot at him a few times to scare him, but he finally got so bad they decided to kill him. They had a small stallion in camp, very gentle; so they got the idea of killing the mustang and turning this saddle stallion in with the mares. They led him out. When the mustang saw them coming and this pet horse nickering to the mares, on he came! Wilkinson shot him and turned the pet loose. When turned loose he ran into the mares, scattering them into half a dozen bunches, and finally ran off with a few. Needless to say, the whole bunch was lost. The sky was blue and sulphur the balance of the day. They had to rest up the saddle horses for a few days before starting another *manada*.

About two weeks later their pet stallion came limping into camp more dead than alive. He was cut and scarred from his head to tail—cuts inches deep in his hips and he was very lame. They thought he would die, but in a few weeks he was well enough to work to their wagon. The wild stallions had just about eaten him up.

A horse-raiser that I knew at the foot of the plains found, while riding out one day, a bunch of his gentle mares with a good-looking mustang stallion. He worked them to the nearest corral and had the luck to pen the stallion. The next day he took a man with him and they roped this horse. The mustang fought them hard, but they finally got him down and put a hackamore on him, then let him up and tied him to a log. The next day my friend tried to rub him on the forehead. When he reached his hand out the horse made a snap at him and bit the first finger off his right hand just above the knuckle joint. He had to ride a long way to a doctor, who took the balance of the finger off at the joint. Probably no more vicious animal lives than a mustang stallion—he bites, strikes with his forefeet, kicks, tries to jump on you or kill you in any way he can. He is the most dangerous animal I ever had anything to do with.

In the fall of 1874 I went to Fort Griffin with the intention of going on the buffalo range. On arriving there I found out there was no sale for buffalo hides in Texas. General McKenzie's expedition was out in the plains country to the west. The Comanche Indians were raiding all buffalo hunters' camps. There was not much doing. Several hunting outfits had just come south from Kansas and were camped, waiting until the Indians were put on reservations. Amongst the hunters from Kansas were White and Russell. I went with them to their camp about sixty miles west of Fort Griffin. They were camped on Deep Paint Creek. It was beautiful country at that time, open, rolling plains country; nothing like a house or any kind of settlement for four hundred miles and then only a few cow camps on the Pecos River in New Mexico, and then nothing for two hundred miles west of the Pecos, except a few Mexican settlements on the Rio Grande —just buffalo and his wild red herder, the Comanche Indian, over the whole Llano Estacado and far out on both sides of it.

Before leaving Fort Worth I had bought a good cow horse. I paid fifty dollars for him, which was a good price for a horse at that time. I should have said I paid fifty dollars in gold. At that time there were three kinds of money, all of different values: gold, silver, and greenbacks. I rode this horse to Fort Griffin and then out to this camp. There was nothing to do but hunt a little, poison a few wolves and coyotes—and wait for a hide market and for McKenzie to get the Indians to their reservation.

There was another ex-cowpuncher with the outfit named Louis Keys. He had been up the trail several times to Kansas and, like myself, wanted to get on the buffalo range. He also had a good cow horse.

Deep Point Creek heads southwest of the Double Mountain and runs in a northeast direction into the Double Mountain Fork of the Brazos. It has deep, steep banks on both sides, flanked by a belt of elm timber on both sides. About a mile below our camp a band of mustangs ranged, sometimes on the south side, and again on the north. If they were on the south side and anything started them, they ran to a certain crossing—an old buffalo trail worn deep in the banks. Buffaloes had crossed here, no doubt, for countless ages on their migrations north and south. If these mustangs were north and ran south, they used another crossing. I might say there were not many mustangs in that part of Texas—nothing like the number above the Cap Rock, on the plains proper.

The master stallion of this band was a big red sorrel horse, from a thousand to eleven hundred pounds. Keys and I decided we would try to rope this stallion as he crossed Paint Creek the first time we saw him on the south side. We had not long to wait. One day we saw the band on the south side. We saddled up. I had the heavier horse; so I was to take a stand on the top of the creek bluff on the north side of the crossing, and when this stallion came out, just drop a loop on him. Keys was to take a roundabout way and come on them from south of where they were grazing, and when they got well started to shoot his Winchester so that I could get ready.

Well, I went to my appointed place. It wasn't long before I heard a shot, and then they came, the stallion behind his *manada*, Keys crowding them all he could. He was to help me if I made a good catch. The band was led by a big mare; they came out just as fast as they could run, up this one buffalo trail, the stallion last. He had just stopped on the south bluff for a look at Keys, who was only a few hundred yards behind. Then he had plunged down and crossed the creek bed, and now up the trail he came like a big buck, in long jumps. Just as he showed up, I let my loop drop over his head. I could not have made a better catch.

I had no intention of trying to stop him suddenly. I thought he would pass me; but, no, he struck with his forefeet and caught me with his teeth on my right thigh. When his teeth slipped off my leg, their hitting together sounded like a sprung steel-trap. Pants, skin and a little flesh came off. I had a six-shooter on, which I grabbed before he could make another bite or strike again.

As he came for the second charge, I shot. I guess the flash of the pistol right in his face scared him. He turned. I had missed his head, but as he turned I shot again. This time I hit him near the root of the tail. He went to the end of the rope with all his might, jerked my horse down. I fell clear, but here he came back full speed, ears back and mouth open, ready for the kill. By then Keys had crossed the creek and was out on top. He jumped off his horse, had his Winchester out and shot. He hit the stallion in the shoulder, breaking it. That stopped him. The next shot hit square in the head. He fell within a few feet of me. My horse was still tied to him.

There's not the slightest doubt that if Keys had not come up at the right time, the stallion would have killed me. There was not much chance for me to get to the bluff.

We went back to camp; by the time we got there my boot was full of blood. Our cook was an old soldier of the Civil War; he got some hot water, well salted, and bathed the wound and kept hot blankets on it. My leg turned black, but I guess the hot salt water and the amount of blood I had lost kept down infection. I limped around for a few days but was soon all right. The scar is still plain to be seen.

I shall never forget seeing this stallion with his mouth open and ears set back and eyes like balls of fire. I have roped some bad grown bulls, but they are nothing to a wild, savage stallion. He was, I believe, the most vicious animal on four legs, the most deadly fighter of them all.

V. THE GHOST OF THE LLANO ESTACADO

In every locality where I rode during mustang days there was always, somewhere in the country, a wonderful stallion. Sometimes he would be a gray, sometimes a paint, or a black with white legs, and nearly all of these noted animals were—according to the accounts—natural pacers. For a hundred years writers have been writing about a pacing white stallion seen in various parts of the West at various times, always out-pacing anything that took after him. I was never acquainted with this fabulous steed, but I did come to know very well a white mustang stallion that ranged on the Llano Estacado in the late seventies and early eighties. He became known as the Ghost of the Llano Estacado. No man's hand ever touched his beautiful hide.

In the spring of 1878 there were few buffaloes left on the Staked Plains, where I had been hunting them for four years. The Indians had been rounded up, too, and now cattlemen from New Mexico, Colorado, Kansas, and all parts of Texas to the south and east began pouring into the finest cow country that ever lay out of doors. I knew the country from the Conchos north to Dodge City and from the upper prongs of the Brazos River west to the Pecos. I hired to Coggin and Wylie to pilot two big herds of Jingle Bob cattle from John Chisum's empire on the Pecos River in New Mexico to the promised land in Texas. We turned them loose on my old hunting grounds along Tongue River in Motley County, and here I remained for three years. Along in March of 1879 I heard that there was a bunch of cattle on Running Water, about seventy-five miles northwest of our range. As we had come this route from the Pecos, I though maybe the cattle might be ours, trying to drift back home. I picked a man named Dick Lane to go with me. We packed a mule and, with two horses each, set out to investigate.

After we got on the plains above the Cap Rock, we were seldom out of sight of bands of mustangs. Riding on past where the town of Plainview now is, we began to see many carcasses of horses along with carcasses of coyotes and lobos. Then about ten miles on up the draw, we came to the camp of Bob Payne, a buffalo hunter I knew well. He told us that the cattle we were after belonged to another outfit, over on the Quitaque. We staked and hobbled our horses and settled down to spend the night. Payne had killed only a few buffalo during the winter and had taken to poisoning wolves for their pelts. Horse meat makes the best wolf bait in the world, and Payne had been shooting mustangs for bait.

That night we all got to talking about mustangs, always a subject for conversation and yarns in camp. Payne said: "There is a young white stallion running from the headwater of this branch to the Black Water Draw south, and over to the Tierra Blanca north. He's the fastest and wildest animal on the plains. He's no native mustang—he's a Thoroughbred; I have been close to him and tried for two years to catch him. I killed his mother near my camp at the head spring."

Here is his account of the Ghost of the Llano Estacado. He was a big stout man of about forty-five—always wore a full beard. No one ever doubted his word.

"I was hunting on this water the winter of 1877. There was a big band of mustangs running near Spring Lake. I noticed particularly a white mare and her yearling, also white. She always seemed to run near the lead but a little to one side. Later she left this bunch of horses and seemed to stay alone most of the time—just her and her white yearling horse colt. I got fairly close to her several times; got a good look at her through my glasses. I then saw she was a saddle mare. The main color was white, but she was 'flea-bitten'—red specks all over her. You could not call her a paint, just speckled all over. She didn't belong to this mane-to-the-knees, tail-dragging-the-ground stock. She looked like a Thoroughbred—thin mane and tail, good legs and feet, a little under fifteen hands. Her yearling was snow white and well-grown for a yearling past—just like the mare—tail thin, short ears, standing well on his legs and keeping them under him.

"I did not get all this the first time I looked at them, but every time I saw them I took another good look. The more I looked, the more I wanted that white colt. I was busy killing and could not take time to try and catch them. Later, when I thought I would try, she had left. The next fall I was there but did not see them. But this last winter she was back. She had a filly, about a yearling, a regular paint. With so few buffalo, I commenced to poison wolves, killing mustangs for bait.

"The stallion colt was still with the mare, past three years old now. He'd grown taller than his mammy, better than fifteen hands. I tried every way to get them to take up with my horses, but no good. That white colt was wild—could run like an antelope."

Here Bob Payne stopped and asked, "Did you every try to crease a horse?"

"Yes," I said, "a good many, but never did. I always either broke their necks or shot too high—through the root of the mane."

"Well, that's my luck," he said. "But I have heard that if you would shoot a horse through the thick of his ham, not too high and behind the thigh bone, and let him run off, he'd be so stiff the next day he couldn't run off, and a man could catch him easy."

I told Payne I had never tried that; it might work.

"Well," he said, "I tried; it didn't work. I went out and maneuvered around until I could get a shot to suit me and not hit the horse colt. I got fairly close, not over two hundred yards. I had my rest sticks, and it looked like I ought to hit a dollar that close. Well, I cut loose. At the crack of the gun the mare fell. I got to her as quick as I could, but she was about dead when I got there. I had hit her thigh bone, mashed it all to pieces. She bled to death."

"How did you come to make such a poor shot?" I asked.

"Damned if I know. Only I guess the yearling filly must have nipped her and she backed up just as I touched the trigger. [All Sharp's rifles had set triggers.] But she was dead. I had a good look at her. Yes, she was a saddle mare, had saddle marks on her back. Well, I went back to camp and cussed the gun, then looked at the sight and cussed all the mustangs on the plains. I would try and crease the next time. Well, I went back. The filly was near the mare; the white colt ran off. So I thought I would try and crease the filly. Which I did; broke her neck. She was a nice filly but not to compare with the horse colt. I went back the next day; thought I would try another shot at the colt. He was watching me a mile off. I started towards him, but he just disappeared. I have not seen him since, never will again unless he goes to Montana or Canada."

I said, "You had a good look at the mare and at the stallion. Was he what they call an albino?"

GEORGE CATLIN IN *North American Indians,* 1841

"What the hell is albino?"

I said, "Was he glass-eyed and his eyes run water?"

"No, his eyes were black. Also his eyelashes. I looked at the mare good and was close to the colt and could see him good. No, in my opinion, some of those Mexican buffalo hunters brought her here from Mexico to run buffalo on. She was fast, but slow to that colt of hers. She might have been what they call a Arab. Bred in Mexico, ran away up here to have her colt, and they never saw her again.

"Do you see that ox wagon loaded ready to start for Dodge? There's three hundred buffalo hides on the wagon and trail. It will take six yoke of cattle to pull that load to Dodge. I would give the whole outfit for that white three-year-old stallion. I do not believe he will ever be caught alive."

Old Bob was right. The next morning I told him good-bye and rode back to Tongue River. It was Dodge City, Kansas, for Payne. From there he went north, and I never saw him again.

I have already spoken of the Trujillo brothers, Pedro and Soledad, and described the way they came out on the plains each spring and captured mustang colts. In May, 1880, I had to go to Fort Sumner, on the Pecos, to pass on some high grade bulls. On the way back to Tongue River, I came upon the Trujillo outfit camped at Los Portales—not a town, just a place marking a pass—The Portals. I stopped to camp with them for the night.

Naturally we talked about mustangs. I asked them how far east they were going—if they got out on the Llano Estacado proper.

"Yes," Pedro Trujillo answered, "I was over on the Cañon Blanco years ago. If the mustangs are ranging east of the New Mexico line, we go where they are most plentiful."

I then said, "Have you been as far as Spring Lake lately?"

"Yes, I was through this spring. Caught a few good colts this side on Black Water Draw." (They called it Agua Negra.)

I said, "Did you ever see or hear of a white stallion that waters in Spring Lake or any place in that part of the country? He should now be going on five years old."

"Yes, I sure have seen that horse, and that's about all. We call him the Ghost. There is not a mustang hunter from Fort Sumner to Puerta de Luna but what has tried to catch him. There's a lot of good fast horses among these mustang hunters, but so far no one has been able to crowd the Ghost. If they do, he just quits the *manada* and disappears. He's the wildest and fastest horse on the Llanos."

I said, "I can't get away at present, but the first time I can, I will come over and we will give him a run for the money."

Pedro said he sure would like to have a regular hunt for him. So we agreed to try, if he was not caught or killed in the meantime.

Well, in May, 1881, the Tongue River outfit sold to the Matador Land and Cattle Company—the only big British ranch left operating in Texas today. My pardners and I bought out a brand of cattle on Duck Creek in Dickens County and added other cattle to the stock. After the fall work was over and everything seemed well located for the winter, I decided to go over to Fort Sumner and arrange with the Trujillo brothers to hunt the Ghost next spring. A man by the name of Dockum who had a small store on what is still called Dockum Flats was operating a mail line to Colorado City and offered to loan me one of his old rattletrap buckboards. We had plenty of good horses; so I put in some bedding and chuck and hitched up and struck out. There never was better grass than on the plains that fall; nobody could need any feed. I covered the two hundred miles in less than a week.

Old Beaver Smith ran a saloon in Fort Sumner and I went to see him to hear all the news and ask if the Trujillos were well. "Yes," he said, "they are all right and they come down here from their little ranch every day or so." The very next day I saw Pedro Trujillo. He was still anxious to go on the hunt. We agreed to meet at a spring he called Gato Montes on Black Water Draw the following March. Pedro said he would have some good grain-fed horses and we'd give the Ghost the run of his life.

Early in March—1882 now—I left our camp on Duck Creek. Dick Lane, who had been with me three years before when Bob Payne told us about the white stallion, was with me again. It was about a hundred and fifty miles to where we were to meet the Trujillos. On two pack horses we carried bedding, grain and a two weeks' supply of grub. Each of us led an extra horse, all four of the mounts being grain-fed.

The Trujillos were waiting for us. They had already located where the Ghost was watering with a big *manada* of mares. Pedro Trujillo thought it best to start the mustangs and first follow them wherever they went. We knew they would circle back, no matter how far they ran. Pedro was to take the first run, the balance of us to keep a lookout, the first to see him, when he circled back, to take his place, and so on until the *manada* commenced to give out. Most of the mares were near foaling time.

Our agreement was that the Trujillos were to have any and all the mares and young stock we got and that I was to have the white stallion if he proved to be the horse he was said to be, by paying half the price we agreed on. If he turned out to be just a common white horse, I did not want him at any price. I had seen the horse several times when out on the plains but never closer than a mile. I was now—within a few days at least—to see him at close quarters. Early on a fine bright morning, we pulled out for his range, soon found the bunch we were looking for, and the chase was on. The mustangs were quickly out of sight, Pedro after them. We scattered around for several miles. Soledad Trujillo had brought a long slim pole, with a red flag on the top. This he stuck up near where the mustangs were feeding when first started.

Well, we saw no more of mustangs or Pedro that day. By daybreak next morning, we were scattered for ten miles or more in every direction. Just about sun-up, Dick Lane and I saw a big dust to the northwest and soon the mustangs came in sight. Dick was anxious to make the next run. Away he went. Pedro reported that the band had run straight north at least twenty miles before they stopped, then circled to the west. It got dark long before they turned back to their own range. He followed them as best as he could. Toward day they stopped, grazed a while. Pedro rested his horse, but by daylight was after them again. He estimated he had followed them at least seventy miles or more. We saw no more of Dick Lane that day. He came into camp late, said the band was stopped near Spring Lake.

I was the next to make the run. I was riding a big bay horse I had bought from a cattle trader the year before. He claimed this horse was the best stayer he ever owned. The only reason he had for selling him was that the horse had thrown him several times, and he was afraid of him. He had once ridden him from Fort Worth to Brownwood and never unsaddled him—a distance on one hundred and forty miles. He was of no particular breeding, just a big, stout, good horse near sixteen hands high. He was grain-fed and had seen a lot of hard riding all winter. So, mounted on this horse, I knew I was good for a hundred miles behind any band of mustangs on the plains.

The Trujillos went with me until we found the horses. Along with the Trujillos, were two *vaqueros* they had working with them and also a half-breed Apache Indian who did most of their roping. He was a light, small man, rode bareback, with just a tanned rawhide surcingle laced tight around his horse, a loop of rawhide laced on each side for stirrups. He stuck his big toes in these loops, and that was all the seat he had. He had a piece of inch rope, wrapped with a strip of old blanket, tied around his horse's neck. To this collar he had one end of his riata tied. The arrangement was all right for colts and small stock, but for this stallion I could not see how it would work. But he was willing to try.

After the mustangs started, the Trujillos and their outfit were to catch any that were too stiff and sore to make much of a run. I did not crowd them for the first few miles, but after my horse warmed up to the run and had pretty well emptied himself, I struck a long lope and kept them going. They crossed Running Water above Bob Payne's old camp and kept on north. About noon we got to Tulia Draw, the south prong of Red River, and went on west. I had seen several bands of mustangs, but they did not mix with the band I was running. It was not a run all the time. The mustangs would slack down, trot a while, then lope, then make another run, and so the day passed. My horse did not appear to tire much. The mares kept falling out.

Towards evening the stallion turned south again, but still kept up the same speed. I had a small compass in my pocket and kept the course we were running all the time. Still the

Ghost kept up his flight. By late evening very few mares were left—not over eight or ten. A little before sundown I could see a ridge of sand hills I knew, west from where Hale Center is now. That was the first sand I had seen that day. After passing through this sand, I followed until I knew we were near Black Water Draw, but well above our camp. The band wanted to stop; so I quit following them, unsaddled and let my horse graze. I had been following them since seven A. M. and it was now near nine P. M. I had traveled at least seventy or eighty miles. I wrapped up in the wet saddle blanket and slept fairly well, but was up and ready to start by the time I could see.

The mares were all lying down, but the Ghost was on his feet and down the draw he led the few mares, mostly in a trot. By nine, I came in sight of the camp. The stallion then took a southeast course toward Eagle Spring, only three mares with him. I told Soledad he had better try them a turn. The stallion, I was sure, would soon be alone. He appeared to be in good shape. Soledad took out after him. I ate a little and changed horses. We all struck south for Yellow House Lake. Near noon we saw the Ghost coming straight west again, Soledad half a mile behind. It looked as if the stallion was trying to go north of the Yellow House, into the Bull Lake country.

We headed him off and he struck due south. We spread out and followed the Indian, now on the fastest horse the Trujillos owned. Pedro was running on the west; I was right behind the Indian, making straight for the Yellow House Lake. This lake is one of the big alkali sinks, or basins, on the Staked Plains. Nothing will drink this water. The lake is white as snow, generally a few inches of water on top. Under this white surface is a black, bottomless alkali bog. Nothing can cross these lakes after a rain but a coyote or wild cat. Broken ridges run right out into Yellow House Lake, the alkali bog coming up to their bases.

The white stallion took right down one of these backbones that stop abruptly in the lake. No doubt he was lost at last, or confused by desperation. Any direction to get away from these pursuers, the only animals he had ever been afraid of. After nearly four days of constant travel, he was still ahead of their fresh horses. I felt sure he would turn back when he saw this big alkali bog hole; but no, on he went, the Indian ready to make a catch whenever he checked.

He came to the bluff, the white bog in front and on each side. He never even checked. He made one tremendous jump, struck this bog at least twenty-five or thirty feet from the foot of the bluff, which was fully twenty or twenty-five feet high. I heard the splash when he hit the white bog. When, a few second later, I got up to where I could see over beneath the bluff, the stallion was nearly out of sight, his head and neck still sticking up, but with every flounder he made, he sank deeper, his nostrils full of the foul alkali mud. He shook his head and coughed a few times and it was all over. The Ghost of the Llano Estacado was dead and sinking out of sight.

By then all hands were on the bluff and I guess they felt as I did, not very proud of our work.

I have seen a good many Arab horses and I believe this white stallion on the Llano Estacado of Texas was a descendant of the true Nefdee strain of Arabian. The Nefdee stallions and mares have a record for keeping up a lope on desert sands for twenty-four hours at a time in hot weather, and for forty-eight hours in cold weather, without a drop of water. The only colors of this strain are, first, sorrel or chestnut;

and, second, white or grey. Very few sorrels were ever exported. The late General Don Luis Terrazas of Chihuahua and Don Carlos Zuluago of the Rancho Bustillos, Chihuahua, both very rich ranchmen when in the heyday of their careers, imported a good many Arabs. There was a friendly rivalry as to which had the best. The dam of this Ghost of the Plains may have come from one or the other of these ranches. I saw several of their importations and hundreds of their own raising.

But I never saw one I liked as I did this wild horse of the plains. He had been foaled on the best natural horse range in the world, the best curly mesquite or buffalo grass that ever grew, in climatic conditions that cannot be equalled in any other part of the world that I ever saw or heard of. He had grown bigger than the ordinary run of his stock. After having been run for about three hundred miles by five or six good grain-fed horses, he could, at the time of his fatal jump into Yellow House Lake, have easily run away from any horse chasing him. Had we taken more time and worn him out, I doubt that we ever could have captured him alive.

I have known several mustang stallions, when they saw their mares giving out and being roped and hobbled, to turn and fight so that they had to be shot. The Ghost did not once offer to fight any of his chasers—perhaps additional evidence of his fine blood.

Mustanging on the Staked Plains, 1887

By Homer Hoyt*

IN THE SUMMER of 1886 Bob and Tom Hightower went to
the Panhandle of Texas, chased around all summer and
caught nothing, although they both were first class wild-horse
men. The reason for failure was shortage of saddle stock. In
the spring of 1887 the brothers asked me to join them, as
I had several saddle horses. We went overland to Tascosa,
Texas, a frontier town on the South Canadian River, where
Bob's wife and baby were. I also took my wife to Tascosa,
where we left our families. Tom was a single man then. There
was no railroad at that time, everything being freighted from
Dodge City, Kansas, two hundred and twenty miles away.
We caught our horses that summer about seventy-five miles
south of Tascosa, south of Tierra Blanca Creek, and south-
west of the present city of Amarillo.

First, I must describe the habits of the wild horses. Nearly
all the stories I have read state that the band was led by a stallion, frequently a pacer that could not be made to break the
pacing gait. Such writers are writing from hearsay or drawing upon their too vivid imagination. I have never seen a
pacer among the wild stallions; and a stallion never leads. He
is a tyrant and goes behind and drives his harem where he
chooses. The harem usually consists of from one to eight
mares exclusive of colts and yearlings. In earlier days, before

*Reprinted in part through courtesy of the State Historical Society of Colorado, from
The Colorado Magazine, Denver, XI, No. 2 (March, 1934), 41-45.

96

my time, the bands were larger. Young males are driven from the harem at the age of two. The sexes are about equally divided. Ninety per cent of the horses are bay, dark brown, or black; other colors are rare.

Only the strongest stallions can maintain a harem. When a stallion begins to get old, some younger one will try to take his harem. Then a bloody battle ensues. If the older horse is vanquished and not killed outright, he will wander away into solitude, crestfallen and broken in spirit. When he is rested and his wounds are healed, sometimes he will hunt up his harem and try to retake it. This he is seldom able to do. He will then wander away into solitude until, when he has grown old and feeble, some younger stallion will kill him. It is a matter of the survival of the fittest. A stallion is the most vicious and cruel fighter that I know.

The Staked Plains of Texas appear to be a vast level expanse; however, every mile or two there are depressions from

STAMPEDE OF THE TRAIN BY WILD HORSES.

A. Hoppen in John R. Bartlett's *Personal Narrative*, 1854

ten to one hundred acres in extent called lake beds. The spring rains settle in these. In the spring of 1887 the water was from six inches to two feet deep in these depressions.

Now for the real campaign. The equipment of the rider consists of a bed blanket of wool used as a saddle blanket and for sleeping purposes when the rider is caught out too far from camp, a thirty-foot saddle rope, a canteen of water, field glasses, sandwiches, and a grass hobble, usually carried around the horse's neck while riding.

The rider is ready to start at daylight after having located the herd the day previous and watched them from a distance through his field glasses until dark. We will suppose that there are twenty in the herd, made up of four or five harems. There will be a little space between each harem. When the rider comes in sight, one or two stallions will advance a few yards, raising their heads as high as possible to get a better look. The stallion is very polite—he will bow two or three times. This is done to focus his eyes on the object of his gaze. He will then give a big snort, almost a whistle, as he starts for the herd. He drops his head to within a foot of the ground, sticks his nose straight out in front, lays his ears flat on his neck, shows his teeth to his harem, and they are off.

The rider had better not be riding a plug draft horse if he expects to keep within sight of the dust. He may start with twenty horses, but before night he may have forty or sixty head. Other horses, seeing the herd running across the plains, will join them. The rider keeps them moving all day, but by mid-afternoon some of the very young colts will begin to lag. The mothers will keep calling to the colts, but if a mare should slip by a stallion and run back to the colt, the stallion will be right after her, bringing her back to the herd and biting her as often as he can get within reach.

Unlike cattle, horses do not like to leave their accustomed range. They seldom go more than ten or fifteen miles in one direction before circling back. Should the herd pass within two or three miles of camp, the rider will go in to get a fresh saddle horse, something to eat, a canteen of water, and more sandwiches. He then overtakes the herd as soon as possible and follows them until dark. Now he lets them drift into a lake bed for the night. The field glasses which he carries are night glasses so that he can watch them until they are well settled. Then he takes the back track a mile or more. If he should bed down near the herd, his saddle horse would whinny and call the wild ones to him in the night. This would stampede them all.

The rider removes the saddle for a pillow, takes the grass hobble from around his horse's neck and puts it on his front legs. One end of his rope is now fastened to his horse; his arm is put through the loop at the other end. But he must be sure that the rope cannot draw tight on his arm. He next wraps up in the saddle blanket, which will be soaked with sweat, and lies down to pleasant dreams—if he can. The next morning he starts the herd as soon as it is light enough to see. If any show signs of splitting off, he hurries them a little faster; the more tired they are, the better they stay together.

The rider should change horses as often as possible and riders should be relieved as often as convenient. After four or five days of about seventy-five miles per day, the horses become tired and will let the rider come within two hundred yards of them. Then every six or eight miles he lets them stop and rest about fifteen minutes. About one day of this and they are ready for a lesson in turning. After a rest, the rider approaches until the horses are about ready to move on; then he rides out at right angles to the general course. The horses will be watching him. He bears in a little closer to them until they turn and start off. Now the rider should drop in behind the horses and follow until they are ready for another rest; then he should repeat the operation but not at too short intervals. Nor should he always turn them the same way; sometimes they should turn to the right, sometimes to the left. As they get more tired, they can be turned more often.

Soon the more exhausted horses will want to stand, while the vigorous ones swing around them. This is called "milling." They should not be allowed to mill long in one direction. They can now be milled all day and all night; but it is necessary to give them a chance to drink occasionally; otherwise they will become unmanageable. When they are very tired, the rider can get close to them. Now is the time for clog-chains to be put on.

A clog-chain is a chain twenty inches long, the links being made of three-eighths inch iron. An iron band which goes around the ankle is made of three-fourths inch iron, flat on one side, half round on the other. The round side goes next to the ankle. The band is made into about three-fourths of a circle, the chain fastened to one end and the ring to the other. When on the ankle, the chain is run through the ring, completing the circle. The band, being of iron and stiff, cannot draw tight and make the ankle sore as a leather strap does. The chain is then allowed to drag or swing. It wraps itself around the forelegs and throws the horse if he attempts to run.

It takes three men to put the clog-chains on. To do this, all the saddle horses not in use should be near a lake bed. The mill herd should be brought near a pile of clog-chains about two hundred yards from the bed. Two men get their ropes ready; a third is detailed to take the herd some distance away when a horse is roped. A horse roped by the neck will choke until he falls. His feet having been tied quickly, a clog is put on one front foot. The other front foot and the hind foot on the same side should be side-lined about three feet apart. The horse can then be released and put with the saddle horses.

The first horse caught should be the stallion with the largest harem. Then his harem should all be caught and put with him. All stallions are castrated at the time the clogs are put on. When all the herd have been clogged except the yearlings and two-year-olds, and some of the weaker ones, the herd is brought to within fifty yards of the tent door at sunrise and kept there until noon. Then the man in charge will whistle to them and start them toward the lake to drink and graze for one hour and a half. He then brings them back to the same place to stand until sundown, when they are started to the lake to spend the night. This procedure is repeated every day, the reason being that if the horses graze all day, they will wander away at night. But if they are kept hungry all day, they will graze at night and not be far away in the morning.

In this manner in the summer of 1887 we made three catches, the first of thirty-three head, the second of fifty-two, and the third of eighty-one. The real wild horse of the Staked Plains in those years was the wildest, hardiest, and fleetest of all the creatures of the earth. No one without experience can easily realize this.

Black Kettle

By Frank M. Lockard[*]

I. Black Kettle Becomes a Legend

O N A DAY in June, 1867, a wagon train owned by Mormons was passing west over the old Smoky Hill Trail. They carried with them a bunch of Kentucky Thoroughbred horses, which they were taking to Salt Lake for breeding purposes. Somewhere near the west line of Logan County, Kansas, Black Kettle and a band of Cheyenne Indians swooped down upon them, stampeded the stock which was grazing near camp, and left the Mormons with their loaded wagons and nothing to pull them.

Among these horses was a fine yearling stud colt that escaped from the Indians and joined the wild horses, which were plentiful on the prairie at that time. In the course of time this colt developed into one of the finest specimens of the equine family. Nothing to compare with him had ever been this far west. The Indians tried many times to capture him, and it was from them that the white men learned his history. The white men around Fort Wallace would speak of him as the Black Kettle colt, a name which stuck during his long life. His range, until he was thirteen years old, was in central Sherman County, where the city of Goodland now stands. During those years the old government road, known

---

*A reprint—omitting some material not pertinent to the subject—of a pamphlet, *Black Kettle* (forty pages), by Frank M. Lockard, published and copyrighted by R. G. Wolfe, Goodland, Kansas, in 1924.

as Custer Road, ran through the center of Black Kettle's range and was much traveled by military authorities and also buffalo hunters, who sold their hides and bought their supplies at Peter Robidoux's store at the old fort. Very few ever traveled that road without seeing Black Kettle, and by the time he was five or six years old he was known to hundreds of men.

I first learned of Black Kettle through a newspaper story written by Honorable W. D. Street, of Decatur County, and published about 1878. From the first I was greatly interested in Black Kettle. Well do I remember clipping that story out of the paper and carrying it in a vest pocket until I wore it out. What I have written concerning the early history of Black Kettle I remember from that clipping. I wish I had it now, as it told many interesting incidents that have passed from my memory.

Street was an old plainsman and buffalo hunter and was well known in Norton County. He died at Oberlin a few years ago. When I first knew him, his long auburn curls reached his shoulders; he was proud of his hair and took as much pains with it as the society belle of the effete East. Dressed in buckskins and wearing Indian moccasins, he was a conspicuous figure in any assemblage. He had been a soldier in the Nineteenth Kansas and was with Custer on the Sweetwater in Northwest Texas when Mrs. Morgan and Miss White, Kansas women, were rescued from the Cheyennes. He served several terms in the Kansas Legislature and was speaker in 1894. He became a buffalo hunter in 1870 and continued in that occupation until the buffalo became extinct fifteen years later.

Black Kettle's chief distinction was his long mane and tail. His heavy tail was so long that more than a foot of it rested on the ground when he was standing still; and when he was running, it stuck straight out behind—making him appear to be about twenty feet long, when viewed from a distance. His mane reached nearly to the ground when he stood erect, and when he was in motion, with his head up, it lay along his back, making him appear about a foot higher than he really was. When he ran he was continually tossing his head. This movement puzzled me at first, but I soon discovered that he was throwing his foretop over his ears so he could see. That foretop, which reached below the end of his nose, completely shut off his vision when in its natural place. He was coal black and his glossy coat glistened like burnished silver; his movements were as graceful as the fawn, while for speed and endurance he excelled any other animal on these plains.

Wild horses ran in small bands, usually eight to ten in a bunch, all of them mares, except one, the leader. I have seen many bunches of twenty or more and when I first saw Black Kettle, in 1879, he had twenty-nine mares, which is the largest band I ever saw. There were only two colors, black and roan. Nearly all the mares were red roan. There was an occasional blue roan, but the latter at a distance looked black; and when on occasion we saw a bay, iron-gray or white, we always knew that they were animals that had escaped from immigrants or cattlemen. Among the females about one in ten was black, while the percentage of roans among the males was a little higher than that. The surplus males were driven out by the leaders and flocked by themselves, usually one, two and sometimes three together. There were hundreds of them on this prairie when I first came. These outcasts were called "dog soldiers" by the Indians, and the white men used the same name in describing them. The same name is used in describing an outcast among the Indians. A dog soldier had only one ambition, and that was to get a family of his own. They haunted the herds day and night, and the stud who had a family was compelled to keep up a continuous fight or lose them. For the most part these dog soldiers were roan and old blacks that could not fight any more. A roan with a bunch of mares was seldom seen. To be born a roan meant that a horse was doomed to celibacy. I suppose that was nature's way of providing for "the survival of the fittest."

For more than ten years Black Kettle was a conspicuous mark on this prairie. He was chased more often than any other horse. I have talked with men who knew him long before I saw him. Most of them had at some time tried to catch him. An early day captain of Fort Wallace, Homer W. Wheeler[1] by name, conceived the idea of using the U. S. cavalry to aid in catching him. He came out with his company and surrounded Black Kettle one night. He had a scope of prairie about the size of a township in the circle with a soldier every half mile. His plan was to chase him inside the circle by sending in a fresh horse every hour and finally late in the day, when he was exhausted, to send in a cowboy and rope him. But Black Kettle went through that circle before he made the first revolution. Then Captain Wheeler marched back to the post. Shortly after this, while in the Robidoux store, Captain Wheeler was telling experiences in the presence of Ame Cole and others and wound up his story by offering two hundred dollars to any one who would bring him that horse, properly attached to the end of a rope. Here is where Ame Cole gets into the story.

---

[1]In 1923 Colonel Homer W. Wheeler's autobiography, *The Frontier Trail, or From Cowboy to Colonel*, was issued in Los Angeles. In 1925 it came out with some changes under the title of *Buffalo Days*. Although Wheeler tells of many episodes connected with horses, cattle, buffalo, etc., during his stay at Fort Wallace, he does not in either edition of his book mention trying to capture mustangs.—Editor.

"By G—d, Captain, I can walk the tail off the G— d—m horse in five days." And as Cole afterwards related the circumstances to me, Captain Wheeler replied by saying: "I consider the tail the most valuable part of the horse and would not give much for him without it." When Cole left Wallace the next morning it was his intention to catch Black Kettle and return in about one week. Many of my readers knew Ame Cole more intimately that I did; however, Cole as I knew him might interest even those who knew him best.

It was about fifty years ago that I first met him. He was then a comparatively young man. His reputation as a buffalo hunter and a long distance pedestrian had already been established. He had hunted the buffalo alongside of Cody and Comstock and other celebrities and beaten them. Only his modesty prevented the whole world from knowing him. After Buffalo Bill and Dr. Carver were known around the globe, Ame Cole said: "I have shot agin 'em both and beat 'em." He seemed to seek solitude. I have heard it said that while hunting he never made camp near other hunters if he could help it. Vanmeter once said, "I have hunted for days within hearing of Ame Cole's gun, yet I never saw him." After the buffalo disappeared, these men lived for many years within twenty miles of each other and never met. This shows the seclusion of Cole, because Vanmeter was a globe trotter and at one time or other had seen every man on the Prairie Dog except Cole.

I loved to hear Cole talk. There was something attractive about his voice. His profanity was so natural and unassuming that it soon ceased to be offensive. I do not think he was conscious of it. He did not know many words in our bully old language or, at least, he did not use many, and it seemed he could not express himself without a swear word in every sentence. It was all a habit and I suppose he acquired it when he learned to talk. It was part of his greeting when he met you and the last thing you heard when he departed. His mind was not well disciplined. I do not know as that expresses exactly what I am trying to tell you or not; anyway if you were trying to discuss something that did not interest him, his mind at times seemed far away. At the time I prepared the "History of Norton County," I went to see him. Jim Hall of Almena went with me. We spent most of the day and ate dinner with him. There were several early day incidents that I knew he was familiar with, but I got nothing from him. When I would ask him something about a certain incident that occurred in 1872, he would say, "Oh, that (accompanied with the usual profanity) don't amount to anything." He then would commence a long story about the Indian war in Minnesota. Of course, I would explain that the Minnesota story was interesting, but that I was trying to write a history of Norton County. "Oh, pitch to it to h-ll," he answered. "Nothing important ever happened here; drop it and write a history of Minnesota and I will tell you all about it." Of course, he told the Black Kettle story, which interested Jim Hall because he had never heard it, but he had told me that story many times before that. . . .

Cole came to Kansas in 1866. He passed up the Prairie Dog on a buffalo hunt and camped for a short time on the land he afterward homesteaded and where he lived for more than fifty years. This was the northwest part of Phillips County. He returned to Minnesota but came back bringing his brother, George, with him. His eccentricities furnished a topic for conversation among the early settlers. His house was part dugout and part logs. On the top of the bank the logs were set back some, making a convenient shelf, on which

he kept a veritable museum. On this shelf he had the skulls
of many Indians. Some of these he had picked up on the Big
Sandy, where Colonel Chivington with the First Colorado had
fought Black Kettle some time previous. Later he got another
supply at Beecher Island. These skulls he used for candle
sticks and at times when lonesome he kept many candles
going the whole night through to drive away the evil spirits.
At other times he would set them up for a target and shoot
at them until he wore them out. He had a footlog across the
creek near his house. This footlog was charmed, and when
the Indians started across they dropped off and rose no more.
Many times he sat in his door which faced the creek and
watched the Indians disappear in the surging waters, which
was about one foot deep at that point. Frank Whitaker tells
this one: "One day as I approached the house I heard shooting. Cole was running around the house at top speed and each
round as he passed the door he would shoot at a tree which
stood near. Afterwards he examined the tree to see if he had
made a hit." He told Frank that old "Blazeface" was watching him from that tree. "Blazeface" was an Indian that Cole
said was spying on him. At another time he cut a hole in
the ice and stuck his gun in and never recovered it. He did
this to compromise with old "Blazeface," who appeared to
him in a dream and ordered it done. The weird stories he told
I always thought were for his own amusement, but many
thought him demented. He seemed to enjoy the discomforts
of his neighbors, especially women and children, but he was
as harmless as a dove. Cole suffered Indian depredations in
Minnesota and never lost an opportunity to show his con-
tempt for the "noble red men." His army service for the most
part was on the frontier in driving the Sioux across the
Missouri into western Nebraska. Frank Whitaker was a small

boy at that time, but he makes a wry face yet when describing the grinning skulls of our aborigine brethren that faced him whenever he entered the Cole dugout in those days.

He was part of the frontier; this country before the white men came here suited him, and if he could have had his way it would not have changed. The dry, lean years that came with the early settlers confirmed him in the belief that this country was made for the Indians and buffaloes; so he sat in his cabin and waited for the settlers to leave and the buffalo to return. Conditions as they exist today could not produce such a man as Cole; his type is extinct and will not be seen again.

Before I tell you of his experiences with Black Kettle, another incident comes to my mind. When I first knew Cole he had a partner by the name of Grant, who owned and drove a four-mule team. Cole did the shooting while Grant and a hired man did the skinning and delivered the hides to market. While they were in camp on the Beaver in Sherman County, a roan dog soldier slipped in and drove away their four mules. The men knew at once that they must shoot that horse before they could recover the mules. Cole started after them on foot, expecting to finish the job in a short time. In telling about it afterwards he said: "I think I walked one thousand miles in the next two weeks trying to get a shot at that stud, but he was smart enough to keep a mule between us, so I dared not shoot." However, he finally killed the horse and recovered the mules, but it was the longest and most tiresome tramp he ever experienced. After that he always shot every dog soldier that came within range. Other hunters and stockmen did the same but still the prairie was alive with them until the settlers came, and then they frequently drove away the work horses belonging to the hunters and settlers and but few of them were ever recovered. Cole thought his experience in recapturing those mules fitted him for the more exciting game of catching Black Kettle.

When Cole left Fort Wallace, his plan was to crease Black Kettle and then hobble him before he woke up. (A shot through the top of the neck just in front of the withers would temporarily paralyze but not permanently injure a horse and was called "creasing.") But his partner, Grant, was opposed to fooling away any time on so uncertain a project. "Buffalo are plentiful on the river and might move on any time. Let us get a load of hides while we can." But Cole was obdurate, and the chase was on.

The wild horse can see, hear and smell a man farther than any other animal, and this country being flat and unbroken, it was only on rare occasions that you could get closer than one mile to a horse. As there were bands of them at frequent intervals, a man would be seen by some of them before he could get very close. And as soon as a man was seen by one, all others within a few miles knew it and were on the alert. Wild horses never move very far from their watering place and when being chased they run in a circle and never leave the home range. Usually that circle was small, as they never went more than ten miles to water. But Black Kettle had been chased so much that he became unusually smart and would sometimes run twenty miles in a straight line when badly scared. Another unusual thing, he had two watering places, one in the Wild Horse Draw, near the Smoky, and the other in a waterhole on the head of the Beaver. These two waterholes were twenty miles apart as the crow flies. Had Cole known this fact on the start, I might have a different story to write, but he learned it later.

I would like to tell you the remaining part of this story in

Cole's dialect but I can't; so I give it in my own poor way. He found Black Kettle on a high prairie about ten miles southeast of Goodland. Black Kettle ran northwest, and in the course of an hour passed out of sight. Cole followed at a brisk walk and at times in a trot, until he felt sure he had gone as far as that band would go in that direction. Far away on the horizon, in all directions, he could see horses, but as he had no field glasses, he was uncertain which was his bunch. So he turned west and, after following a band until late in the afternoon, he found he was after the wrong horse. He turned toward camp feeling sure that Black Kettle would come to the Smoky for water sometime during the afternoon. Cole reached camp late, hungry and nearly famished for water; and as he put it, "the only real quarrel I ever had with my partner occurred that night."

Early next morning he started out to locate Black Kettle. All day he tramped up and down the Smoky watching for him to come down, but night finally came and Black Kettle had not been seen, although many bands were sighted. That night Grant said: "Tomorrow we leave for the Republican," and Cole reluctantly gave in. The next afternoon as they drew near the Beaver, they unexpectedly came upon Black Kettle. Cole wanted to try him again, but Grant would not stop. Other hunters joked Cole about it afterward. He took it in good part but insisted that but for Grant he would have got Black Kettle. Cole intended to come back later and catch Black Kettle, but he never found time when he was in the mood.

II. TRIAL-AND-ERROR MUSTANGING

My partner in these days was the late William Simpson. We were dealing in ponies quite extensively, and during the

year of '78-'79 we spent most of our time around Wakeeney.
The first settlement of Trego County came during that time,
and a bunch of Chicago capitalists started the town of
Wakeeney. Warren and Keeney were the promoters and by
putting their names together the name Wakeeney was coined.

New settlers were arriving every day, and the demand for
saddle ponies was brisk. We kept a supply on hand which sold
readily at good prices. We talked of Black Kettle many times
and whenever a buffalo hunter came in from the west our
first inquiry was whether he had seen the horse or not. Our
plans to capture him were discussed a thousand times, for we
were cocksure of getting him later. Our experience in handling broncos had given us a conceited idea that no wild horse
had any show whatever when we started after him.

During the time that we were at Wakeeney, word reached
us that a pair of wild horses ranged on the high plateau, between the South Solomon and Saline. The center of their
range was about twenty-five miles northeast of the town, not
far from the northeast corner of Trego County. We went out
to look them over. We did not expect to catch them but
wanted to study them at close range, hoping to learn something that might be useful later when we got ready to catch
Black Kettle. We found a beautiful pair of roans with a young
colt following them. We chased them for two days but never
got nearer than one mile of them. Their watering place was
at the head of Wild Horse Creek, a tributary of the Solomon.
Because of this the first settlers gave this creek its name. Some
boys from down the river came out later and caught the colts,
but the old ones were still there the last I knew of them,
which was in the fall of 1880.

Late in the fall we returned to our home in Norton and at
once began our preparations for the big wild horse chase.

About December 10, 1879, we started following the Prairie Dog to where the city of Colby now stands. Here we struck a dim road leading southwest which had been made by buffalo hunters going to and from Wallace. We followed this road until we came to a waterhole in a draw, some two or three miles before we reached the Smoky. This was the first water we had seen since leaving the headwater on the Prairie Dog, just north of Dresden. As we had been without water for nearly three days for our horses, we laid up for a day to give them a chance to recuperate. Neither of us had ever been that far west except on the railroad. We had but little idea where we were. The weather had been cloudy with a good deal of fog, with the result that we differed about the direction in which this road was leading us, but while in camp at this waterhole we heard a train pass on the old K. P. and we then knew that we were pointing in the right direction.

Early next morning we came to the Smoky. We turned upstream, knowing that the headwater, which was to be our destination, could not be far off. Late that evening we came to an abandoned frame house, sitting back under a bank. It was only a shell without doors or windows. We afterwards learned that this house belonged to the X Y cattle outfit. There was no one about, and from appearances there had not been for some time. Here we made camp and decided we would investigate. About three miles below we had crossed a wagon road which proved to be the old Custer Road, although we did not know that at the time; in fact, we did not know there was a Custer Road there, or elsewhere, but later discovered that it was the only landmark on this prairie. It served us many times afterward by pointing the way when we became bewildered on this vast expanse of level, flat country. Late that evening we sighted a bunch of buffalo coming into the draw south of camp. Simpson killed one, which supplied our wants in the line of fresh meat for the balance of the trip. This draw, we learned later, was called Wild Horse Draw, and it carries that name today. Next morning we rode south to a high point from which we could see over all the prairie north of the river, and with aid of field glasses we counted more than fifty herds of wild horses. There were more wild horses in Sherman County that day than there are tame ones today. This high point south of the Smoky we named Point Lookout, and it served us in several ways afterward.

Later, we set a post on this point from which waved a red undershirt, which could be seen through a field glass from the high points on the north prairie fifteen miles away. And during the following months signal fires burned many nights near this post to guide us to camp when darkness had caught one of us on the prairie.

We returned to camp, and after dinner we rode out north for the purpose of familiarizing ourselves with lay of the country. We felt sure that we were on Black Kettle's range and expected to see him any time. Several small bunches of horses were scared up and we watched them through the field glass as long as they were in sight. We then observed for the first time that the mares were all roans with a black leader—and each leader looked like Black Kettle to me. But later in the evening, after we had started for camp, Black Kettle himself came in sight. We had heard him described so often that one flash through the field glass settled his identity. That long mane and tail were plainly visible, although he was a mile off. I wanted to start right there and then but Simpson said, "No, it is late, and your horse is jaded now. Wait until morning." This I reluctantly did.

Just what our plans were, if we had any, I have forgotten. We had, in a way, studied wild horses and I suppose we had in mind a complete plan which we thought could not fail, but what it was has escaped my memory. Green and inexperienced as we were, I don't think we expected to rope him on the open prairie; so I think probably we intended to run him down and then drive him to Norton without catching him. So far as we knew, there was no corral within one hundred miles of us and I do not think it ever occurred to us that we would need one. We had talked to many men who had run wild horses but had never heard of anyone catching them except an occasional colt or cripple, but these stories did not discourage us in the least. On that first afternoon we had seen two or three hundred horses in the course of our twenty-five mile ride, and I think we expected to drive them all into our home corral at Norton before spring.

That night at camp our arrangements were gone over for the steenth time and Simpson decided to haul a load of cow chips out to Point Lookout, so that if I failed to return before dark, a signal fire would be burning to light my way home. I weighed one hundred and forty pounds at that time and was hardened to the saddle. I could ride a hundred miles without tiring, and I had corn-fat horses that were as tough as I. At daylight next morning I was in the saddle, and two hours later I found Black Kettle. I started after him on a stiff lope, going at about ten miles an hour and held that same rate of speed for the next ten hours. As darkness closed down around me, I observed I was getting colder. A brisk wind was blowing and I noticed occasional snow flurries, which lasted for a moment. In order to make the load on my horse as light as possible, I had left my overcoat in camp. My plan was to drive Black Kettle toward camp in the late afternoon, and when night came, I expected to go in and get something to eat and mount a fresh horse in the morning. I had crossed the Custer Road two or three times that day but had paid no attention to it, as I felt sure that I knew in what direction I was going. The weather had been pleasant and I was delighted when I thought how easy it was to follow and finally catch a herd of wild horses. But even in fair weather the nights are cold in this altitude. After I stopped and got off my horse, I walked briskly to warm my stiff legs. It occurred to me that possibly I did not know the direction in which camp lay. I fed the horse some corn that I had in the saddle pockets and ate some cold biscuits that I had had for my noonday lunch, and as I was eating I walked around and around the horse to keep warm. When he finished his grain I was uncertain which direction I had come from; so I decided to remain there until morning.

I unsaddled my horse, and wrapping the saddle blanket around me, lay down. The blanket, being wet from the perspiration of the horse, was frozen stiff in a few minutes and I was not long in discovering that I would freeze to death if I remained there. So I put the saddle on the horse and started for camp on foot, leading the bronco. I had not gone but a short mile until I came to a shallow ravine. I supposed this led to the Smoky but could not recall having seen a draw in these parts before. I walked fast all night as I had to keep warm, but I was sure I was going toward camp and expected to arrive there any minute. When daylight came I found myself going down a broad valley with the bed of a dry creek through its center. I then supposed I had struck the Smoky above headwater and would soon come to water and camp.

It was cloudy and I had not realized that I was lost. I

mounted the pony and urged him into a trot and kept up that gait most of the day, until, just as night was closing down, I came to the ranch of Johnny Buck on the Sappa, which I afterwards learned was near the southeast corner of Rawlins County. Here I spent the night and got food for myself and Mr. Buck explained that the Custer Road ran from Fort Wallace straight north to the Republican and directed me to follow the Sappa until I came to that road and then follow it to the Smoky. I reached the road that evening just at dark and got to camp at daylight. I walked most of the way, for my horse was completely exhausted.

Simpson was just coming in from Point Lookout, having spent most of his time up there for the three days I had been absent. He was so delighted at seeing me that he wanted to embrace and kiss me. "I had given you up," he said. "I supposed you were lost and probably dead." He had kept a fire going on the point for three nights and had spent most of his time during the day up there scanning the prairie with the field glasses, hoping I would come in sight. He had scarcely closed his eyes in sleep during the time, and I was in nearly the same condition, but it took us most of the day to recount to each other our experiences for the past three days. Finally I said, "If I had had a pocket compass I would not have got lost." "Sure," he said, "and we will have one before we start out again. I was going to start home today if you had not come, but we will go anyway," he said.

I protested and told him that I had Black Kettle jaded and now was the time to finish him, but he thought his nerves needed a rest; so back we went to Norton. During my three days' absence he had found the XY corral, which was only three miles west of camp. I don't remember that we had thought of a corral before but now that we had found one, we felt sure that all we needed was a pocket compass; so we went one hundred and twenty-five miles to Norton to get one.

III. Black Kettle Saved by a Blizzard

We reached Norton late in December and spent the holidays at home. About the 10th of January, 1880, we came back and camped at the XY corral, beside the headwater of the Smoky, at the point where the Dyatt ranch is now. We brought a wagonload of corn drawn by four horses, with Ed Maple as driver and cook; also six corn-fat saddle horses, and a pocket compass. Our previous experiences satisfied us that we knew the game perfectly and that all the loose horses on this prairie were soon to be decorated with our well-known brand.

One of our delusions was that a tired horse meant a tame horse, and, the wild horse being weak at that season, we had no doubt that our corn-fat saddle horses would soon make them tired.

A wise philosopher once said, "Experience teaches a dear school." During the following weeks we learned many things that can't be found recorded in Kansas history.

A few miles west of our camp on Goose Creek lived one Mr. Johnson, known as Wild Horse Johnson. We heard that he was the only man in the West who had successfully caught and tamed a wild horse. So, before starting after Black Kettle again, we paid him a visit. We found about fifty wild horses grazing contentedly around his corral. We found him a very courteous gentleman and he explained his system both of catching and taming. Before that time we had supposed that a wild horse could be run until exhausted, but he explained that to run them down was impossible, and even if you could, he said, they were worthless ever afterwards. "I follow them in a buckboard," he told us, "until they become sore-footed and then corral them. Once in the corral, I catch them and tie a clog to the front foot." A clog is made of a forked cottonwood limb about two feet long; this is slipped over the foot just above the hoof and tied with a rawhide thong from the points of the fork. He would turn them out and once or twice a day drive them into the corral to keep them tame. After wearing the clog a few days they were again caught and the clogs removed.

Mr. Johnson drove his captives into the corral, thus giving us an opportunity for close inspection. Only a few of the leaders were wearing clogs at the time and all of them seemed as tame as the ordinary range horse. The wild horse at a distance looked much larger than these did from a close-up view, and this accounts for the many stories of large twelve hundred pound horses seen on the range in the early days. We inquired of Johnson if he had ever seen Black Kettle.

"Yes, and run him, too," was his quick response. "I chased him once for two days and then lost him; he has been run so much that he is very wild and cunning." He then admonished us not to bother with Black Kettle. "There are hundreds of horses on the prairie that are worth as much as Black Kettle," he told us. "There is nothing to him but his mane and tail. He weights about eight hundred pounds and is getting old. Let him alone."

He told us many interesting incidents of cowboys chasing Black Kettle, and explained that by reason of this the horse was very wild and had a wide range. He had seen him often twenty miles from his usual watering place, which was Wild Horse Draw. He also told us the same story about Lieutenant

Wheeler's chasing him with the United States cavalry that we had learned from Bill Street.

On our way back to camp we had a good laugh over Mr. Johnson's warning us not to bother with Black Kettle. We felt sure he wanted the horse for himself and greatly under-estimated his size and value. Having seen the horse, we knew his size and value, or thought we did. We learned later that what Mr. Johnson told us was true in every respect, but it cost us much time and labor and some little humiliation to admit it.

We killed a buffalo and two antelope in the breaks of North Smoky that evening on our way to camp, which sup-plied us with fresh meat for some weeks.

The only way to make the business of catching wild horses profitable was to drive the whole bunch. Even if your saddle horse had bottom enough to overtake them, the weak ones would drop out, and if any were captured it would be those of no value.

A man on horseback in the rear can't hold them together; that is always done by the leader. When the leader is crowded to fatigue, the bunch scatters and the first thing you know you are only driving one or two at most, and of course, if you catch one the others get away. Mr. Johnson explained this, but it did not impress me at the time. That night our arrangements for capturing Black Kettle were complete.

Early next morning we left camp, going north toward the point where Goodland now stands. I was mounted on a fleet, fat horse and was to do the running, Simpson following slowly on a big twelve hundred pound draft horse, carrying a half bushel of corn for the horses and a few biscuits for ourselves. A short five miles from camp we sighted through the field glasses Black Kettle with his bunch of roan mares quietly feeding on a piece of high ground about two miles northeast of us.

Simpson was to take up as a permanent position on some high point, and I was to run Black Kettle in a circle around him. Knowing that these horses never went far from water, I felt certain I could hold them within bounds until they were exhausted and then the two of us would drive them into the corral. Keeping the high ground between us as much as possible, I approached the herd, riding slowly. While I was still a mile off, they saw me and moved away to the north.

I followed on at a stiff lope, going about ten miles an hour, but Black Kettle was going faster than that and gained on me rapidly and after a two-hour chase they disappeared in the brakes of the Beaver. An hour later I came to a waterhole where they had watered and from there turned west.

This waterhole is on the section line between sections 24 and 25, township 6, range 39, and had been a noted camping ground for buffalo hunters in past years, but I did not know that at the time; in fact, I did not know what stream I was on but supposed it was the Sappa. Little did I think that some day I would be farming in that neighborhood.

This famous waterhole has made a history to which I will refer later. Many an Indian fight occurred there; white men whom I knew were buried there. That land is now owned by Oscar Ramsey. I watered my horse and started southwest, and in a short time I saw Black Kettle quietly grazing about two miles west of me on the high prairie on the land now owned by Mr. Fixsen. From there he ran south and crossed the Beaver, I following as fast as my bronco could run, being determined not to lose sight of him again. About mid-afternoon I came in sight of Simpson a little northeast of the present site of Goodland. The watcher had been cold and crisp but not very uncomfortable.

About noon it became cloudy and a strong wind arose. By the time I reached Simpson, snow flurries were in the air and in a very short time the worst blizzard I ever experienced was upon us. We abandoned the herd and started for camp, but the fury of the storm became so intense that we soon lost all sense of direction. We came to a lagoon and decided to stay there. We began to gather chips but they were scarce and for the most part hid by the snow; yet we succeeded in piling up about one bushel and then decided to keep them until morning. We removed the saddles and fed the horses some corn; then, taking the saddle blankets, we wrapped ourselves as best we could and sat down on our

"Frontispiece," WILLIAM YOUATT's *The Horse*, 1852

small pile of fuel in an endeavor to keep it dry for future use. In those days men wore boots exclusively and cowboys shunned the hand-me-downs kept for sale by the frontier merchants and wore the fancy high-heel variety, made to order by the village shoemaker. A cowboy with high heels and a Stetson hat was dressed up. In the way of clothing nothing else mattered.

Simpson wore a pair of high-top alligator boots that fit the foot snug, and as we had no overshoes he was complaining of cold feet before darkness settled and the storm had reached its worst. Fearing we should lose our hats, we put them in the saddle pockets. To replace them we cut two strings about one foot wide off the end of a saddle blanket, each of us wrapping one around his head. Then, drawing the saddles over our laps and feet, we sat there eating frozen biscuits, contemplating what our fate was to be.

Whether I had any premonitions about our future during the long arctic night I don't remember, but at one time Simpson said, "I wonder how long our cadavers will remain here before we are found." Simpson had the appearance of a perfect specimen of physical perfection, but he was not; whether it was cold or heat, hunger or thirst, he tired out quickly.

I always thought if he had been alone, he never would have left that camp alive. He died a few years later while still a young man. He talked very little that night and I don't think I said anything. Like James Whitcomb Riley, "I just kept a-thinking." When daylight came, the fury of the storm increased, the air was full of icicles that cut like a knife. After making several attempts we finally started a fire, which only lasted a few minutes. Simpson wanted to remain right there, but I went to work and saddled up both horses while he stood in the ashes of our small fire, trying to warm his feet.

Fortunately we were north of our camp and could go with the wind. (It was impossible to go against it.) I started on foot, leading the horses and thus breaking a path through the snow, Simpson rather reluctantly following. We had taken but a few steps when I heard him yell, "Stop."

When I turned back he was sitting down, the soles of both boots gone; he had burned them out while I was saddling up. We both wore corduroy pants and in addition I wore overalls. These I removed, cut them in two from crotch to waist, and tied the legs around his feet; then, taking a double blanket from under my saddle, I laid it across his horse and tucked the ends around his feet and slipped the stirrups over them. About mid-afternoon we reached camp. I had walked all the way and was not very cold, but Simpson was so cold and exhausted that he had lost all ambition and interest. We were stopping in a dugout near the XY corral and we found a good dinner awaiting us. Simpson's feet were so badly frozen that the loss of his boots made no difference, because he could not have worn them anyhow. He had a high fever that night and was threatened with pneumonia.

All interest in Black Kettle had passed out of my mind as we set about our preparations for returning home. As soon as the storm was over, we set out for Norton. The cook and I walked and as we passed along we gathered chips from the bare spots on the prairie and threw them in the wagon so that we could have a fire at night. The snow was deep and badly drifted, and our progress was slow. On the second day we reached the dugout of Andrew Jardine near where Colby now stands. We had passed near there on our way out but did not see it.

IV. BLACK KETTLE'S CAPTURE

Early in May we left Norton for the annual round-up and proceeded to Pawnee Grove, where we spent the next ten days in gathering cattle, but before leaving home I had gotten together my supplies for another wild horse chase and, of course, took them with me to Pawnee Grove, as I planned to proceed from there to Sherman County and make one more attempt to capture Black Kettle. Having learned that the weakness of the wild horse was in his feet, I secured a buckboard, as I felt sure the practical way to follow them on this smooth prairie was in a light buggy, which enabled me to carry food and water for myself and team.

I started from Norton with three driving teams (good ones) and one saddle horse, a wagon of corn, and supplies for myself and cook, sufficient to last sixty days. During the round-up at Pawnee Grove there were present ten or twelve cattlemen with about forty saddle horses, and when they discovered my load of corn, they of course helped themselves and nearly all my groceries and flour were consumed by that outfit before we finished working the cattle. So it came to pass when I was ready to move on to Black Kettle's range I found it necessary to send my cook, Ed Maple, to Wallace for corn and provisions. These he secured from Pete Robidoux's store and then met me with the balance of the outfit at the XY corral on the Smoky.

There was considerable speculation at the camp at Pawnee Grove about Black Kettle, and the probability of my catching him. So when I started for the Smoky several of the men decided to go also. Marsh Parker of Jewell County had cattle on the Sappa that winter and was present at the round-up. He said: "If I ever see that celebrated horse, I will have to go to his range; you will never catch him." So he came along.

My youngest brother, Allen, had just arrived in Kansas that spring. Before taking up his work as a cowboy at Pawnee Grove, he decided he wanted to see a buffalo and the wild horses; so he came along. There were two or three other men in the party who had never seen a buffalo or wild horse, and as we neared the old camp ground on the Smoky there was considerable speculation among them about the probability of seeing a buffalo or getting a close view of the wild horse.

Somewhere in the Sappa draws near where Brewster now stands, we came suddenly onto two old buffalo bulls and after a five or six mile chase killed one and wounded the other.

This satisfied the boys so far as the buffalo was concerned. Later the same evening we sighted Black Kettle. He, with his fine bunch, was grazing on the high prairie near the old Custer Road. Although he was more than a mile away, all the men got a good view of him through the field glasses.

When we got to the XY corral, my cook was just driving in from Wallace with the supplies. I observed that he was leading behind the wagon a strange horse, which he said belonged to a cattleman at Wallace. "They are starting for Texas in the morning to meet three thousand cattle which are at this time on the trail coming to Kansas, and I have a job with them." So after supper he mounted his horse and rode away and I have never seen or heard of him since. He was a fine cook, and I was sorry to lose him but glad to see him get a position on the trail, as that had been his ambition.

His going was a disappointment in another way. My nerves were keyed up on the Black Kettle chase and I was anxious

to be off but I could not leave camp until I had some one
to care for the stock while I was out. So I was compelled to
lie there and do nothing until the party who came with me
returned to Pawnee Grove and sent a man back a week later.
Billy Rogers of Norton came and remained with me the
balance of the season. That week seemed long to me. Each
day I rode out and took a look at Black Kettle and hundreds
of other horses and wondered if I was ever to catch them.

I had so far received little encouragement. Not a man in
Pawnee Grove believed I would succeed. Simpson had abandoned me and discouraged the enterprise as foolish, but I
never worried for a minute. I was young and full of energy.
I knew if I followed that horse long enough and far enough,
some time he would give up and I meant to do that very
thing, and did it.

Now a word descriptive of my equipment. In my open
buggy I carried a five-gallon keg of water for the team, a
gallon jug of water for myself, a frying pan and coffee pot.
I brought a supply of bread from camp but made coffee
and fried bacon each time I camped. I carried a Springfield
rifle and a field glass, a pair of blankets and a slicker. When
night came, unless I was near the home camp, I made camp
on the prairie, put my team on the picket rope and went
to sleep.

The next morning after the arrival of Billy Rogers, I set
out for the chase. This was on June 2, 1880, but as the chase
progressed, I lost track of the day of the week and month—
when I got in, Billy set me right.

Within two hours after leaving home camp that morning
I found Black Kettle, and the chase was on. I had learned
that speed was not necessary; that if a horse was kept moving
constantly his feet soon gave out. So I jogged along at the

rate of about five miles an hour. For the first two or three days the herd ran away at sight of me and left me many miles behind, but on the fourth day I could see them limping along and only half a mile away at times. Late that afternoon they went to water in Wild Horse Draw, and I went to the home camp for a change of horses and a fresh supply of bread.

During the night it hailed and rained, which made it disagreeable. We had no fuel but buffalo chips and the reader will understand how near the impossible it was to build a fire with that kind of fuel when it was wet. So I went to the old corral and got some boards with which we cooked breakfast and baked a supply of sourdough biscuits for me to carry along.

This made me late in getting started and I drove many miles before I sighted Black Kettle again. The prairie was covered with water, the lagoons and draws were full. But late that afternoon and about fifteen miles northeast of the home camp, I found Black Kettle and his little herd quietly feeding near the old Custer Road. All signs of tender feet has disappeared, and he apparently was as wild as at the beginning and I followed him for five days before I saw home camp again.

The soft ground made it easy on the horses' feet and, there being an abundance of water everywhere, they moved back and forth half way between the Smoky and the Beaver. Try as I might, I could not get them within ten miles of the home camp. On the afternoon of the fourth day, the prairie having dried up, they began to go lame again.

They had been running nearly due east and west. After running about fifteen miles west, they would turn and go back over the same ground. I had been experimenting with them by driving them farther each day than they wanted to go. Late on the fourth day I had driven them east until we were ten or twelve miles east of the Custer Road. When darkness came, I made camp with the horses about a quarter of a mile east of me. I had killed an antelope that day; so I gathered some chips and cooked an antelope steak, which I found an appetizing supper, as I had been living on cold biscuits and bacon and only a limited supply of these.

Black Kettle had wanted to turn back for some time before we stopped. I had learned to read his movements, as he would stop and loiter a considerable distance behind the bunch when he wanted to change his course. His movements always indicated on which side he intended to pass when he turned, but I had kept them moving in the direction he expected to use when turning.

Early dawn next morning found me up and cooking another antelope steak. When it was light enough to see, I discovered they had gone around me during the night but had gone but a short mile west of me, where some of them were lying down, the others standing around, all of which indicated they were very tired. As I started after them they moved west, first in a walk but a little later as I drew near they broke into a trot, but did not appear to be excited or afraid.

This was the most beautiful morning I ever experienced. The atmosphere seemed to be impregnated with sweet perfume. I seemed to see hundreds of miles and on the high spots I could see clear across Sherman County.

I had driven only a short two miles when I heard something that sounded like distant thunder; the earth seemed to tremble, and as I looked about me, I discovered wild horses coming from all directions. Black Kettle broke into a wild run and other bunches fell in alongside of him. My team wanted to run and I let them out at full speed.

There was a magnificent scene spread out before me and I wanted a close view of it. I was also curious to know the cause, and as I looked out on that panorama, I could see horses coming from everywhere. The herds from each side came in close, then turned west alongside of Black Kettle. We had only run a short time when there were hundreds of them all abreast and running their best. Such a sight I shall never see again. The studs were busy keeping their bunches from mixing, although they were very close together. The almost military discipline of each bunch counted and each herd maintained its own individual number. There were many dog soldiers darting here and there, but they were driven off, and antelope by the hundreds joined in the chase.

After I crossed the Custer Road, I looked to the right and saw a herd of buffalos, about fifty in number, running parallel with the horses and a short time afterwards off to the left there was a small bunch, probably ten or twelve, which soon crossed over behind the horses and joined the other herd. They ran along in this direction for about ten miles and then bore off toward the northwest. These were the last wild buffalo that I ever saw.

Black Kettle was near the center of the long line, which extended half a mile on either side of him. Presently a young colt fell and dropped behind, and when the mother tried to turn back to it Black Kettle put her back in her place and kept her there. As I cast my eyes down the line I could see the little colts dropping behind. The studs paid no attention to them but kept the mares in the bunch by simply shaking their heads at them with their ears back.

We were going very fast. My team soon began to weaken

but I applied the whip and kept as near them as I could. About this time I noticed the strangest mirage that I had ever seen. Those horses at times looked to be fifty feet high and then a golden mist would hide them completely; when I was on low ground, the mist seemed to lift so that I could see their legs, which appeared as long as telephone poles. This would only last an instant. Just a flash, and everything changed again and then for a minute the mist shut off the view of the horses, but on beyond I could see towers and spires of a great city.

When the mirage dissolved, I found the horses had separated; some went southwest and other bands were moving toward the northwest. Black Kettle had been in a pocket. He could not run fast enough to go around in front and I kept so close that he dared not drop back. Although he was weary and wanted to stop, he had held his place at the front. My team was exhausted and stopped as soon as I laid the whip away. I must have run thirty miles that morning and probably crossed Sherman County quicker than has ever been done since with a team and buggy. I had killed a team that was worth more than a hundred wild horses.

As I turned back I could see many little colts coming. I suppose some of them found their mothers, but the coyotes got a few of them.

After I had gone about ten miles, I came in sight of a horse standing on the prairie with two colts standing near him. As I came closer, I discovered the horse wore a harness. Then the mystery of the stampede was explained. Had I looked behind me early that morning I might have seen him coming, but I had no time to look anywhere but straight ahead. He had followed until he came to those little colts and had stopped with them, and as I drew near he came to my team. I tied him alongside and moved on toward camp. One of those colts followed for several miles and then turned back.

I moved along on a slow walk because my team could go no faster. Late in the afternoon I met a man on horseback riding bareback. I had been thinking as I rode along, "If I don't catch Black Kettle, I have found a pretty fair horse that will help pay expenses," but the man claimed the horse and soon satisfied me he was the owner.

I asked him his name and he said, "Call me Boney Joe; that's all the name I use in this country." He was camped at a waterhole in a Sappa draw near the east line of the county and only four or five miles from where I had camped the previous night. He had harnessed his team before breakfast and left one of them loose to graze. While he was eating, a bunch of wild horses crossed just below and his loose horse followed them. The rattle of the harness has caused their stampede.

Boney Joe said, "I knew if that old chain harness stayed on him I would get him again, because no wild horse would go near him." He went with me to my camp and spent the night there. Boney Joe lived at Wallace and was gathering buffalo bones for the market. A week later he moved up to my camp and remained there several days.

Well do I remember his description of the mirage. I must have been twenty miles ahead of him when that mirage showed the best. Yet he said he could see those horses running and hear them plainly. There must have been five hundred of them.

The next morning after the mirage I went northwest from camp and met Black Kettle as he was returning to his home range. I came onto him about twelve or fifteen miles from camp at a point near where Ruleton now stands. The horses ran for a couple of miles and then slowed down to a trot and kept that up during the day. They moved around in a circle on ground that was familiar. Toward evening I was driving close up to them, but that night it rained and the soreness in their feet seemed to disappear and they were nearly as wild as on the first day. During the next week it rained every night and their tender feet seemed to improve. I would probably have caught them just as soon if I had laid up during that rainy week, because as long as the ground was soft they could travel about as well as at the beginning.

When the prairie dried off, they soon showed sore feet and I was again driving them about where I pleased. I had now followed them more than twenty days and they were so tame I kept within one hundred yards of them and closer at times. I would drive them close toward camp each evening and spend the night with Billy, and as I would drive away next morning I would tell him I expected to corral them that day. Every day I would get them in sight of the corral but could not get them in. They would break back and run a mile or so and then stop until I came up again.

My best team was out of commission since the big stampede and my other teams were tired and slow. Wild horses are always led by the same mare, and right here I must tell you about Black Kettle's leader. When we had first looked them over the previous winter, Simpson had named the old mare Aunt Susan. He said she reminded him of an old lady by that name he once knew. She was a beautiful blue roan and about twelve years old and during her remaining years she was widely known as Aunt Susan. I shall have occasion to mention her often as my story nears the end. When the wild horse is excited, the male always remains between the herd and danger; so it happens that as you follow them he is always in the rear, except that on occasions he will run around in front to drive off dog soldiers or other danger that may appear, but he soon takes up his position behind and remains there. In all their movements he is in supreme command. By some signal which mystifies me Black Kettle would turn his mares in any direction he chose without seemingly making a move. I always thought he made the signal with his ears but was never sure. He could increase or lower their speed by a slight movement of the head, which was imperceptible unless you watched him very close. The lead mare kept her eye on him at all times but the balance of the herd had no responsibility except to follow the lead mare, and if one of them dropped out of place even for a few steps, the male was right there to put her back.

The XY corral was in a bend of the creek and I had difficulty in getting the horses to it. I had been holding them near it for several days but had not had them nearer than two hundred yards of the gate. One morning as I was getting ready to start, Billy said, "This is the thirtieth day you have run Black Kettle; if you don't get him today, you had better quit him and try another bunch." I told him I would corral him before night.

When I got out on high ground, I saw my bunch going up the slope on the south side of the river. I had never seen them on that side before, although I had tried to put them there several times. They were moving along in a slow walk, Black Kettle in the lead. Fifteen minutes later I was in front of them trying to turn them toward the corral, but, try as I might, I could not turn them. They would walk around me, part on one side and part on the other. I rode close enough to touch them with my whip. They would trot around me and move on in a walk. Black Kettle had lost all interest. His feet

were so sore that he would stop for a moment once in a while
and hold up one foot while part of the bunch had stopped
and was acting as though they did not intend to follow; so I
got behind and drove them along. I knew that if they separated they were lost. Black Kettle and Aunt Susan kept
moving slowly toward Lake Creek, while I was doing my best
to keep the balance with them. I lost several that day, mostly
old mares and yearlings, because each wanted to go his own
way, but I saved the best ones and might have saved them all
if I had driven my best team that morning.

I was now in strange country. I did not suppose there was
a corral between me and Fort Wallace, but no matter, my
mind was clear: I was going to stay with them and trust to
luck. Late that afternoon I came to a house and a corral. I
afterwards learned this was the Bar Lil ranch owned by
Kibbe and Edwards. Although I had never heard of their
ranch, I was delighted to find it. After a few trials and as the
sun was going down, I got the horses into that corral.

Could you have seen me then, you would have seen a
proud boy. I would not have changed places with the presi-
dent of the United States, although I had had no dinner and
my team was jaded. I felt like singing the national anthem
and did it. I unhitched my team and put them on the picket
rope and went to the house. There was no one about, and
from appearances had not been of late. I looked around for
something to eat but found nothing; however, in one corner
was a comfortable bed. I turned in at once and was sound
asleep. Some time later I was awakened by some one getting
into bed with me. I did not suppose there was a man in many
miles of me. The first conscious thought was that some high-
wayman was there to hold me up; the next was that the
proprietor had come to throw me out, and as I began to

apologize a voice said it was all right, sleep as long as you want to. I felt relieved but he talked a little. I don't remember whether I told him I had a bunch of wild horses in the corral or not, but suppose I did.

V. Black Kettle's Life in Town

The first thing I did when I came out that morning was to take a peep into that corral to see if Black Kettle was still there. The horses were standing close together in one corner, seemingly contented and enjoying their rest. It then occurred to me that I had not eaten anything for twenty-four hours, and I felt the need of something stimulating; so I set about getting some breakfast. After drinking a pot of black coffee and eating a couple of sour dough biscuits, I felt better. The puzzling thing to me was what I was going to do with those horses, now that I had them. So far as I knew there was no one in twenty miles of me and for me to catch and hobble that bunch alone was impossible. So I decided to turn them out and drive them to the home camp. As Black Kettle had led them in the wrong direction all day coming back, I decided to tie him up and drive the mares alone and come back and get him. I was not an expert roper, but I caught him the first throw. He made a lunge at the fence and landed on top with his head and front feet on the outside. After struggling for an instant, he slid down on the outside and started north dragging my forty-foot lariat.

I hitched my team to the buckboard as quickly as possible and turned the bunch out. Aunt Susan led them straight north, and when I came up to them they were walking peaceably and slowly towards the Smoky. You would have supposed that drag rope would have kept them excited, but except when it touched one of them they paid no attention to it. Aunt Susan was in the lead, and Black Kettle brought up the rear; so it was seldom they noticed the rope at all. We reached the Smoky about noon and turned upstream towards the XY corral and camp. I had difficulty at times in steering them in the right direction but succeeded late that day in driving them into the big corral at the home camp.

So it was the end of the thirty-first day before I had them safe. I called Billy to bring the saddle. Although I was very tired and hungry, I decided I would ride Black Kettle that night; so we both got hold of the rope and snubbed him to a post and saddled him. I got on and rode him for a few minutes inside the corral. We left the saddle on him for the night and went to camp. The next morning we caught and hobbled a few of the leaders and turned them on the grass. We took Black Kettle to camp and kept him on a picket rope. Within a week they were all tame and never made us any trouble. Billy had Black Kettle eating corn from the start and within two days he was as gentle as a plow horse. Billy cut some horseshoes from a piece of rawhide and nailed them on Black Kettle with shingle nails. He wore those shoes for some time and they were a great help to his sore feet.

I had a saddle horse that was afflicted with Texas itch, and when we saddled Black Kettle we used a blanket that had been worn by that horse. Black Kettle was jaded and weak and the powers of resistance were low; so it came about that one week later Black Kettle had the itch. His hair began to slip and nearly all, including that mane and tail, came off. He was a sorry looking specimen. I worried about it, and told Billy no one would ever recognize that horse, and the boys back home would never believe it was he. Billy thought that the hair would grow back and he would look natural when we got home. Billy applied a coat of bacon grease and had him cured in a short time.

Billy was an expert at making lariat ropes from rawhide, also quirts and horsehair bridles. He made a fine bridle out of the hair of Black Kettle's mane and tail, which I used for several years. Black Kettle's new mane and tail were never long afterwards; they were short and coarse, and his appearance was changed very much.

There were twenty-nine head in the Black Kettle herd when I started after them but only seventeen when I finished. I had lost twelve, but I had saved the seventeen best ones. After resting a couple of days, I started out again and was soon running another bunch. In the next two months I caught six more herds, averaging ten to fifteen in the bunch. The prairie had dried up and I had ideal weather for that kind of work. I had now learned the trick and would pen them in seven or eight days. I have forgotten the exact number caught, but I suppose about seventy-five. Among those I caught later was a black stud that was a good mate for Black Kettle. I named him Black Hawk, but Billy insisted on calling him Black Pot. I told him when we had them broke to harness I should call them Hawk and Kettle, but he insisted on calling them Pot and Kettle. Try as I might, I could not make my name stick. The public took an interest in them, and the first thing I knew everybody was calling them Pot and Kettle. By that name they were known ever after.

We started home late in October. A prairie fire had run through our camp a few days before and burned up our bed and harness, which lay on the grass near the wagon. The nights were getting cold, and we had no bed except the saddle blankets. That was another reason for our being in a hurry to get home. We shot and skinned a wild horse and made a set of harness; for collars we filled some empty corn sacks with buffalo grass and used them. They were not very handsome harness but we pulled the wagon home with them.

Markers were plentiful on the prairie. I have seen them all the way from Norton to the Colorado line. Buffalo heads were used by driving the horns in the ground, leaving the nose pointing straight up; across the face of the skull would be written the direction and distance to water and sometimes other information. The first markers were put up by government surveyors, and later others were added by government scouts, hunters, and trappers, but when the bone pickers came, they were all gathered in. I saw many piles of bones that summer along the Beaver. There was one big pile on the point just north of the old waterhole at what is now the corner of George Bigelow's pasture fence. Joe Collier afterwards told me that he gathered those bones the same summer I was here, but I never happened to meet him.

Two incidents occurred on our way home that I will always remember. On the second evening after leaving the head of the Smoky Hill River, we camped at the home of my old friend, Andrew Jardine, near Colby. Billy was leading Black Kettle behind the wagon. We always led him with the saddle on because he led better that way. We had an extra saddle that was used for that purpose. Black Kettle became frightened at Mr. Jardine's dog, broke his halter and started back toward the Smoky as fast as he could run. I saddled a fresh horse and while I was doing so Mr. Jardine said, "You will never catch that horse, and the only way you will ever recover the saddle is to shoot him." I confess that I was a little uneasy, as that was the first time he had been loose since I drove him into the corral, nearly four months before.

However, when I caught up with him about five miles out he stopped. I got off my horse and walked up to him.

The other event occurred as we neared Norton. Several of the horses were lame, some of them so lame that we left them and drove on. I asked Billy to make camp and stay there until morning and let me go on in, but he refused. He was just as homesick as I. One beautiful filly refused to go any farther; so we backed the wagon up to a bank in a draw and loaded the filly in and drove on home. The next morning that filly was dead. I always thought we killed that mare by driving too fast.

We arrived in Norton on election day in November, 1880—just in time for me to cast my vote for James A. Garfield. We had fifty-five head of horse stock at the finish, having lost a few on the way. Shortly after we got to Norton with the herd, William Case came to see them. Mr. Case lived on Dry Creek in Furnas County, Nebraska, near the Kansas line. He was contemplating a visit to his old home in New York state and wanted to get a pair of wild horses to take back just for the novelty of the thing. He picked out Aunt Susan and a younger mare that looked just like her, and was probably her colt, and bought them. He broke them to drive, and, taking his wife in the buggy with him, drove to Little Valley, New York, his old home. He sold them there for a big price just because of their history. The balance of that herd was sold around Norton and Almena during that fall and winter.

Bill Street and Ame Cole both came to Norton to see Black Kettle, and, although that mane and tail were gone, they recognized him but seemed a little disappointed about his size. They both thought him much larger than he was.

I have never been back to the old Bar Lil ranch since I penned Black Kettle there in July, 1880.

I sold Black Kettle and Black Hawk—Pot and Kettle, as their names came to be called—to Jesse S. Wright, who drove them on a milk wagon for some time. Later they were owned by Jim McGinnes, who farmed with them several years. They were equally at home on the breaking plow or freight wagon. Most of the farming in those days was done with ponies and small horses. Such horses could not handle the improved machinery in use today. Some years later they were owned by Henry Howard; and sometime in the nineties they were owned by Harlan Dey and remained his until they died. They were about thirty years old and died within a few days of each other.

Only a few years back Bill Street came to Goodland with his lecture and magic lantern display of early days. I took him out to the old waterhole on the Beaver. Parson Stewart went along. Street had spent three winters at the hole, but had not been here since the country was settled. He said he could point out the spot where Bob Canfield and other frontier men were buried, but time and the elements had done their work and no trace of a grave was visible. He seemed to enjoy the two hours we spent there and told us many things about the surroundings that he had witnessed and that should be preserved, and possibly sometime will be written. This was the last time I ever saw Bill Street. He promised Parson Stewart to write a history of that old water-hole for the *Republic,* but death intervened before he got to it. The house in which this chapter was written stands only a few rods from that old waterhole.

The wild horse never emigrates or leaves the home range. He remains on the same range through life. The wild horses remained here until the settlers came; many of them were shot and many others died during the hard winters of '85 and '86. There were still a few of them here after the railroad came.

Comanche Horses

I

By Thomas James*

[Having fallen into the power of the Comanches, James was adopted as the *moneta,* or brother, of the One Eyed Chief, the greatest brave of the tribe. In his company James was traveling through the country of the Osage Indians about 1823.]

ABOUT the middle of the day I noticed preparations making by the warriors as for battle. I asked the One Eyed what this signified, and before he could reply Alasarea rode up and exclaimed, "Osages, Osages, a heap," and asked me whether I would stay or go over to them. "I will stay," said I. "Will you fight for us?" "I will," said I, and the One Eyed laughed and said they were only wild horses that had caused the alarm.

I ascended a mound with him, whence I could observe the manner of catching these animals. In an incredibly short time one hundred were captured and tamed so as to be nearly as subject to their masters as domestic horses reared on a farm. A small party of less than a hundred well mounted Indians were in ambush, while a multitude scattered themselves over the prairie in all directions and drove the wild horses to the place where the others were concealed, which was in a deep

---

*Three Years Among the Indians and Mexicans, St. Louis, 1916, 213-215.

ravine. As soon as the wild drove were sufficiently near, these last rushed among them and every Indian secured his horse with his lasso, or noosed rope, which he threw around the neck of the animal, and by a sudden turn brought him to the ground and there tied his heels together. This was the work of a few minutes during which both horses and men were intermingled together in apparently inextricable confusion.

The whole drove was taken at the first onset, except a fine black stud which flew like the wind, pursued by a hundred Indians, and in about two hours was brought back tamed and gentle. He walked close by the Indian who captured him, and who led him by a rope and wished to sell him to me. I feared his wild look and dilated eye, but his Indian master and protector said he was gentle and gave me the end of the rope with which he led him, when the noble animal immediately came near to me as to a new friend and master. He seemed by his manner to have ratified the transfer and chosen me in preference to the Indian. In twenty-four hours after their capture these horses became tamed and ready for use, and kept near to their owners as their only friends. I could perceive little difference between them and our farm horses. The Indians use their fleetest horses for catching the wild ones, and throw the lasso with great dexterity over their necks, when by turning quickly round and sometimes entangling their feet in the rope, they throw them on the ground, and then tie their legs together two and two, after which they release the neck from the tightened noose, which in a short time would produce death by strangling. The sport is attended with the wildest excitement, and exceeds in interest and enjoyment all other sports of the chase that I ever saw.

II

By GEORGE CATLIN*

[Together with thirty Indian guides of various tribes and a war party of ninety Comanches, the artist Catlin, in company with a troop of cavalry, crossed the country between the False Washita and Red River about 1838.]

There is no animal on the prairies so wild and so sagacious as the horse, and none other so difficult to come up with. So remarkably keen is their eye, that they will generally run "at the sight," when they are a mile distant, being, no doubt, able to distinguish the character of the enemy that is approaching when at that distance, and when in motion they will seldom stop short of three or four miles.

I made many attempts to approach them by stealth when they were grazing and playing their gambols, but only once succeeded. In this instance, I left my horse, and with my friend Chadwick, sulked through a ravine for a couple of miles; I used my pencil for some time, while we were under cover of a little hedge of bushes. In this herd we saw all the colors, nearly, that can be seen in a kennel of English hounds. Some were milk white, some jet black—others were sorrel, and bay, and cream color—many were an iron grey; and others were pied, containing a variety of colors on the same animal. Their manes were very profuse, hanging in the wildest confusion over their necks and faces, and their long tails swept the ground.

After we had satisfied our curiosity in looking at these proud and playful animals, we agreed that we would try the experiment of "creasing" one, as it is termed in this country, which is done by shooting them through the gristle on the top of the neck, which stuns them so that they fall, and are secured with the hobbles on the feet; after which they rise again without fatal injury. This is a practice often resorted to by expert hunters with good rifles. Chadwick and I had each a light fowling-piece, which has not quite the preciseness in throwing a bullet that a rifle has. Having both leveled our pieces at the withers of a noble, fine-looking iron grey, we pulled trigger, and the poor creature fell, and the rest of the herd were out of sight in a moment. We advanced speedily to him, and had the mortification of finding that we had never thought of hobbles or halters to secure him. In a few moments more we had the still greater mortification, and even anguish, to find that one of our shots had broken the poor creature's neck, and that he was quite dead.

The usual mode of taking the wild horses is by throwing the *lasso* whilst pursuing them at full speed, and dropping a noose over their necks, by which they are "choked down." The lasso is a thong of rawhide, some ten or fifteen yards in length, twisted or braided, with a noose fixed at the end of it.

The Indian, having roped a wild horse, instantly dismounts, leaving his own horse, and runs as fast as he can, letting the lasso pass out gradually and carefully through his hands, until the horse falls for want of breath, and lies helpless on the ground. He keeps his lasso tight upon its neck until he fastens a pair of hobbles on the animal's two forefeet; then he loosens the lasso (giving the horse chance to breathe), and fixes it around the under jaw, by which he gets great power over the affrighted animal, which goes to rearing and plunging when it gets breath. [Again the Indian advances, hand over hand, up the rope holding the horse by the jaw. He may throw the plunging animal down again more than once.]

Finally he is able to place his hand on the animal's nose, and over its eyes; and at length to breathe in its nostrils, when it soon becomes docile and conquered; so that he has little else to do than to remove the hobbles from its feet, and lead or ride it into camp.

This "breaking down" or taming, however, is not without the most desperate trial on the part of the horse, which rears and plunges in every possible way to effect its escape, until its power is exhausted, and it becomes covered with foam; and at last yields to the power of man, and becomes his willing slave for the rest of its life. Great care is taken not

GEORGE CATLIN IN *North American Indians,* 1841

to subdue the spirit of the animal, which is carefully preserved and kept up, although they use them with great
severity, being, generally speaking, cruel masters.

The wild horse of these regions is a small but very powerful
animal, with an exceedingly prominent eye, sharp nose, high
nostril, small foot and delicate leg; and undoubtedly has
sprung from a stock introduced by the Spaniards, which,
having strayed off upon the prairies, have run wild and
stocked the plains from this country to Lake Winnipeg, two
or three thousand miles to the north. There are many traditions about the first appearance of horses among the different tribes.

This useful animal has been of great service to Indians
living on these vast plains, enabling them to take their game
more easily, to carry their burthens, etc.; and no doubt
render them better and handier service than if they were of
a larger and heavier breed. Vast numbers of them are also
killed for food by the Indians, at seasons when buffaloes and
other game are scarce.

Whilst on our march we met with many droves of these
beautiful animals, and several times had the opportunity of
seeing the Indians pursue them and take them with the lasso.
The first successful instance of the kind was effected by one
of our guides and hunters by the name of Beatte, a French-
man, whose parents had lived nearly all their lives in the Osage
village, and who himself had been reared from infancy among
them. In a continual life of Indian modes and amusements
he had acquired all the skill and tact of his Indian teachers,
and probably a little more; he is reputed, without exception,
the best hunter in these western regions.[1]

---

[1]Beatte was a noted character. His capture of another mustang is described by Washington Irving in *A Tour on the Prairies*, chapters XIX and XX. Irving was in the Indian
Territory in 1832.—*Editor*.

When the bugle sounded for the noon halt one day, Beatte and several other hunters asked permission of Colonel Dodge to pursue a drove of horses a mile or more from us. The permission was given and they started off, and by following a ravine approached near to the unsuspecting animals, when they broke upon them and pursued them for several miles in full view of the regiment. Several of us had good glasses, with which we could plainly see every movement. After a race of two or three miles, Beatte was seen with his wild horse down, the band and other hunters rapidly leaving him.

Seeing him in this condition, I galloped off to him and had the satisfaction of seeing the whole operation of "breaking down" and bringing in the wild animal. When he had conquered the horse in this way, his brother, who was one of the unsuccessful ones in the chase, came riding back, leading up the horse of Beatte which he had left behind. After staying with us a few minutes, he assisted Beatte in leading his conquered wild horse towards the regiment, trembling and covered with white foam. When the bugle sounded the signal for marching, all mounted; and with the rest rode Beatte, astride his wild horse, which had a buffalo skin girted on its back, and a halter, with a cruel noose around the under jaw. Beatte rode quietly and without difficulty until night. The whole thing, capture and breaking, had been accomplished within the space of one hour, our usual halt at midday.

Several others of these animals were caught in a similar manner during our march. They were by no means very valuable specimens, being rather of an ordinary quality. The finest of these droves can never be obtained in this way, as they take the lead at once when they are pursued, and in a few moments will be seen half a mile or more ahead of the bulk of the drove they are leading off. There is not a doubt that there are many very fine and valuable horses among these herds; but it is impossible for the Indian or other hunter to take them, unless it be done by "creasing" them, which is often done, but it always destroys the spirit and character of the animal.

Legendary Wild Horses

WILL JAMES IN *Cowboys North and South*

Adam and Eve of the Mustangs

(Texas, 1540)

By Hortense Landauer Sanger

THE Spanish camp lies sleeping,
  The horses hobbled and fed,
And by his fire the sentry droops
  With Aragon in his head.

The captain enters kingdoms,
  The soldiers finger gold,
But the Spanish horses stamp and sweat
  In the dreamed-of galleon hold;

They whinny for far-off pasturage
  And farther desert sands,
For the white-robed desert riders
  With naked heels and hands;

Their days of freer journeying
  Have never been forgot,
The saddle-bags being heavy
  And the gilded trappings hot:

The gilded trappings irksome
  And the rider closed in steel,
With conquest on the bridle
  And agony at his heel.

153

, . . Snap! Like a bough in winter
   Abruptly from the tree,
The Arab stallion's broken
   His tether to go free.

He stretches to the gallop
   And feels the prairie grasses
Crisply give to his going
   And spring up as he passes;

A wind from the western mountains
   Tangles his wayward mane;
He caracoles where no other hooves
   Have touched the naked plain,

And all night flees. At morning
   He wheels around to stare
Where with a light step following
   He sees the Barbary mare.

—HAROLD BUGBEE

The Ghost Horse

By Chief Buffalo Child Long Lance*

With the first touch of spring we broke camp and headed southwest across the big bend of the upper Columbia, toward the plateau between the Rockies and the Cascades. It was on this lofty plateau that the world's largest herd of wild horses had roamed during the last hundred and fifty years. Several hundred head of them are still there, where every summer efforts are being made to exterminate them by the provincial government of British Columbia. It was these horses that we were after, to replace the herd which the storm had driven away from our camp.

We struck the herd in the season of the year when it was weakest: early spring, after the horses had got their first good feed of green grass and their speed had been slowed by dysentery. Since these wild creatures can run to death any horse raised in captivity, it is doubly a hard job to try to ensnare them on foot. But, like wolves, wild horses are very curious animals; they will follow a person for miles out of mere curiosity. And, when chased, they will invariably turn back on their trails to see what it is all about; what their pursuers look like; what they are up to.

The big timber wolves would do the same, when we were traveling in the North Country. They would trot along behind us all day. When we would stop, they would stop, and

*By arrangement with Farrar and Rinehart, Publishers, New York, reprinted from *Long Lance*, by Chief Buffalo Child Long Lance, New York, 1928.

stand motionless and look at us with one foot raised; and when we would start again, they would continue to follow us. If we made a noise at them, they would jump back and hide behind the nearest bush. From then on, they would keep out of sight, but whenever we looked back we would see them peeping at us from behind the farthest bush.

They used to scare us children, but our fathers told us not to be scared; the wolves would not hurt us; they were just curious about us—although, they said, if the wolves followed us all day, they might try to snatch off our dogs when we camped that night. So they told us boys who were traveling in the rear to keep trying to "shoo" them away before we should make camp for the night. Wolves like dog meat better than any other, though male wolves will never harm a female dog.

But with the wild horses it was different. They always traveled ahead of us, but they had a way of turning back on their own trails and coming upon us from the side or the rear, to keep watch on us. It was this never-satisfied curiosity of the wild horse that enabled our braves to capture them on foot.

The method of our warriors was to locate a herd and then follow it unconcernedly for hours, and maybe for days, before making any attempt to round it up. This was to get the horses used to us and to show them that we would not harm them.

We had been trailing fresh manure for five days before we finally located our first herd away up on the expansive Couteau Plateau of central British Columbia. There they were: a herd of about five hundred animals grazing away over on the side of a craggy little mountain on top of the plateau. Their quick, alert movements, more like those of a deer than those of a horse, showed they were high-strung beings that would dash off into space like a flock of wild birds on the slightest cause for excitement. There was one big, steel-dust stallion who grazed away from the rest and made frequent trips along the edge of the herd. It was obvious to our braves that this iron-colored fellow with the silver mane was the stallion who ruled the herd, and our warriors directed all of their attention to him, knowing that the movements of the entire herd depended on what he did.

When we had approached to within about five hundred yards of the herd, our braves began to make little noises, so that the horses could see us in the distance and would not be taken by surprise and frightened into a stampede at seeing us suddenly at closer range.

"Hoh! Hoh!" our braves grunted softly. The steel-dust stallion uttered a low whinny, and all the herd raised their heads high into the air and, standing perfectly still as though charmed, looked intently over at us with their big, nervous nostrils wide open. They stood that way for moments, without moving a muscle, looking hard at us. Then, as we came too near, the burly stallion tried to put fear into us by dashing straight at us with a deep, rasping roar.

Others followed him, and on they came like a yelling war party, their heads swinging wildly, their racing legs wide apart, and their long tails lashing the ground like faggots of steel wire. But before they reached us, the speeding animals stiffened their legs and came to a sudden halt in a cloud of dust. While they were close they took one more good look at us, and then they turned and scampered away with the rest of the herd, which had already begun to retreat over the brow of the mountain.

But the big steel-dust stood his ground alone for a moment

and openly defied us. He dug his front feet into the dirt far
out in front of him, wagged his head furiously, and then
stopped long enough to look and see what effect his mad
antics were having upon us. Around and around he jumped
gracefully into the air, swapping ends like a dog chasing its
tail. Then again he raised his head as high as his superb stature
would carry him, and with his long silver tail lying over his
back, he blazed fire at us through the whites of his turbulent
flint-colored eyes. Having displayed to us his courage, his
defiance, and his remarkable leadership, he now turned and
pranced off, with heels flying so high and so lightly that one
could almost imagine he was treading air.

Our braves laughed and said: "Ah, *ponokamita,* vain elk-
dog, you are a brave warrior. But trot along and have
patience. We shall yet ride you against the Crows."

WILL JAMES IN *Man, Bird, and Beast*

For five days we chased this huge herd of horses, traveling along leisurely behind them, knowing that they would not wander afar; that they would watch us like wolves as long as we were in the vicinity.

By the fifth day they had become so used to us that they merely moved along slowly when we approached them, nibbling grass as they walked. All during this time our braves had been taming them by their subtle method. At first they just grunted at them. But now they were dancing and shouting at them. This was to let the horses know that although man could make a lot of noise and act fiercely, he would not harm them; that no injury could come to them through closer contact with man.

Nothing scares a horse quicker than a quiet thing that moves toward him and makes no noise. He will jump and break his neck at a noisy movement of a rodent in the grass or a falling twig, while a roaring buffalo or a steaming train will pass him unnoticed. That is because he has the same kind of courage that man has: real courage; the courage to face any odds that he can see and hear and cope with, but a superstitious fear of anything ghostlike. The mountain-lion, and most other animals of prey, have courage of a different kind. A slight unexplained noise will bring them to a low, crouching, waiting position, while a loud noise will send them scurrying for cover. They have more discretion and less valor than man or the horse.

On the tenth night of our chase our warriors made their final preparations to capture the herd. They had maneuvered the horses into the vicinity of a huge half-natural, half-artificial corral which they had built of logs against the two sides of a rock-bound gulch. From the entrance of this corral they had built two long fences, forming a runway, which gradually widened as it left the gate of the corral. This funnel-shaped entrance fanned out onto the plateau for more than a half mile, and it was covered over with evergreens to disguise its artificiality. It was a replica of the old buffalo corral which we used to build to round up the buffaloes when they were plentiful on the plains.

The mouth at the outer end of this runway was about one hundred yards wide. From this point on, the runway was further extended and opened up by placing big tree tops, stones and logs along the ground for several hundred yards. This was to direct the herd slowly into the mouth of the fenced part of the runway, where, once wedged inside, they could neither get out nor turn around and retrace their steps. They would be trapped; and the only thing left for them to do would be to keep on going toward the corral gate.

Subdued excitement reigned in our hidden camp on this tenth night of our chase; for it was the big night, the night that we were going to "blow in" the great, stubborn herd of wild horses. No one went to bed that night. Shortly before nightfall more than half of our braves, comprising all of our fastest-traveling scouts and young men, quietly slipped out of our camp and disappeared. According to prearranged directions, they fanned out to the right and left in a northerly route and crept noiselessly toward the place where the herd had disappeared that afternoon. All during the early night we heard wolves calling to one another; arctic owls, night hawks, and panthers crying out mournfully in the mystic darkness of the rugged plateau. They were the signals of our men, informing one another of their movements.

Then, about midnight, everything became deathly quiet. We knew that they had located the herd and surrounded it;

and that they were now lying on their bellies, awaiting the first streaks of dawn and the signal to start the drive.

One of our subchiefs, Chief Mountain Elk, now went through our camp, quietly giving instructions for all hands to line themselves along the great runway to "beat in" the herd. Every woman, old person, and child in the camp was called up to take part in this particular phase of the drive. We children and the women crept over to the runway and sprawled ourselves along the outside of the fence, while the men went beyond the fenced part of the runway and concealed themselves behind the brush and logs—where it was a little more dangerous.

Thus we crouched on the ground and shivered quietly for an hour or more before we heard a distant "Ho-h! . . . Ho-h!" It was the muffled driving cry of our warriors, the cry which for ten days they had been uttering to the horses to let them know that no harm could come to them from this sound. Thus, the horses did not stampede, as they would have done had they not recognized this noise in the darkness.

We youngsters lay breathless in expectancy. We had all picked out our favorite mounts in this beautiful herd of wild animals, and to us as we lay there it was like the white boy lying in bed waiting for Santa Claus. Our fathers had all promised us that we could have the ponies that we had picked, and we could hardly wait to get our hands on them. My favorite was a beautiful calico pony, a roan, white and red pinto—three different colors all splashed on his shoulders and flanks like a crazy-quilt of exquisite design. He had a red star on his forehead between his eyes, and I had already named him *Naytukskie-Kukatos*, which in Blackfoot means One Star.

Presently we heard the distinct rumble of horses' hoofs—

a dull booming which shook the ground on which we lay. Then "Yip-yip-yip, he-heeh-h-h," came the night call of the wolf from many different directions. It was our braves signaling to one another to keep the herd on the right path. From out of this medley of odd sounds we could hear the mares going, *"Wheeeeh-hagh-hagh-hagh"*—calling their little long-legged sons to their sides that they might not become lost in the darkness and confusion.

Our boyish hearts began to beat fast when we heard the first loud "Yah! Yah! Yah!" We knew that the herd had now entered the brush portion of the runway and that our warriors were jumping up from their hiding-places and showing themselves with fierce noises, in order to stampede the horses and send them racing headlong into our trap.

Immediately there was a loud thunder of pattering hoofs —horses crying and yelling everywhere, like convulsive human beings in monster confusion. Above this din of bellowing throats and hammering feet we heard one loud, full, deep-chested roar which we all recognized, and it gave us boys a slight thrill of fear. It sounded like a cross between the roar of a lion and the bellow of an infuriated bull. It was the massive steel-dust stallion, furious king of the herd. In our imagination we could see his long silver tail thrown over his back, his legs lashing wide apart, and stark murder glistening from the whites of those terrible eyes. We wondered what he would do to us if he should call our bluff and crash through that fence into our midst.

But, now, here he came, leading his raging herd, and we had no further time to contemplate danger. Our job was to do as the others had done all along the line: to lie still and wait until the lead stallion had passed us, and then to jump to the top of the fence and yell and wave with all the ferocity that we could command. This was to keep the maddened herd from crashing the fence or trying to turn around, and to hasten their speed into our trap.

"*Therump, therump, therump.*" On came the storming herd. As we youngsters peeped through the brush-covered fence, we could see their sleek backs bobbing up and down in the star-lit darkness like great billows of raging water. The turbulent steel-dust stallion was leading them with front feet wide apart and his forehead sweeping the ground like a pendulum. His death-dealing heels were swinging alternatingly to the right and left with each savage leap of his mighty frame.

Once he stopped and tried to breast the oncoming herd, but these erstwhile slaves of his whims struck and knocked him forward with terrific force. He rose from his knees, and like something that had gone insane, he shot his nostrils into the air and uttered a fearful bellow of defiance at any and everything. He seemed to curse the very stars themselves. Never before had he tasted defeat, utter helplessness. The loyal herd that had watched his very ears for their commands was now running wildly over him.

I believe that, if at that moment there had been a solid iron wall in front of that stallion, he would have dashed his brains out against it. I remember looking backward into the darkness for a convenient place to hop, if he should suddenly choose to rush headlong into the noise that was driving him wild with helpless rage. But, even as I looked back, I heard a whistling noise, and my eyes were jerked back to the runway just in time to see the steel-dust king stretching himself past us like a huge greyhound. With each incredible leap he panted a breath that shrieked like a whistle.

No one will ever know what was in his brain; why he had

so suddenly broken himself away from his herd. But on he went, leaving the other horses behind like a deer leaving a bunch of coyotes. A few seconds later the rest of the herd came booming past us. As we went over the fence, shouting and gesticulating, we looked into a blinding fog of sweat and breath, which fairly stung our nostrils with its pungency.

I thought that herd would never stop passing us. I had never seen so many horses before, it seemed. We stuck to our posts until it was nearly daylight, and still they came straggling along; now mostly colts limping and whinnying for their mothers.

When we climbed down the fence and went down to the corral at daylight, the first thing we saw was four of our warriors lying on pallets, bleeding and unconscious. They were four of the best horsemen in our tribe: Circling Ghost, High Hunting Eagle, Wild Man, and Wolf Ribs. When our mothers asked what was the matter, someone pointed to the corral and said: *"Ponokomita—akai-mahkah-pay!"* ("That very bad horse!")

We looked and saw a dozen men trying to put leather on that wild steel-dust stallion, who, with his heavy moon-colored mane bristling belligerently over his bluish head and shoulders, looked now more like a lion than a horse. He was splotched here and there with his own blood, and his teeth were bared like a wolf's. Four men had tried to get down into the corral and throw rawhide around his neck. While the other wild horses had scurried away to the nethermost corners of the corral, this ferocious beast of a horse had plunged headlong into them and all but killed them before they could be dragged away.

He had proved to be one of the rarest specimens of horse known to man—a killer—a creature that kicked and bit and tore and crushed his victims until they were dead. One might live a hundred years among horses without ever seeing one of these hideous freaks of the horse world, so seldom are they produced. He had already killed two of his own herd, young stallions, right there in our corral. Little did we wonder, now, that he was the leader.

Our braves were taking no more chances with him. They were high up on top of the seven-foot corral fence, throwing their rawhide lariats in vain attempts to neck the murderous monstrosity. But this devil disguised as a horse had the reasoning of a human being. He would stand and watch the rawhide come twirling through the air, and then just as it was about to swirl over his head, he would duck his shaggy neck and remain standing on the spot with his front feet spread apart, in devilish defiance of man and matter. None of our oldest men had ever seen anything like him.

It was finally decided to corner him with firebrands and throw a partition between him and the rest of the herd, so that our braves could get busy cutting out the best of the animals, before turning the rest loose. This was done, and by nightfall we had captured and hobbled two hundred of the best bottoms anywhere in the Northwest.

The next day our braves began the arduous task of breaking the wild horses to the halter. They used the Indian method, which is very simple and methodical. While four men held on to a stout rawhide rope which was noosed around the animal's neck, another man would approach the horse's head gradually, "talking horse" to him and making many queer motions and sounds as he went nearer.

"Horse talk" is a low grunt which seems to charm a horse and make him stand perfectly still for a moment or so at a time. It sounds like "Hoh-hoh," uttered deep down in one's chest. The horse will stop his rough antics and strain motion-less on the rope for a few seconds; while he is doing this and looking straight at the approaching figure, the man will wave a blanket at him and hiss at him—"*Shuh! Shuh!*" It takes about fifteen minutes of this to make the horse realize that the man is harmless; that no motion which he makes, no sound that he utters, will harm him in any way.

It is a strange fact that a wild horse, of either the ranch or the open ranges, will not react to quiet kindliness at first. He must first be treated gruffly—but not harshly—and then when he is on a touching acquaintance with man, kindness is the quickest way to win his affections.

When the man has reached the head of the horse, his hard-est job is to give him the first touch of man's hand, of which the horse seems to have a deathly fear. He maneuvers for several minutes before he gets a finger on the struggling nose, and rubs it and allows the horse to get his smell or scent. When this has been done, the brave loops a long, narrow string of rawhide around the horse's nose and then carries it up behind his ears and brings it down on the other side and slips it under the other side of the nose loop, making some-thing like a loose-knotted halter, which will tighten up on the slightest pull from the horse.

This string is no stronger than a shoe-lace, yet, once the warrior has put it on the horse's head, he tells the other men to let go the strong rawhide thong, and from then on he alone handles the horse with the small piece of string held lightly in one hand. The secret of this is that whenever the horse makes a sudden pull on the string, it grips certain nerves around the nose and back of the ears, and this either stuns him or hurts him so badly that he doesn't try to pull again.

With the horse held thus, the warrior now stands in front

of him and strokes the front of his face and hisses at him at close range. It is the same noise that a person makes to drive away chickens—"*shuh, shuh*"—and perhaps the last sound an untrained person would venture to use in taming a wild, ferocious horse; yet it is the quickest way of gaining a horse's confidence and teaching him not to be afraid.

When the warrior has run his fingers over every inch of the horse's head and neck, he now starts to approach his shoulders and flanks with his fingers. The horse will start to jump about again at this, but a couple of sharp jerks on the string stop him, and as he stands trembling with fear, the warrior slowly runs his hand over his left side. When this is finished he stands back and takes a blanket and strikes all of the portions of his body that he has touched, and shouts, "*Shuh!*" with each stiff stroke of the blanket.

When he has repeated these two operations on the other side of the horse, he now starts to do his legs. Each leg, beginning with his left front leg, must be gone over by his hand, with not an inch of its surface escaping his touch. This is the most ticklish part of the work; for his feet are the horse's deadliest weapons. But two more jerks on the string quiet the horse's resentment, and within another fifteen minutes every square inch of the horse's body has been touched and rubbed, even down to his tail and the ticklish portions of his belly and between his legs.

Now the job of breaking the horse is all but finished. There is just one other thing to do, and that is to accustom the horse to a man hopping on his back and riding him. This is done very simply, and within about five minutes.

The warrior takes the blanket and strikes the horse's back a number of blows. Then he lays the blanket on his back very gently. The horse will be first to buck it off, but another jerk on the string, and he is quieted. The warrior picks the blanket up and lays it across his back again. The horse will jump out from under it perhaps twice before he will stand still. When he has been brought to this point, the man throws the blanket down and walks slowly to the side of the horse and presses down lightly. He keeps pressing a little harder and harder, until finally he places his elbows across his back and draws his body an inch off the ground, putting his full weight on the back of the animal. A horse might jump a little at the first experience of this weight, but he will stand still the next time it is tried.

After the warrior has hung on his back by his elbows for several periods of about thirty seconds each, he will now very gradually pull himself up, up, up until he is ready to throw his right foot over to the other side. It is a strange fact that few horses broken in the manner ever try to buck. He will stand perfectly still, and the man will sit there and stroke him for a moment and then gently urge him to go; and the horse will awkwardly trot off in a mild aimless amble, first this way and that—so bewildered and uncertain in his gait that one would think it was the first time he had ever tried to walk on his own feet.

The reason a horse can be broken in the above manner is that he is a remarkably intelligent being with rationality. A chicken has no reason; therefore it goes through its life running away from "*shuhs*" that will never harm it. This keeps it from getting many extra crumbs that it could leisurely eat if it only had the reason to learn from experience as the horse does.

Four months later we were again back on our beloved plains in upper Montana. Our horses were the envy of every tribe who saw us that summer. They all wanted to know where we got them. Our chief told the story of this wild-horse hunt so many times that it has since become legend among the Indians of these prairies.

But at the end of the story our venerable leader would always look downcast, and in sadly measured words he would tell of the steel-dust stallion with the flowing moon-colored mane and tail, which he had picked out for himself. He would spend many minutes describing this superb horse; yet he would never finish the story, unless someone should ask him what became of the spectacular animal.

Then he would slowly tell how our band had worked all day trying to rope this beast, and how that night they had decided to leave him in the little fenced-off part of the corral, thinking that two or three days contact with them might take some of the devil out of him. But the next morning when they visited the corral he had vanished. The horse had literally climbed over more than seven feet of corral fence, which separated him from the main corral, and there, with room for a running start, he had attacked the heavy log fence and rammed his body clear through it. Nothing was left to tell the tale but a few patches of blood and hair and a wrecked fence.

That should have ended the story of the steel-dust beast, but it did not. On our way out of the camp on the wild-horse plateau we had come across the bodies of seven wild stallions and a mare, which this fiend of the plateau had mutilated in his wake. He had turned killer through and through, even unto the destruction of his own kind. Our old people said that he had been crazed by the fact that he had lost control of his herd in that terrible dash down the runway. This blow to his prowess and pride of leadership had been too much for him; it had turned him into a destructive demon, a roaming maniac of the wilds.

This horse became famous throughout the Northwest as a lone traveler of the night. He went down on to the plains of Montana and Alberta, and in the darkest hours of the night he would turn up at the most unexpected points in the wilderness of the prairies. Never a sound from him; he had lost his mighty bellow. He haunted the plains by night, and was never seen by day. His sinister purpose in life was to destroy every horse he came across.

This silent, lone traveler of the night was often seen silhouetted against the moon on a butte, with his head erect, his tail thrown over his back like a statue, his long moon-colored mane and tail flowing like silver beneath the light of the stars. Owing to his peculiar nocturnal habits and to the fact that his remarkable tail and mane gave off in the moonlight something like a phosphorescent glow, he became known throughout the Northwest as the *Shunka-tonka-Wakan—* the Ghost Horse. The steel-blue color of his body melted so completely into the inky blueness of the night that his tail and mane stood out in the moonlight like shimmering threads of lighted silver, giving him a halo which had a truly ghostly aspect.

The Deathless Pacing White Stallion

By J. Frank Dobie

THE great horse went under various names—the White Steed of the Prairies, the Pacing White Stallion, the White Mustang, the Ghost Horse of the Plains. There were, in fact, several extraordinary white mustang stallions scattered far apart, living at different times. In tradition they all blended into one, the stories about them combining to make the greatest horse legend of North America. The stallion's fire, grace, beauty, speed, endurance, intelligence were supernal, making him admired and sought by all men in an age when every man was a horseman. His passion for liberty was the passion that his admirers and pursuers idealized and were ready to die for. In body and in spirit he represented horse ranges stretching from far down in Mexico to the Bad Lands of Montana, and from the Brazos River in eastern Texas to the Rocky Mountains in Colorado.

In *Tales of the Mustangs* (published by the Book Club of Texas in 1936) and elsewhere I have traced this super-equine over an empire of range lands and through more decades of time than nature has allotted to any other terrestrial horse. The earliest notice I have found of him is in Washington Irving's *A Tour on the Prairies*, which tells how in 1832 this mustang had for six or seven years been "setting at naught every attempt of the hunters to capture him" on his range in what is now Oklahoma.

171

When J. L. Rountree came to Texas and settled in Milam County on the Brazos River, in 1839, the White Pacer was ranging the prairie lands—much less extensive than those to the west—of that region.[1] It was not long before Rountree joined with two other men to run him down. The horse's circuit was well known. The mustangers placed three relays of horses along it and added three packs of hounds. On the third day an expert Mexican roper on the fastest horse in the country was brought into the chase, but the White Stallion could not be made to break his pace. He simply tired down everything after him. His hunters set snares for him under trees where he was accustomed to stand in the shade in the heat of the day, but no device known to man ever succeeded with the wary animal. He disappeared finally without anyone's knowing whether he had been killed, had died a natural death, or had left the country.

White Horse Plains, in Colorado, southward from Cheyenne, is said to have taken its name from a noted mustang stallion that roamed that region some time before 1890. "This horse was supposed never to have broken a pace, and at this gait was able to outdistance all pursuers, though many traps were placed for him and many a horse hunter gave chase."[2]

The White Steed came into fame, however, through the description that George W. Kendall wrote of him in *The Texan Santa Fé Expedition*. Kendall heard of the horse while, in 1841, he was on the Staked Plains of Texas, that vast land then being the noble animal's home—and security. "As the camp stories ran," wrote Kendall, "he has never been known to gallop or to trot, but paces faster than any horse that has

---

[1]Information received in 1929 from L. S. Rountree, Austin, Texas, son of the original settler.

[2]Kupper, Winnifred T., *Sheep and A Sheepman of the Southwest*, M.A. Thesis, The University of Texas, 1938, p. 209.

been sent out after him can run. Some of the hunters go so far as to say that the White Steed has been known to pace his mile in less than two minutes. Large sums have been offered for his capture and the attempt has often been made. But he still roams his native prairies in freedom."

But there is no point in reviewing what has already been written. It is all wrong anyhow. I have just learned the true history of the immortal white horse.

John R. Morgan, who lives near Wichita Falls and is past his eighty-sixth birthday, came to Travis County, Texas, from Kentucky in 1868. He was soon riding with his uncle, John W. Young, who had been a range man for going on a quarter of a century. From him and from other men who were then old-timers, Morgan learned the detailed history of the wonderful horse. I will try to give his story.

While mustangs were still plentiful in all the prairie country, there appeared among them in the vicinity of what is now called McKinney Falls, on Onion Creek in Travis County, an extraordinary stallion. This was in the early 1840s. The animal had the markings of a pure-bred Arabian. His form was perfect; his alertness and vitality were superb. He was pure white. His tail brushed the tall mesquite grass that carpeted the earth, and his tossing mane swept to his knees. His only gait out of a walk was a pace, and it was soon found that he never, no matter how hard pressed, broke that pace. His *manada*, or bunch of mares, normally numbered from fifty to sixty head—double the size of the ordinary mustang *manada*.

His favorite watering place was on Onion Creek near the McKinney Falls, but he led his *manada* over a great range, southwest across the Blanco, the San Marcos and to the Guadalupe. It was known that he even at times ranged down as far as the Nueces, though this was not on his accustomed round. He kept clear of the timbers, never crossed the Colorado to the east, and did not range into the rocky cedar hills to the west; he seemed to like the rich mesquite grass of rolling country edging the blacklands better than that on the blacklands themselves. His habits were closely studied. He was the most magnificent horse known between the Colorado River and the Rio Grande, and many men, alone and in parties, tried to trap or walk down or otherwise catch him.

It was observed that when persistently chased, the White Stallion usually moved southward. It was generally supposed that he had come up from that direction. There was some evidence that he had been imported to Mexico, had been brought up as far as the Texas border by one of the owners of the great horse ranches occupying that country, and then, after being established on this ranch, had quit it and the semi-domesticated horsestock to run with the mustangs. Many a good ranch stallion in those days answered the call of the wild mustangs, some of them never to be recovered.

The White Stallion, no matter how chased, always in time came back to the water of, and the mesquite grass along Onion Creek. The favorite point of view from which to see him and his *manada* was Pilot Knob, about four miles from McKinney Falls. From this eminence John W. Young himself saw the stallion and his *manada* several times. Any mustanging party that proposed a chase generally sent a scout to Pilot Knob to locate their quarry. The White Stallion's color, his alert movements and the large size of his *manada*, all made him and the bunch he led conspicuous. If started, he would lead out pacing — single-footing — the *manada* following at a dead run. In a mile's distance he would gain at least a hundred and fifty yards on anything behind him.

Then he would stop and look back, and wait while his bunch approached. If pursuers were still following, he would pace on, gaining and gaining, but again would stop and look back, thus keeping out of shooting, as well as roping, distance.

The Indians had spotted him and they gave him a few chases, but the most persistent chasers were from San Antonio, then a horseback town. A certain doctor of San Antonio who was a horse fancier heard of the White Stallion, saw him in action, and offered five hundred dollars for him if delivered in "sound condition." Five hundred dollars in those days amounted to a small fortune.

A Spanish-born rancher named Santa Ana Cruz determined to win the prize. He had a ranch on Onion Creek, near McKinney Falls, and had numerous peon vaqueros under him. He was associated in a business way with Samuel A. Maverick, and in putting down desperados had led a desperate life; it is said that he kept as many as ten guards around his house every night. His men had chased the White Stallion numerous times. One day they ran him seventy-five miles south, and when they got back home two days later, found him grazing with his mares on the accustomed range.

Now, to win the five hundred dollars, Santa Ana Cruz picked twelve riders, furnished each of them with two horses selected for speed and endurance—particularly endurance—and disposed them in the direction that the White Stallion might be expected to run after he was started. A scout on Pilot Knob saw the *manada* go in to water. After they had drunk, the nearest of the twelve men began the chase. The White Pacer took out in the direction of San Antonio. That first day, however, he did not keep his direction and before the morning of the second day he had circled back into his favorite range. He was crowded harder, his mares lagged

more, and on this day he crossed the Guadalupe, going southwest. For three days and three nights the Santa Ana Cruz
men ceaselessly pursued him. The time picked for the chase
was in the full of the moon in June, and the country covered
was, in those days, nearly all open prairie.

Before the end of the third day, every animal in the *manada*
following the White Stallion had been run down. He himself, however, had not once lagged, had not once broken
his single-footing, except to change from right to left and
left to right. Two of Santa Ana Cruz's relay men trailed him
across the Frio River. Then they quit. The White Stallion
was still pacing toward the Rio Grande.

He never returned to his old range. In time the Onion
Creek country learned why.

Going on south, the Pacing Mustang no doubt drank at
the Nueces River. Before modern ranchmen built tanks,
drilled wells and put up windmills, the wide country between
the Nueces and the Rio Grande was very sparsely watered.
In some places it is a level country, all brushed today; in other
places it is crumpled into high, rough hills and cut by deep
canyons. About three miles from a waterhole in one of these
canyons there was in the forties a Mexican ranch called
Chaparro Prieto. The low rock house, with portholes against
Indian attacks, and the adjacent corrals were located in a
wide draw matted with mesquite grass. Near by was a hand-

FROM C. W. WEBBER'S *Wild Scenes and Wild Hunters*, 1856

dug well that supplied water for the ranch people and for the saddle horses. All stock loose on the range watered at the big hole in the canyon, the only watering within a radius of many miles.

The hole was boxed in by the canyon walls on both sides and by a high bluff above it, leaving only one entrance— from the north. One hot afternoon a vaquero from the Chaparro Prieto while riding near the waterhole saw a lone white horse approaching in a slow pace from the north. At the instant of observation he was hidden by some black chaparral and was considerably to one side of the trail the horse was traveling. The animal's behavior indicated that he had smelled the water. He was very gaunt, indicating that he had not drunk for a long while; he was evidently jaded, but his footing, though weary, yet seemed secure, and he maintained an alertness in ears, eyes and nostrils. The wind was in the vaquero's favor. He cautiously slipped a hand over his mount's nostrils to prevent a possible whinny. As the horse passed nearer, he recognized him from descriptions he had often heard as the Pacing White Stallion of the Mustangs.

Here was a chance to rope what so many riders had tried and failed to capture. As has been said, there was but one entrance and exit to the boxed waterhole. The vaquero knew that the thirsty stallion would drink deep and come back up the bank loggy with water. After the mustang had gone down the trail out of sight, the vaquero placed himself in position for a sure throw when the animal should emerge. He was riding a fresh pony. He did not have long to wait. Within a few minutes the long-sought-for lover-of-freedom emerged, his ears working, his body refreshed, his senses more alert. He saw the trap and made a dash so cunning that he eluded the rope's throw. Quickly recoiling his riata for

another cast, the vaquero spurred in pursuit. The Steed of
the Prairies had come two hundred miles or more from his
range on Onion Creek, besides pacing in great circles before
he had finally headed straight for the Rio Grande. His marvelous endurance was at last wearing out; the water that had
refreshed him now also loaded him down.

The second loop thrown by the fast-running vaquero went
over his head. But he did not run full speed on the rope and
jerk himself down. His response showed that he had been
roped before. He wheeled just as the rope tightened and with
wide-open mouth rushed at his captor. He did not seem to see
the horse ridden by the vaquero. He was after the man. He
nearly seized him, but the agile cow pony had wheeled also.
Fortunately for the vaquero's life, some scattered mesquite
trees grew just ahead of him. Guiding his well-reined pony,
he managed to get one of these mesquites between himself
and the roped stallion. The mesquite served as a snubbing
post for him to halt and then tie the magnificent horse. Magnificent, for, unlike many mustangs appearing magnificent
at a distance, this one remained so at close quarters, even
though worn by his long war of defense.

Tying him up as close as he could and leaving him to lunge
at the rawhide-strong riata, the vaquero left in a long lope
to get help at the Rancho Chaparro Prieto. He returned in
less than an hour with two other vaqueros. With three ropes
on the White Mustang now, thus checking his attempts to
fight, they led and drove him to a spot on the prairie near
the ranch corrals where the mesquite grass was particularly
fine. There they threw the proud King of the Mustangs, tied
ropes on him so that he could not choke himself to death,
fixed a clog on one of his forefeet, and staked him. When

night came, he was standing where they left him, not having taken a mouthful of grass.

The next day they carried a sawed-off barrel, used as a trough, within the horse's reach and filled it with water. He did not notice it. For ten days and ten nights he remained there, grass all about him, water at his nostril's tip, without taking one bite to eat or one swallow out of the trough. Then he lay down and died. He fulfilled the ringing cry of Patrick Henry, "Give me liberty or give me death." As he had lived, he died noble.

Certain black mustang stallions achieved fame also, but no one of them ever became so famous as the Pacing White Mustang, and they did not add themselves together to make one, single, continuous tradition.

In the early days of Parker County a beautiful black leader of the mustangs became the object of desire by many men. After they had tried in various ways to catch him, two or three persistent mustangers dug a hole, large enough to contain a man, out in a prairie where the black and his *manada* frequently used. Grass made it invisible except to eyes almost over it. Day after day one of the men rode to this hole, gave his horse to a partner to lead out of sight, and, with loaded rifle, waited for the mustang to approach within shooting distance. His object was to crease the mustang—shoot him through the top of the neck so that the tendon running there would be so injured as to paralyze the animal temporarily. Creasing took an expert shot; a fraction high, and the bullet would be harmless; a fraction too low, and it would be fatal.

After the concealed mustanger's patience was about exhausted, his companions managed one day to haze the black

stallion within rifle-shot. The bullet paralyzed the beautiful
stallion all right—paralyzed him permanently.[3]

Among the thousands of mustang horses grazing in the
San Joaquin Valley of California in early days, the one that
lives strongest in stories yet told was a black stallion.[4] Because
he was the most beautiful and the fleetest animal in all the
manadas ranging around Tulare Lake, he was the most sought
for. Pens were built with long wings to catch him; while
many other mustangs were captured in these pens, the black
never allowed himself to be hemmed in. His fame spread.
Finally two cowboys spied him feeding out of the point of a
long tongue of land jutting into the lake. Loosening riatas
and yelling, they rode toward him. At last they had the stallion cut off! He snorted and plunged into the soggy-bot-
tomed lake. When he got out to where the water was about
half way up his sides, he began floundering in the mud. The
men retreated, so as to give him a chance to get back on the
land—and come by them on his way out. The black paused,
seemed to consider, and then plunged farther out from the
peninsula, his struggles growing more desperate. It looked as
if he designed drowning rather than risking capture. He did
drown.

The action of the captured White Stallion in standing on
grass and beside water for ten days without touching either
appears to have been as deliberate as the self-starvation of any
hunger-striker in India. Though his captors may have in-

---

[3]Neelley, Mrs. C. L., "Known as Pioneers," in the *Dallas Semi-Weekly Farm News*,
April 29, 1938.
    [4]Latta, F. F., *Uncle Jeff's Story*, Tulare, California, 1929, 42-43.

jured him internally, the injury could hardly have destroyed his thirst. Certainly they "broke his heart." The manner in which the Tulare black chose the fatal mud rather than safe footing on man-dominated land looks like another case of wilful suicide, though terror may have driven him to death—terror at a threat to his wild, free way of living. The range has many stories of wild horses—and wild cattle, too—that have preferred death to capture.

In the fall of 1882 W. K. Shipman, who now lives out from the edge of San Antonio, was an eighteen-year-old cowboy ranging on Jim Ned Creek in West Texas. He had already bossed a herd up the trail. (The sparsity of men on the frontier and the opportunities for self-reliance made boys develop early.) Except for drift fences, the range was still open, and many mustangs yet ran on the vast, broken prairies east of the cap rock. Shipman had noted especially one band, led by a blood-bay stallion with black mane and tail. He got six other cowboys to go in with him to capture this band, all agreeing that Shipman himself should have the stallion if they ever got him within reach of a rope.

After some preliminary running, the mustangers managed to work a belled mare into the wild band. The stallion adopted her, and her bell proved to be a considerable help to the pursuers at night. After the first circle, they followed the mustangs in a buckboard, drawn by a pair of tough ponies, which, with driver, were relayed three times every twenty-four hours. The mustangs were accustomed to watering in Jim Ned Creek, to which they had to descend from prairie country down trails through the roughs. Now they seemed afraid to enter the rough land and thus get cut off from their open running grounds, though by crossing the breaks they might have cut the buckboard off from pursuit.

Like antelopes, they relied for safety on their running power in clear country. For three days and nights the cowboys kept so close behind them that they took no chances in going down to water and, of course, ate very little. At the end of this time they were near enough "walked down" that they could be thrown in with some manageable range horses and hazed into a big cow pen. During the pursuit they had run around Tecumseh Peaks several times, keeping within the range familiar to them.

In the pen, the blood-bay stallion, his black mane and tail marking Spanish ancestry, showed up as beautiful, as well proportioned and as desirable as he had appeared while running in the distance on the prairies. During the long chase he had exercised much more than the other animals in his band, sometimes leading them, often driving them, frequently racing up one side of them and down the other. Now he stood gaunt, jaded, but still with plenty of life in him, and apparently as sound as a dollar. He was about four years old, an age at which any horse is still comparatively green, two or three more years being necessary to bring him to his toughest stage. But the bottom of this young blood-bay stallion had stood the test.

When roped, he struggled but did not fight. When mounted, he did not pitch. Guiding him with a hackamore and accompanied by two other men, Shipman rode out of the pen toward Jim Ned Creek, some distance off, and into water not more than eighteen inches deep. The reins of his hackamore loosened, the mustang thrust his muzzle into the water up to his eyes. Then suddenly he lay down, his muzzle still submerged. His rider quickly loosened the girth and all three men struggled to force the mustang's head out for air. He would not submit. He drowned himself right there. No doubt he was dazed, past the stage of using clear-headed judgment. Certain psychologists say that no man who kills himself is entirely sane at the time. However that may be, the process of taking the mustang stallion's liberty from him took also his instinct for life.

Caballos

Antonio de Espejo

The Horse of the Pampas

By R. B. Cunninghame Graham*

SHORT-TAILED, long-tailed, in cart or carriage, ridden by 'Arry or by Lord Henry, the horse of Europe (excepting always the coster's pony) delights me not, or very little. He seems to me a species of property, a sort of investment for capital, precarious sometimes, unsatisfactory too often.

If he is ill, his malady must be ministered to in the shape of beer to his groom; does he die, my equine investment is lost; I must try another.

On the pampas it is different. He is part of me, I live on him, and with him; he forms my chiefest subject of conversation, he is my best friend, more constant far than man, and far exceeding woman.

What wonder, therefore, that a letter from an Argentine friend should bring back to me the broad plains, the countless herds of horses, the wild life, and the camp-fire.

Most people know that there are great plains called pampas. Books of travel more or less authentic have informed them that these are roamed over by countless herds of horses.

As to what these horses are like, where they came from, and if there are any special peculiarities that distinguish them from other horses, few have inquired.

---

*From *Father Archangel of Scotland and Other Essays*, London, 1896. Some few changes in the text here printed, as compared with the original, were made in a transcript generously sent by the author to the present editor. The Spanish horse of South America was essentially the same animal as the mustang breed of North America. Hence, Graham's essay throws a peculiar light on our original range horses.

It seems to me that there are certain differences between the horses of Spanish America and the horses of any other country.

That they should more or less resemble those of the south of Spain, from whence they came, is nothing to be wondered at. That special conditions of food, climate, and surroundings should have produced a special type is nothing extraordinary.

What, then, are the general characteristics of these horses?

That which specially attracts the attention of all those who see them for the first time is the great difference to be observed betwixt them when in motion and at rest. Saddled with the *recado*, the American adaptation of the Moorish *enjalma*, the heavy bed on horseback, with its semi-Moorish trappings, standing patiently before the door of some gaucho's house from morn till sunset, they appear the most indolent of the equine race. But let the owner of the house approach with his waving poncho, his ringing spurs, his heavy hide and silver-mounted whip, and his long flying black hair; let him by that mysterious process, seemingly an action of the will and known only to the gaucho, transfer himself to their backs, without apparent physical exertion, and all is changed. The dull, blinking animal wakes into life, and in a few minutes his slow gallop, regular as clockwork, has made him and his half-savage rider a mere speck upon the horizon.

In a country where a good horse costs a Spanish ounce (£3.15s), it is not wonderful that all can ride, and all ride well. In a country where if you see a man upon a plain, you are always certain that it will be a man on horseback; in a country where the great stock-owners count their *caballadas* by the thousand (Urquiza, the tyrant of Entre Rios, had about one hundred and eighty thousand horses), it is to be supposed that much equine lore, "hoss sense" the Texans call it, has grown up. It is to be looked for that a special style of riding has arisen, as that what we in Europe think strange is there regarded as an ordinary occurrence of everyday life.

It would indeed be as impossible to measure the pampas horse by the standard of an English horse as to measure a gaucho by the standard of an ordinary city man. Each man and each animal must be estimated according to the work he is required to do. Putting aside cart horses and those employed in heavy draught, almost every horse in England, except the cab horse, is an object of luxury. He has a man to look after him, is fed regularly, is never called on to endure great fatigue, carry much weight, still less to resist the inclemency of the weather. He is valued for his speed, for his docility, or merely for his pecuniary value in the market. In the pampas none of these things is of prime importance. We do not require great speed from our horses, we care nothing as to their docility, and their pecuniary value is small. What we do look for is endurance, easy paces, sobriety, and power of withstanding hunger and thirst. A horse that will carry a heavy man seventy miles is a good horse; one that can do ninety miles with the same weight is a better horse, and if he can repeat the performance two or three days in succession, he is the best, no matter if he be piebald, skewbald, one-eyed, cow-houghed, oyster-footed, or has as many blemishes as Petruchio's own mustang.

As I was talking with some gauchos, seated on the ground one starlit night, before a fire of bones and dried thistles, the conversation fell as usual upon horses. After much of the respective merits of English and Argentine horses, after many of the legends as closely trenching on the supernatural as is befitting the dignity of horsemen in all countries, an ancient, shriveled gaucho turned to me with, "How often do you feed your horses, Don Roberto, in England? Every day?" Thereupon, on being answered, he said, with the mingled sensitiveness and fatuity of the mixed race of Spanish and Indian, "God knows, the Argentine horse is a good horse the second day without food or water, and if not He, why then the devil, for he is very old." In all countries the intelligent are aware that you can estimate a horse's goodness by his stature. The average stature of the pampas horse is about fourteen and one-half hands—What we should call a pony in England. In his case, however, his length of loin, his lean neck, and relatively immense stride, show that it is no pony we have to deal with, but a horse, of low stature if you will, but one that wants a man to ride him.

Intelligent and fiery eyes, clean legs, round feet, and well-set sloping shoulders, long pasterns, and silky manes and tails, form the best points of the pampas horse. His defects are generally slack loins and heavy head, not the "coarse" head of the underbred horse of Europe, but one curiously developed that may or may not be, as Darwin says it is, the result of having to exert more mental effort than the horse of civilization.

Of his color, variable is he; brown, black, bay, chestnut, piebald, and gray, making a kaleidoscopic picture as on the dusky plains or through the green *monte* (wood) a herd of them flash past, with waving tails and manes, pursued by gauchos as wild and fiery-eyed as they. As on the steppes of Russia, the plains of Queensland and Arabia, the trot is unknown. To cross a pampa loaded with the necessaries of desert life, without a path to follow, it would be a useless pace. The slow gallop and the jogtrot, the Paso Castellano of the Spaniards, the Rhakran of the Turks, is the usual pace. The pacer of the North American, the ambler of the Middle

Ages, is in little esteem upon the pampas. You spur him, he does not bound; he is a bad swimmer. As the gaucho says, "He is useless for the *lazo,* though perhaps he may do for an Englishman to ride." *"Manso como para un Ingles"* (tame enough for an Englishman to ride) is a saying in the Argentine Republic.

Where did these horses come from, from whence their special powers of endurance? How did these special paces first characterize them, and how is it that so many of the superstitions connected with them are also to be found amongst the Arabs? My answer is unhesitatingly, From the Arabs. All the characteristics of the Arabs are to be observed in the Argentine horses; the bit used is that of Turkey and Morocco, the saddle is a modification of the Oriental saddle, and the horses, I think, are in like manner descended from the horses of the East.

It is pretty generally known that the conquest of America was rendered much easier to the Spaniards by the fact that they possessed horses, and the natives had never seen them.

Great, well-watered, grassy plains, a fine climate, and an almost entire absence of wild beasts—what wonder, therefore, that the progeny of the Spanish cavalry horses has extended itself (in the same way as did the horses turned loose at the siege of Azov in the sixteenth century on the steppes of Russia) all over the pampas, from the semi-tropical plains of Tucuman and Rioja right down to the Straits of Magellan? Spanish writers tell us that Cordoba was the place from which the conquerors of America took must of their horses. To ride like a Cordobese was, in the Middle Ages, a saying in Spain, and such it has remained unto this day. Cervantes makes one of his characters say, "He could ride as well as the best Cordobese or Mexican," proving the enormous increase of horses in the New World even in his time, not much more than a hundred years after the conquest. In the plains of Cordoba, to this day, large quantities of horses are bred, but of a very different stamp from their descendants of the pampas. Whence, then, did the original stock come from? Cordoba was the richest of the Moorish kingdoms of Spain in the thirteenth century. It was directly in communication with Damascus. Thus, there is little doubt that the Cordobese horses were greatly improved by the introduction of the Arab blood. However, Damascus was a long way off, and the journey difficult and dangerous. It therefore seems more probable to me that the most of the Cordobese horses came originally from Barbary. A remarkable physical fact would seem to bear out my belief. Most horses, in fact almost all breeds of horses, have six lumbar vertebrae. A most careful observer, the late Edward Losson, a professor in the Agricultural College of Santa Catalina near Buenos Aires, has noted the remarkable fact that the horses of the pampas have only five. Following up his researches, he has found that the only other breed of horses in which a similar peculiarity is to be found is that of Barbary.[1]

Taking into consideration the extreme nearness of the territories of Andalucia and Barbary, and the constant communication that in Mohammedan times must have existed between them, I am of opinion that the horses of the pampas are evidently descended from those of Barbary.

It is not within my knowledge whether a similar configuration is to be observed in the Cordobese horses of today. But this is a point very easily cleared up.

The genet, too (the progeny of the ass and horse), has the same number of vertebrae. Is it impossible that in former

---

[1] I think it is also the case amongst the Arab horses of the Anazch and other tribes.

times the union of an African mare and a genet may have produced the race of Berber horses which were taken by the Moors to Spain, and hence to the pampas? The genet and the mule are not characterized by the same infecundity. During the last fifty years, in the south of France, many cases have been observed of the reproductiveness of the former animal.

The following story may serve to show that the idea of a mixed race of horses and asses that were not mules has been considered by the Arabs from the remotest ages as possible.

In the western Soudan there are three celebrated breeds of horses, according to the Emir Abd-el-Kader—the Hâymour breed, the Bou-ghareb, and the Meizque. Of these, the Hây-mour breed is considered the best, and possesses many of the same qualities that are so striking in the horses of the pampas —speed, bottom, and robustness. The Emir says that it is not uncommon for them to perform a journey of one hundred and thirty kilometers in twenty-four hours. I myself have frequently ridden horses of the pampas ninety miles, and on one occasion one hundred and three miles, in the same time.

THE CASTILIAN CABALLO.

SWEET AND KNOX, *On a Mexican Mustang,* 1892

The origin of the Hâymour breed is thus related. An Arab chief was obliged to leave a wounded mare in a small oasis, where there was grass and water, but near which no tribes ever passed. About a year afterwards, happening whilst hunting to pass the oasis, he saw his mare, well, and about to foal. Having taken her to the tents, her foal proved of singular excellence, and became the mother of a famous desert stock. The Arabs, knowing that no horses ever passed there (the wild horse is unknown in these deserts), believed that the foal was the progeny of a wild ass, Hamar-el-omâkheh, and to the foal they gave the name of Hâymour, the foal of the wild ass or onagar.

Be this as it may, whether Pegasus or an onagar was the progenitor of the horses of the pampas, the fact remains that they are renowned for the same qualities that made the horse of Barbary famous in the Middle Ages. Nothing is more enjoyable on a frosty morning than to career over the plain, hunting ostriches on a good horse; nothing more fascinating (at twenty-two) than to rattle along behind a good *tropilla* of ten or twelve horses, following their mare with tinkling brass bell. Then indeed, with silver-mounted saddle and toes just touching the heavy silver stirrups (the gaucho rides long and never puts his feet home, for fear of sudden fall), you bound along over the grassy seas, and cover perhaps one hundred or one hundred and twenty miles a day.

It is not only necessary in La Plata to ride well; a man must always fall well, that is, on his feet. Standing once watching the always interesting spectacle of a *domador* on horseback, with bare head and red silk handkerchief laid turbanwise round it, struggling with a violent colt, I rashly remarked that he rode well. "Yes, he sits well," was the answer; "let us see how he falls." Fall he did, after one or two more plunges, and his horse, a blue and white (*azulejo*) colt, on the top of him. The colt, after a struggle or two, regained its feet; the man never stirred again. His epitaph was, "What a pity he did not know how to fall!" "But, after all," remarked a bystander, "he must have died *de puro delicado*" (of very delicateness), so incredible did it seem that a man could have been fool enough to let a horse fall on him.

The same superstitions exist amongst the Arabs and the gauchos as to horses and their colors. Thus, the horse with a white fore and white hind foot is sure to be fast. The gauchos say he is crossed, *cruzado,* and that accounts for it. In the same way the Arabs say he is sure to be lucky. Both peoples unite in praising the dark chestnut. *"Alazan tostado, mas bien muerto que cansado,"* says the proverb. The Arabs have a similar one. Both unite in distrusting a light chestnut with a white tail and mane. "He is for Jews," say the Arabs. The gauchos also assign him to an unlucky caste. *"Caballo ruano para las putas."* A dun horse, unless he have a black tail and mane and red eyes, can never be good. Only a madman would ride a horse of any color that had a white ring round its fetlock. It is unlucky. In peace it will stumble, in war fail you. Greys will not stand the sun. The roan is slow. One striking difference, though. The Arab dislikes the piebald. "He is own brother to the cow." The gaucho esteems him highly. The object in life of a rich gaucho is to have a tropilla of piebalds. The author of "El Fausto," a well-known gaucho poem, makes his hero ride a piebald.

Like the Arab, the gaucho uses long reins, open at the end, to hold a horse by if he is thrown. Like the Arab, he rides upright in the saddle. Like him, too, he stands at the horse's head to mount, looking toward its tail, and catching the saddle by the pommel, instead of the cantle, like Europeans

and Australians, and throws himself at one motion into the
saddle without pausing in the stirrup, his horse in the meantime going on, for no one has his horse held in the pampas
from one end of the nine hundred miles of territory from
Buenos Aires to the Andes. From the frontier of Bolivia to
Patagonia you will never find a man with the heavy hands so
common in Europe. This I attribute partly to the severe bit
and partly to the fashion of never passing the reins through
the fingers, but holding them in the hollow of the hand,
which is carried rather high with the elbow turned down,
and not at right angles to the body, as with us. The Arab
habit of mounting on the off side has been dropped by the
gaucho, but it is practised both by the Indians of the pampas
and those of the prairies of North America. I had once to
mount an Indian's horse. It proved unmanageable till the
owner called out in bad Spanish, "Christian frightening
horse, he mount quiet on Indian side." In the pampas he who
is not an Indian is a Christian. . . .

Horse Lore of the Conquest

By Robert M. Denhardt

I

Most of the early Spanish chroniclers have handed down stories concerning the horses of the Conquest. A few, either because of their love of horses, or their ear for a story, are outstanding. Chief among the authorities for the conquest of Anáhuac is, naturally, Cortés,[1] for not only was he the first to land on the North American continent with cavalry, but he loved good horseflesh. Cortés was born in Estremadura, a blue-blood on all sides, as the Spaniards said, an *hidalgo de los cuatro costados.* Although trained for the law, he soon found a calling more suited to his abilities. His letters are generally terse and emphatic, as a military man's should be, but also reveal a sense of natural beauty. Cortés was rather well caricatured by Bernal Díaz,[2] who said that although he spoke Latin he was somewhat of a poet.

Bernal Díaz was the most voluminous writer and in many respects is the best single authority on the Conquest. Although he wrote in his old age, while governor of Guatemala, his retentive mind and facile pen sketched all the important

---

[1]Cortés wrote five important letters to his Emperor, from which we get most of our information. The first four may be found in Pascual de Gayangos, *Cartas y Relaciones de Hernán Cortás* (Paris, 1866); the fifth is in the *Colección de documentos inéditos para la historia de España* (Madrid, 1844). The best English version is probably F. A. McNutt's *Letters of Cortés* (New York, 1908).

[2]Bernal Díaz del Castillo, *Historia Verdadera de la Conquista de la Nueva España* (México, Garcia, 1904). Best English version, Alfred Percival Maudsley, *True History of the Conquest of New Spain* (London, Hakluyt, 1908-16).

men as well as dozens of the horses with all their colors and individual qualities. As Graham[3] says, Díaz was a brave, truthful, and unlettered soldier, all the prejudices of his race coming to light on every page he wrote. History written impartially is apt to be as dry as pemmican, and as indigestible; Díaz is never dry.

The third authority is the Inca Garcilaso de la Vega,[4] the product of a conquistador of noble birth and an Inca princess. This romantic union produced a historian with certain advantages found in no other chronicler. He saw the Spaniard's side, and at the same time his native blood made him sympathetic to the point of view of the natives. He left Peru when twenty, and never returned to his native land. When he finally settled in Cordoba after military service, his retentive memory and his many chats with retired *conquistadores* gave him a unique opportunity to write the history of the occupation of the New World.

References to horses also abound in Acosta's[5] history. There is a passage from an unnamed writer in his work which portrays unusually well the native regard for Spanish horses. Speaking of a certain advance at the time of the Mexican conquest, he says that although the people of the country resisted, they were soon defeated by the cavalry, which they held in great fear. One evening when the troops were quartered near a village, several of the horses broke loose, running, jumping, and neighing through the village. The natives felt that if the dogs were ferocious, how much more fierce must be these larger animals. The next day the horses were found in an Indian hut, which they had probably entered for shelter or to eat the maize stored in it.

---

[3]Robert B. Cunninghame Graham, *Bernal Díaz del Castillo* (New York, 1915).
[4]Inca Garcilaso de la Vega, *La Florida del Inca* (Madrid, 1723).
[5]Fr. José de Acosta, *Historia natural y moral de las Indias* (Seville, 1890).

Perhaps the Inca has preserved the best records for actual performance of the horses, even giving the distance covered on many occasions, but only Bernal Díaz writes of them always as friends and comrades.

Díaz may have had, with the rest of the conquerors, a lust for gold, a blind faith in religion, and a pride of race; he may have been cruel and arrogant, yet he had the courage and ability to tell the story as he had seen it, and the product is a

Diego de Vargas Zapata Lujan Ponce de Leon

masterpiece. From the very beginning, he talks about horses. After speaking of the difficulty of obtaining good mounts he sets out to give a complete list of the horses embarking for Mexico with characteristic comments on their individual abilities:

The horses were divided up among the ships and loaded; mangers were erected and a store of maize and hay put on board. I will place all the names of the mares and horses down from memory.

Captain Cortés had a dark chestnut stallion which died when we reached San Juan Ulua.

Padre de Alvarado and Hernando López de Avila had a very good sorrel mare, turning out good both for tilting and for racing. When we arrived at New Spain, Pedro de Alvarado took his half either by purchase or by force.

Alonzo Hernández Puertocarrero had a swift grey mare which Cortés bought for him with his gold [shoulder?] knot.

Juan Velásquez de León also had a sturdy grey mare which we called "La Rabona" [bob-tailed]. She was fast and well-broken.

Cristóval de Olid had a dark brown horse that was quite satisfactory.

Francisco de Montejo and Alonzo de Avila had a dark sorrel, useless for war.

Francisco de Morla had a dark brown stallion which was fast and well reined.

Juan de Escalante had a light bay horse with three white stockings. She was not very good.

Diego de Ordas had a barren grey mare, a pacer, who therefore seldom ran.

Gonzalo Domínguez, an excellent horseman, had a dark brown horse that was spotted, but he turned out worthless.

Lares, a fine horseman, had a very good bay horse who was a good runner.

Ortiz, the musician, and Bartolomé García, who had gold mines, had a black horse called "El Arriero" [he probably had driven a pack train], and he was one of the best horses taken in the fleet.

Juan Sedeño, a settler of Habana, had a brown mare that foaled on board ship. Sedeño was the richest soldier in the fleet, having a vessel, a mare, a negro, and many provisions.[6]

_____
[6]Díaz, *Historia verdadera*... (García edición), I, 65-66.

Thus did the rugged old conqueror recall the sixteen horses that first went to Mexico, leaving us a record that Prescott characterizes as "minute enough for the pages of a sporting calendar."[7]

Cortés in the conquest of Mexico used his horses for many things besides transportation. At every opportunity he would utilize them to further his designs, either by intimidating the natives or inspiring his soldiers.

When he arrived on the mainland Juan Sedeño's brown mare had by her side the colt foaled on board ship. During their stay at a hostile Indian village, he made the mare neigh by taking the colt away from her. The Indians, hearing the neighing in the courtyard, asked what ailed the fearful *Tequanes,* as they called the animals. Cortés told them that the mounts were angry because he had not punished the Indians severely enough for making war on the Christians. The natives immediately ordered many cotton clothes for the horses to lie on and fowls for them to eat, that their anger might be appeased.

Another time, when in a precarious position, Cortés utilized his horses in an old trick. Bernal Díaz tells the story in this fashion:

> As Cortés was in all a very clever man, he said, laughing, to us soldiers who happened to be in his company, "Do you know, gentlemen, it appears to me these Indians have a great fear of our horses. They really think they are the ones who make war upon them, and the same with the cannon. I have an idea which will further this belief. Let's take Juan Sedeño's mare, who foaled the other day in the ship, and tie her here where I am. Then, we'll take Ortiz, the musician's horse, which is *muy rijoso,* and let him smell the mare. After he has scented her we will lead them apart so that the *caciques* [Indian chiefs] who are coming will not hear them until they arrive and are talking to me." We did this just as he had commanded, and the

---

[7]William H. Prescott, *History of the Conquest of Mexico* (New York, 1844), I, 262.

stallion scented the mare in Cortés' quarters. We also loaded a
cannon, as ordered, with a large ball and a goodly charge of powder.

It was about noon when forty *caciques* arrived, in friendly manner
and wearing their rich garments. Saluting Cortés and the rest of us,
they covered us with perfume and asked our pardon for what they
had done, saying that in the future they would be good. Cortés
responded somewhat slowly, as though angry, through Aguilar, our
interpreter. He told them how again and again he had spoken for
peace, how they were to blame, and ought to be put to death. However, they were servants of the great king and emperor, Don Carlos,
who had sent us to that place, ordering us to help and favor all who
would enter his service. If they were disposed as they said they were,
we would take this course, but if they were not, some of the *tepuzques*, as they called the cannon, would jump out and kill them. The
tepuzques were mad because of the war made on us in the past.
Cortés then secretly gave a sign to fire the cannon, which was loaded,
and it thundered through the hills. As it was midday and very quiet,
it made a tremendous noise. When they heard it, the *caciques* were
terrified. Since they had never heard anything like it, they believed
what had been told them. Cortés then advised them, through Aguilar,
to fear not, for he had given orders they were not to be harmed.

At that instant they brought the stallion and tied him near. As the
mare was tethered at the same place where Cortés and the *caciques*
were talking, the stallion looked at them and then, scenting the mare,
began to paw the ground, roll his eyes and neigh, wild with excitement. The *caciques*, thinking he was roaring at them, were petrified
with fear. When Cortés saw the ruse had worked, he arose from his
seat, went to the steed, and commanded two servants to take him
away. He then informed the Indians he had told the horse not to
harm them, since they had come for peace and were friendly.[8]

Between these men and their mounts there was the
strongest sense of kinship. Their horses were, as Cortés himself reiterated, their companions and their salvation. In the
following incident we get a glimpse of the relationship between these intrepid men and their faithful horses.

Cortés, amid the strain of war, politics, and administra-
tion, had little time to write to his king and emperor about
his horses, but in telling of the siege of Mexico, in the third
letter, he must linger on the death of a mare:

---

[8]Díaz, *Historia verdadera* ... (García edición), I, 96-97.

Our people were in no danger that day, except during the time when we left the ambush. Some horses collided and a man fell from his mare. She galloped off toward the enemy, who severely wounded her with arrows. When she saw the bad treatment she was receiving, though badly hurt, she came back to us. That night she died. Although we felt her death deeply, for the horses and mares were our salvation, our grief was less because she did not die in the hands of the enemy, as we had feared would be the case.[9]

Graham says that Cortés looked on the mare as a friend and companion, and therefore was thankful that the last words she would hear spoken would be in the tongue she had heard—and no doubt in a vague way understood—since the day she had been foaled. Very likely, also, Cortés did not wish the Indians to know they could kill the fearful animals.

Francisco López de Gómara, one of the few eye-witnesses of the conquest of Mexico who wrote, recounts a story concerning a vision seen by many of the Conqueror's men. Cortés, according to Gómara, when he heard of the vision, used it as a means to encourage his men to fight. The apparition appeared as a mounted man, in the form of San Diego, the patron saint of Spain. This presence drove back the fighting natives and won the battle for the Spaniards. Bernal Díaz out and out ridicules Gómara on this point, saying that although he took part in the battle he did not see the vision. In fact, he continues, he had never heard the story until he read about it afterwards in Gómara. Then, with the thinly veiled sarcasm the man of action so often has for the man of letters, he added that perhaps he was too great a sinner to be allowed to see the glorious apostle. Gómara's account follows:

The Spaniards were in difficulties and imminent danger, since they had no room to use their artillery or cavalry to open a way through the enemy. While hard pressed and about to seek flight, Francisco

[9]Gayangos, *Cartas y relaciones* . . . , 245.

Morla appeared on a dapple-grey horse and attacked the Indians so they were thrown in disorder. The Spaniards, thinking Cortés had come up with the cavalry and as there was now room, charged the enemy and several were slain. Then the horseman left and the Indians again threw themselves upon the Spaniards and pressed them as closely as before. The horseman returned immediately and joined our men. He attacked the enemy and made them retreat. Our men utilized the advantage given them by the man on horseback and hurled themselves on the natives, killing and wounding many. As soon as the tide turned the horseman left.

As the Indians did not see the horseman who caused them to flee in terror and confusion, thinking him a centaur, they again attacked with heathen audacity, treating the Spaniards worse than before. The horseman reappeared now for the third time and dispersed the Indians, terrified and suffering losses. At the same time, the foot soldiers attacked, wounding and killing many.[10]

Gómara up to this point in the story implies that the horseman was Francisco Morla on a dapple-grey horse. But Morla's horse was dark brown; so that if that is who it was, he must have been riding the horse of either Hernández Puertocarrero, Veléasquez de Leon, or Diego de Ordás, as they were the only men amongst the cavalry whose horses were grey. Gómora continues:

Cortés then arrived. . . . They asked if the man on horseback had been one of his men. Cortés replied it was not, as he had not been able to get there sooner. So they concluded it was Saint James the Apostle, patron saint of Spain. Thereupon Cortés cried, "Forward, comrades, for God is with us and the glorious Saint Peter."

This might seem to indicate that Cortés was confusing Saint James and Saint Peter. Perhaps, since San Pedro was his patron, he felt he could not diplomatically commend San Diego for his assistance. So by giving credit to God and at the same time mentioning the name of his patron saint, he forestalled any future difficulties with his patron. Then

. . . he and his men dashed among the enemy, driving them before, out of the maze of ditches to a place where the lances could be freely

[10]Francisco López de Gómara, *Historia de México* (Anvers, 1554), fol. 32b.

used. . . . The Indians . . . fleeing into the dense forests, scattered in all directions. . . .

Everyone declared they had seen the rider on the dapple-grey, three different times fighting against the Indians, as had been stated above, and that it was Saint James, the Patron Saint of Spain.[11]

Díaz' account of the same battle does not tally with Gómara's. Díaz says that during the fierce battle Cortés and his horsemen did not appear, although they wished for him and were afraid some disaster had overtaken him. They fought most of the day with no help but their own arms. He says toward the end of the account of the battle:

Just at this time we saw our horsemen, and as the mass of Indians were wildly attacking us, they did not see them approaching the rear, and, as the ground was level and the horsemen were good, with horses well-trained and fine gallopers, they soon encountered the natives and speared them as they desired.

This is a typical Díaz statement—"speared them as they desired." It tells so much. In another place he says, "as was convenient at the time." Díaz was almost without a particle of humor, but so human. In another place he makes this laconic remark: "After the battle we seared the wounds of ourselves and our horses with the grease we took from a fat Indian." Again,

As soon as the horsemen dismounted in the shade of some trees and huts, we returned thanks to God for bringing us the victory. As it was the day of *Nuestra Señora*, we afterward gave to the town the name of Santa Maria de la Victoria, because of the great victory won on Our Lady's Day.

Díaz specifically differs with Gómara concerning the appearance of the vision of Saint James:

It may be as Gómara says, that the glorious apostles *Señor San Diego y Señor San Pedro* came to our aid and I, being only a poor sinner, was not worthy to see them. What I saw was Francisco Morla on a brown horse who came up with Cortés. . . . There were in our company over four hundred soldiers, including Cortés himself, and

---

[11]Gómara, *Historia de México*, fol. 32a.

many other gentlemen, and it [the vision] would have been talked
about.[12]

So we have the two sides of the argument. Possibly Gómara
was a little skeptical of the story as told, and so added Morla
at the start to appease doubters. On the other hand, he may
have had a failing, common to story tellers, and embroidered
the tale as he progressed by bringing in the saints.

II

Following the route of the preceding expedition, Cortés'
troops finally reached the coast of Mexico. The presence of
foreigners on the coast of Mexico was noted by the subjects
of Moctezuma, the Mexican ruler. Almost as soon as the
Spaniards landed, they were received by representatives of
this powerful king of Anáhuac.

Cortés saw here an opportunity to display before the
astonished eyes of the natives the power of the Spanish forces.
He ordered the artillery to fire, the cavalry to maneuver,
and then had Alvarado on his sorrel mare cavort back and
forth on the sandy shores of the beach displaying his abilities as a fine rider. This, combined with the cannon's roar,
the rattles and bells attached to the horsemen, and the stirring notes of the bugles, presented such a strange and aston-
ishing spectacle that the natives felt they must in some way
report the whole scene faithfully to their emperor. To sup-
plement the oral version, they carefully sketched many of
the scenes; consequently, there were some remarkable repro-
ductions made of the ships, the captains, the horses, and even
of two greyhounds taken by the soldiers. These have been
retained and they may still be seen. After the review Cortés
started his long march westward to reach the Aztec capital.

---

[12]Díaz, *Historia Verdadera* ... (García edición), I, 92.

All along the way toward the imperial city of Tenochtitlán, the natives gathered and discussed the strange new
creatures which had so suddenly descended on their land. The
Zempoaltecas said that the horses were so ferocious that the
Spaniards had to put bridles on them to keep them from
devouring humans. It was commonly believed that they ate
the metal bits. The Indian allies of the Spaniards told how
the animals could run as fast as deer, nothing being able to
escape them. Whenever the horses neighed, the natives, quak-
ing with fear, would run for feed and water. They would
feed the horses, since they were even more afraid not to.

The inevitable happened in the battle between the Tlaxcaltecos and the Spaniards, when the natives, probably acci-
dentally, killed a horse. The horse was decapitated by a
single stroke. Later, at Zempoala, Cortés' chestnut stallion
was killed, and he took El Arriero, the fine dark horse belonging to Ortiz, the musician, and Bartolomé García. After
a fierce battle the Tlaxcalans were defeated, and thereafter
gave their support to the Spaniards, sending many warriors
with Cortés to fight against their traditional enemies, the
Aztecs.

Riding this horse and heading his troops, Cortés entered
the island city of Tenochtitlán before the eyes of tens of
thousands of astonished native inhabitants. The Mexicans
believed the Spaniards were sons of their famous god
Quetzalcoatl, and consequently, since they too must then
be gods, housed them in the palace of Atzaycatl, where Emperor Moctezuma had his principal shrines and idols. A large
number of servants and priests were put at the service of the
Spaniards. These servants were instructed not to forget to
have a sufficient supply of fresh green fodder to feed the
horses. The Spaniards always rode on horseback while in

Mexico City, even using their horses when they went to Moctezuma's residence, which was not much more than across the street.

Cortés had not been long on the mainland when Velasquez, governor of Cuba, sent Pánfilo Narváez to bring Cortés back to Cuba. When Cortés heard that Narváez had arrived at Vera Cruz with a fleet, he decided he had best handle this emergency himself. He left Pedro de Alvarado in Tenochtilán as commander during his absence, and with some of his best soldiers and finest horses started back to Vera Cruz.

As Cortés and his little army approached Vera Cruz, Gonzalo de Sandoval, a lieutenant and personal friend of Cortés, sent two Spaniards with dark complexions to spy within the encampment of Pánfilo Narváez. These two Spaniards disguised themselves as Indians, and carrying baskets of native fruits, mingled with the enemy.

Salvatierra, one of Narváez's officers, arrogantly ordered the disguised Spaniards to go and bring some grass for his horse. The Spaniards, disguising their personal feeling, went and brought back the feed. When they had returned they remained in a squatting position while in the presence of the Spaniard since this was the custom of the natives. Salvatierra paid his unknown countrymen for their service with a string of cheap yellow beads.

The two disguised Spaniards were allowed complete freedom in the camp, and when night came, while one was on guard, the other saddled a horse. Then they quietly stole to the patio where the horses and saddles were kept, and after a few minutes' work hurried away at full speed. Luck was with them, as they came across another horse that was picketed and grazing along a little stream. With two horses now they hurried back to Sandoval, reporting all they had seen, heard and done. Salvatierra must have been angry when he later learned how he had been tricked.

Cortés, upon learning that Narváez had ninety horses, had his allies, the Chinantecas, make copper spears and explained to them how to hold the spears if attacked by cavalry, butts to the ground, heads about one foot apart and some four feet from the ground. With the help of God, and a little ingenuity, Cortés with his few men defeated Narváez, though he had the largest expedition which up to that time had been collected in the New World. Tápia tells us the story which not only explains what the two disguised men had done in Narváez' camp, but also accounts for Cortés astounding victory over the superior forces. Sandoval had had the cinches on the saddles of Narváez' men cut practically in two, so that when the battle started the cavalry soon became footmen, and in the dark, Cortés and his few soldiers came away with the victory.[13] Cortés had gained sorely needed supplies, horses, and fresh men for his conquest.

When he had persuaded the defeated men to accompany him, Cortés returned to Tenochtitlán, where Alvarado's ill-advised actions had created a delicate situation for the Spaniards. The Mexicans let the Spaniards enter, but it was soon to be seen that they were little better than captives within the city. The many outrages of Alvarado had made it unsafe to remain in the city or to travel in small groups. After some deliberation, Cortés decided to leave the city quietly during the dark of the night.

Plans for the exit were carefully laid. First the booty— the treasure of Axayacatl—was distributed by Cortés. Each individual soldier was given a portion, the horses receiving

---

[13]Andrés de Tápia, *Relación*, in García Icazbalceta, *Colección de Documentos*... (Mexico, 1866), II, 590.

shares equal to those given a foot-soldier. Cortés, as befitted his rank, received more, and a fifth part belonged to the crown. The treasure proved no little problem. Don Hernando placed six of the slowest horses and a pregnant mare at the service of the royal officers, to be used as pack beasts, the best horses naturally being reserved for battle.

With the greatest of caution, at midnight of June 30, 1520, the proud army which only a few months before had so triumphantly entered the city, resplendent in their shining armor and colorful clothes, quietly stole from their quarters, heading for the country and trusting in God to lead them safely.

Most of the cavalrymen, led by Cortés and supported by Spanish and Tlaxcalan infantry, headed the procession, carrying the bridges which were to furnish passage across the gaps which cut the causeways leading to and from the island city. Part of the cavalry under the doughty Sandoval were to guard the treasure and the prisoners. The remaining few horsemen, under Pedro de Alvarado, were to cover the retreat of the fugitive army. To avoid as much noise as possible during the retreat, the Spaniards wrapped cotton cloths around the feet of the horses and the wheels of the cannons.

In spite of their precaution, they were detected, and in an incredibly short space found themselves surrounded by furious Mexicans. The bridge they carried slipped from the causeway into the lake, hindering them from crossing the rest of the causeway on the road to Tlacopan. From every side the Spaniards were attacked. The cavalrymen tried to escape by jumping across the cut, but in the dark of the night, and crowded by their soldiers, most of those who attempted jumping fell, horse and all, into the blood-stained waters. According to the account, it was not long until the bodies of the slain filled in the causeway to the level of the road and those men left, although greatly reduced in number, now succeeded in reaching the village of Tlacopan. Don Hernando, wounded and exhausted, waited in this village for those few men who might straggle in. Many of his bravest and most loyal friends were no longer at his side. Afflicted by his grief and pain, both physical and mental, and hardly knowing what he was doing, he turned back to search for those left behind. After having walked for some time, he met Pedro Alvarado muddy and covered with blood, still carrying a spear in his hand. Four Spanish and eight Tlaxcalan soldiers accompanied him. All were wounded. Alvarado was particularly sad. He had left his beautiful sorrel mare dead in the canal.

Others listed among the missing were Velásquez de León with "La Rabona," that sturdy grey mare; Morla, with the dark brown stallion of which he was so proud, since it was the fastest horse in the army; Lares, who next to Sandoval was the best rider in the army, with his beautiful bay horse which was so well reined; these and many more brave soldiers and horses paid dearly with their lives for the temerity of their enterprise. Botello, the astrologer who had proposed the retreat, and his stallion were both missing. Bernal Díaz says Botello had predicted that he would die at the same time as his horse. He proved a good prophet.

The dawn following that sad night— the Noche Triste— came, and the remains of the little army gathered to take stock. Truly, their state was deplorable. All were wounded, some still bleeding. By the grace of God, and Sandoval's clever leadership, the horses which carried the gold were there. Of all the horses which Narváez and Salcedo had brought when they came after Cortés, as well as those first

sixteen to tread on the American continent, there remained
only twenty-three—almost all wounded.

To Don Hernando, all those dreams of conquest which he
had cherished, his glory, his prestige, his best friends—all
seemed lost. Fortune, so long his friend, had turned its back
on him for the first time. Tears, despite his efforts to the
contrary, appeared in his eyes.

When the sun rose, the Mexicans renewed the onslaught.
They followed hard at the heels of the Spaniards, throwing
rocks and arrows and shouting, "Not a single one shall
escape!" The most severely wounded Spaniards were tied
on the horses and retreat continued. To add to their difficulties, they missed the trail which led them to the friendly
land of their Tlaxcalan allies. Hunger struck next. Prickly
pears and *capulines* (wild cherries) provided the only food
available. Their pursuers harried them constantly. They had
killed four more Spaniards, and were just waiting for the
opportune moment to deliver the final blow. Weariness and
discouragement filled the stout hearts of the slowly retreat-
ing and broken army. Even the horses, half dead with exhaustion, seemed discouraged. Martín Comboa's horse died;
and while at other times its body would have been decently
buried, now it was eaten by the hungry Spaniards. Truly
they were in desperate straits—even Cortés was too hungry
to refuse.

The following day the most discouraging spectacle of the
conquest presented itself to the weary and broken army. On
the Plains of Otompan, and on the small hills which surrounded the plains, across the very road they had to follow,
were thousands of savage warriors waiting for the kill, resplendent in their colorful feathers and showy dress. The
fierce hostility of the Indians seemed now to be fanned into

a new white-hot heat as they gathered to rid themselves
of the hated Spaniards. The battle, if it might be so called,
which followed was the most terrible of the Conquest. The
Spaniards, feeling already doomed, fought with reckless
abandon. With bandaged hands they grasped their weapons,
ignoring the old wounds which opened with the violent
exercise. Despite hopelessness, once they started fighting, it
seemed strength and courage replaced their weariness. The
horses, apparently sensing the mood of their riders, began to
prance, perk their ears and raise their tails, and generally
show they sensed the coming struggle and were ready to
fight with their masters.

In the midst of the battle Don Hernando was wounded.
A rock struck him on the head. Almost immediately thereafter an arrow wounded him on the hand. His black horse, the
proud Morzillo, was struck in the mouth at the same time
by another arrow. Cortés dismounted. Morzillo, finding
himself without his master and mad with pain, furiously
attacked the enemy, kicking and biting the Indians, who
gave way panic-stricken at this unparalleled onslaught. The
two Spaniards who were sent after the charger were scarcely
able to control Morzillo and bring him back. Had they not
secured him, Morzillo would not have become an immortal,
as the Indians would probably have succeeded in killing him.
Morzillo was spared for a more glorious fate.

The cavalry was responsible for the ultimate victory on
the Plains of Otompan. The perspicacious Cortés boldly
decided to attack the Indian leader himself, though he was
surrounded by countless warriors. Mounting once again the
faithful Morzillo, and with a handful of picked horsemen,
he fought his way toward the chieftain. It was Cortés who
knocked the Indian chief from his palanquin with his spear,

and Juan Salamanca beheaded him. This broke the spirit of
the natives and they soon retired in confusion, leaving a
practically defeated enemy. Thus ended the historic battle
of Otompan; the Spaniards were saved from what seemed
certain death. Had it not been for the horses, and Morzillo
in particular, who fought his way through the Indian ranks
with tooth and hoof, the outcome would have been very
different. Had the Spaniards lost here, the Conquest might
have been delayed indefinitely.

   While the battle on the Plains of Otompan was in progress,
Juan de Yuste y Morla, with ten cargas of gold, supplies,
and forty-five men and five horses, left Vera Cruz, headed
for Mexico City. They went by Tlaxcala, where three hundred allies joined them. Without knowing anything about
the happenings during the Noche Triste, Morla entered the
territory of Anáhuac. Taken completely by surprise, they
were captured by a group of Mexicans, who sacrificed them
to their gods in Texcoco. The horses (who if they knew,
undoubtedly were grateful), were sacrificed beside and with
their masters. Their hides were carefully packed with dry
grass and placed in the main temple. A similar fate had
already met the horses killed on the Noche Triste. The heads
of these horses had been hung in the temples, carefully
alternated with those of the Spaniards. Even in death horse
and master were not separated. The Indians thought that if
the invaders should return, their horses would be frightened
and run away upon seeing the heads of their dead colleagues,
and that the thrice-hated Spaniards would not be able to
handle them.

   When Cortés, wounded, defeated, and discouraged, finally
reached Tlaxcala, he had only twenty horses left. Now once

again fortune was to smile on him. Unexpectedly he received a supply ship from Cuba. These supplies were sent by Diego Velásquez and were intended for Narváez, whom he believed victorious. The ship landed, commanded by Pedro Barba, and contained soldiers, weapons, a horse, and a mare. Barba was skillfully drawn into a net, and he, with all his supplies, fell into Cortés' hands. Shortly afterward, three more ships arrived; all these were the property of Francisco de Garay, conqueror of the Pánuco. The first ship was headed by Rodrigo de Morejon and it brought guns, ammunition, men, and a mare. A few men succeeded in reaching the shore from the wreck of Camargo's ship. A second boat, commanded by Ramirez and called *El Viejo,* well equipped with supplies, also arrived. It brought fourteen horses, plenty of food and reinforcements. Immediately after this ship, came a third under Miguel Díaz de Auz, which brought seven additional horses and more supplies. Díaz de Auz's men, veterans in the wars in the Indies, had clothing padded with cotton as a protection against arrows. Consequently, they were nicknamed *"los de las albardas,"* the cotton boys. This armor protected the wearer from the powerful Indian arrows better than the second-grade plate carried by most of the Spaniards.

Cortés was jubilant. He had suddenly once again acquired an army. With typical sagacity he decided to march immediately on Mexico City. The first step was to review his troops, which he did on the main patio of the principal Indian temple of Tlaxcala. Wearing clean armor, shining like silver, under a crimson velvet cape and mounted on the coal black Morzillo, he must have been a striking sight as he reviewed his newly acquired cavalry, which now included some forty men divided into four squads of ten men each. The army was soon marching back on the return trip to Tenochtitlán, accompanied by innumerable Tlaxcalan allies.

Once in Texcoco, the welcome news of the arrival of still another ship reached the Spaniards. This ship was owned by Juan de Burgos, who offered for sale gunpowder, crossbows, muskets, and three horses. Cortés sent some of his men to buy everything they could. Before they were done, even the shipmen, including Francisco Medel, the pilot, and all the crew, had joined the Cortés expedition. Furthermore, another ship with more supplies reached San Juan de Ulua. This was probably commanded by Solis de la Huerta, whom Cortés had dispatched to Jamaica for supplies. Through these fortunate arrivals the lucky Cortés was once again well equipped and supplied.

In the final siege and capture of Mexico City there was not a single move in which the horses were not of utmost value. In one of the attacks led by Don Hernando, he was repelled with heavy losses. Forty-three Spaniards, a large number of Indian allies, and five horses were captured, all alive. The allies were taken to the various temples to be sacrificed. The forty-three whites and the five horses were taken to the main temple, honored by a special ceremony.

The next morning Cortés, furious with his losses, viciously attacked the enemy, leading the army in person. The Indians succeeded in killing the horse he was riding and captured Cortés himself, but he had left Morzillo in camp to rest. They did not kill Cortés, because they wanted to take him to one of the temples and sacrifice him there. "*Malinche, Malinche,*" the Indians shouted when they had Cortés in their hands, for that was their name for him, derived from the name of his charming Indian mistress, Doña Marina. Cristóbal de Olea made a solitary, brave, but rash, attack on Cortés' captors. Although Cortés did his best to help, Olea and his horse were soon killed. Another rider tried to reach Cortés and give him a horse to escape on, but he too fell, an arrow in his throat. Finally some *Tlaxacaltecos* succeeded in freeing Don Hernando, who escaped on the horse of the brave dead soldier.

Seeing his forces weakened day by day because of the disloyalty of his allies, the Mexican leader Cuactemoc, Moctezuma's successor, sent messengers to the near-by towns announcing that the gods promised an early victory. To convince the Indians that the invaders were mortals, the messengers carried with them the heads of five Spaniards and two horses.

In one of the last attacks on the city, a rider going at full speed threw his spear at an Indian, piercing him from one side to the other. While the Spaniard was trying to extract his weapon, his horse stumbled on the body and fell. Immediately a shower of missiles rained over the soldier, instantly killing him. The Indians captured the wounded horse and sacrificed it.

It became not uncommon to see the Mexicans with horse tails tied to the headdress they wore in battle. They did this to show their bravery in attacking and killing the terrible beasts of the Spaniards. Most of the horses killed were slain with knives and swords taken from the dead Spaniards and tied to long sticks. Many were also killed with Spanish spears which the Indians had succeeded in taking away from their enemy in battle.

When one reads the story of the Conquest, he cannot but be impressed by the important place the cavalry had in every move. It was always at the head and rear of the expeditions to protect the infantry. When not bathed with mud and blood, the Spanish horseman reflected every ray of the sun, and, with the hawkbells tied to the saddles tinkling merrily, presented to the astonished eyes of the natives a fabulous and fearful apparition. The Tabasqueños called the horses *tequanes,* meaning monsters. The Tlaxcaltecos thought the horses were deer, which by some magic power permitted themselves to be mounted. They believed these animals flew and even talked. Moctezuma believed the same when he first saw the horses. For a long time the natives thought the steeds gained nourishment from the iron bits. Scarcely less superstitious were the Spaniards, who one time declared the Indians' witchcraft had made five horses fall sick. If one factor could be singled out which contributed most to the successful conquest of Anáhuac, surely it was the horses.

III

The difficulties that Cortés later had to face on his trip from Mexico to Honduras defy exaggeration. No one knew better than he that the success of his desperate intentions lay upon his horses. It is from the fifth letter, telling of this trip, that we get our first hint of the singular story of Morzillo, the horse that became a god.

When Cortés left for Honduras in 1524, he was riding Morzillo, who had performed nobly during the Battle of Otompan and the siege of Mexico. By his side rode the intriguing Doña Marina, on her last adventure with Cortés, whose wife came to the New World soon after. Their only guide was a crude compass, supplemented by an occasional Indian captured by the way to lead the party to a village and food. Since they had slight idea where they were going, and less of what awaited them, they relied on the horses to carry and protect them.

One day during the march, Cortés came upon the lovely valley of Tayasal, whose green slopes led to an island-studded lake. Upon its quiet waters the tall white walls of an island city glimmered in the afternoon sun, doubtless bringing to the veterans memories of their first glimpse of Tenochtitlán nestled in the lake at México. Around the shores of this sequestered lake countless deer grazed, still happily unacquainted with Christian sports. Cortés and his men, with typical enthusiasm, gave merry chase, disregarding the afternoon sun, shooting and lancing the deer until satiated with the sport. The chase was not without its ill effects. The horse of Palacio Rubias died; Bernal Díaz tells us that it was because the fat in his body melted,[14] but since it was early afternoon in the tropics, sun-stroke would probably suffice as an explanation. After the hunt, camp was made on the shore of the lake.

In the island city of Tayasal lived the Maya tribe of Peten-Itzás. They were living quietly, tending to their sacred deer and honoring their gods, when strange rumors began to drift in. Then one afternoon they beheld with their own eyes a most bewildering sight. Awe-inspiring creatures were pursuing their deer, and slaying them as they spat thunder and lightning. Although the Itzás were shocked at the inhuman barbarity of these new creatures that killed their harmless deer, they decided discretion was the better part of valor and invited them to visit the island.

Cortés and his company made camp near the lake to rest after the fatigue of the chase. Presently canoes were seen approaching, and an invitation was extended to visit Tayasal. Cortés, against the wishes of his companions, who feared a

---

[14]Díaz, *Historia verdadera*... (García edición), II, 299.

trap, took twenty men and Morzillo and went out to visit Tayasal.[15] He was well received. When night drew near, he felt it best to leave; prudence told him he must get back to his men before dark. But he was compelled to leave Morzillo. In the simple words of Cortés, the horse had "got a splinter in his foot and was unable to go on. The chief promises to cure him but I do not know if he will succeed."[16] As he was destined never again to set foot in the province, Cortés never knew of Morzillo's fate.

The Itzás were awed by the responsibility entrusted to them. Eager to gain the favor of their new god, they decorated Morzillo with garlands of flowers and brought chickens and other like delicacies for him to eat; in short, they treated their hippomorpheus deity with every honor within their ken. Morzillo, either from grief over losing his old master or perhaps from this change of diet, wasted away until only the bones of the apotheosized charger remained to his worshipers.

Some hundred years later, Father Barolomé Fuensalida and Juan de Orbita made a missionary trip to the Peten-Itzás. They were not a little surprised to see temples of a size equal to any in the Christian province of Yucatan. Twelve would hold over a thousand people.[17] In the center of the largest temple, to the utter amazement of the *padres*, there stood a large statue of a horse, seated on his haunches.

No sooner did Padre Orbita catch sight of the idol than it seemed as though the spirit of the Lord descended on him. He seized a stone, and, climbing to the top of the heathen idol, battered it to pieces.

Thus we have the story of Morzillo, the horse that became

---

[15]Gómara, *Historia de México*, 262.

[16]*Colección de documentos ... de España*, IV, 69.

[17]Fr. Diego López de Cogolludo, *Historia de Yucathan* (Madrid, 1688), 492.

a god. Even today, if you ask a native canoeman of the city of Remedios, which has grown up on the ruins of Tayasal, he will tell you that on clear moonless nights you may see him deep in the waters of the lake, tolerantly receiving the worship of the Itzás while he awaits Cortés' return.

With the legend of Morzillo we close the story of the famous horses of the conquest of Anáhuac, and although they have long been dead, as long as men admire horses, stories of these faithful animals will survive.

IV

The horses of Cortés have more fame than those of any other *conquistadores'*; but others had similar experiences. The Inca, Garcilaso de la Vega, gives us the best account of the horses of Hernando de Soto. An example of the horse lore to be found in the writings of the Inca follows.

The story takes place some two hundred and fifty years before Paul Revere cantered across the New England countryside and concerns the ride of one Gonçalo Silvestre and Juan López for help through the Everglades of Florida. They were riding for God and their king, as well as to succor de Soto, who found himself in a rather awkward situation. He had moseyed off into the swamp and became separated from the main body of his troops. With hostile Indians on all sides and with insufficient provisions, he deemed it wise to send for reinforcements.

De Soto knew of a certain young man who was always in the front line of battle, and though he had barely reached his majority, was *muy jinete,* as the Spanish phrase for a good horseman goes. This was Gonçalo Silvestre. De Soto called Gonçalo before him, and in front of his men explained what he wished done. After saying he might choose a companion, he gave minute directions for the perilous trip. Realizing then that the mission amounted to little less than a death sentence, de Soto explained that the reason he was choosing Gonçalo was that he had the best horse in the army—*el mejor cavallo de todo nuestro exercito.*[18] De Soto was human.

After Gonçalo had heard the orders, he turned and walked to his horse without a word. What he may have said to the animal while he was saddling is something else. Mounting Peçeno, he jogged through camp in search of Juan López Cacho, one of his chums.

De Soto's great name had attracted some of the best families in Spain for his expedition to the land of the "Fountain of Youth." Juan was one of these, as well as de Soto's favorite page. Gonçalo found Juan asleep under a tree. Awakening his companion, he told him that the chief had commanded that he should come with him for a ride for help to the main army. Juan, who was worn out with marching and fighting, and who perhaps saw more peril than adventure, said he was too exhausted to make the trip. Gonçalo, a little tired himself, said sharply, "Soto said for me to pick a companion, and I pick you. Now either you come with me or stay in God's name, for the dangers will not be the less for your absence." In this he was entirely correct. With these words Gonçao mounted Peçeno and rode on down the path. Juan, wearily saddling, followed.

The first four or five leagues, on an Indian trail, were fairly smooth, but before they had gone much farther their difficulties commenced. They encountered mires, streams and lowlands, which announced they were approaching the main body of the swamp. Fresh Indian signs were also prevalent.

---

[18]Garcilaso de la Vega, *La Florida* . . . , 43.

At the edge of the swamp the trail ended, and, as the Inca
Garcilaso de la Vega tells the story, they could never have
continued had it not been for God and their horses' instinct
(the latter element doubtless being the more apparent). The
horses put their heads down and trailed their own scent back
the way they had come. At first the youths endeavored to
guide them, but then, showing a wisdom worthy of men
years their seniors, allowed the animals a free rein. Like
bloodhounds on a warm scent, the horses moved along with
noses close to the trail. When they would occasionally inhale
some dust or loose grass and blow, the sound scurried fear
through the riders, who imagined Indians behind each
shadow.

Gonçalo's horse was by far the best tracker. But that was
not surprising to the Inca. Was he not the perfect color both
for war and peace? He was a deep chestnut, so dark brown
as to be almost pitch colored; hence his name. He had a white
stocking on his near front foot and a blaze on his forehead,
which he seemed to drink as it went down to his lips (ser
bueno en estremo, porque era castaño escuro, peçeno, calcado
el pie izquierdo, y lista en la frente, que bebia con ella).[19]

The color of a horse very often gave the Spaniards a name
for the animal. Thus we have lobuno (wolf-colored),
gateado (cat-colored), and pardisco (greyish brown). Cortés'
horse was called simply Morzillo, as he was black. Sandoval's
horse, considered by Bernal Díaz as the best in either the Old
or New World, was called Motilla, meaning a tuft, although
we don't know where it grew. De Soto's horse was Azeitunero
because of his olive-colored coat. Velásquez' mare was called
La Rabona because of her short tail. The conquistadores loved
colorful horses, whether that color lay in their coats or their

---

[19]Garcilaso de la Vega, La Florida . . . , p. 44.

actions. If anything, they were partial to color, allowing a horse was as good as his coat, just reversing the old Western proverb which says no off color can be on a good horse. Don Bernardo had the answer when he said, *"Pero en este de colores, camina cada uno a su gusto."*[20] (As far as color goes, let each suit himself.)

Juan López had a buckskin with a beautiful black mane and tail. He, too, was an unusual horse, although not to be compared with the chestnut of his companion.

All through that night they kept on their way, guided by their steeds. Two days passed in this manner. The only diversion was the occasional twang of a bowstring and the whistle of an arrow. As the chronicler says, "They continued on their way with difficulties easier to imagine than to write."[21]

They had no food other than some corn they were able to pick up at a deserted Indian village. Since they did not dare build a fire, they had to eat the kernels as they were, cold and hard. Three days passed, while hungry and exhausted they rode on. Time and again they passed close to the fires of Indian camps. The savages were feasting and dancing, and though an occasional dog barked, divine providence closed the ears of the natives.

After having traveled in this state for ten leagues, Juan López gave out. Stopping and turning to his comrade he said, "Either let me sleep a moment or else run your lance through me here on the trail, for I can go no farther." Gonçalo, with a youth's disgust at weakness (he had refused the same request many times during the last few days), said, "Get off and sleep if you must, but if the sun rises and the

---

[20]Don Hernando de Vargas Machuca, *Libro de Exercicios de la Gineta* (quoted in Graham, *Horses of the Conquest*, 126).

[21]Garcilaso de la Vega, *La Florida* . . . , 44.

Indians see us, all is lost."[22] Juan, when he heard these welcome words, relaxed and fell to the ground like dead. Gonçalo
dismounted wearily and retrieved his fallen comrade's lance,
then stood holding the horses while he waited for Juan to
awake.

Before many moments had passed it started to sprinkle; a
cloudburst followed. Just as suddenly, the downpour ceased.
The sun came out before the last drops fell. Gonçalo had
been dozing, but when he felt the sun he awoke with a start
and called guardedly to his companion. Juan did not awaken.
Gonçalo finally succeeded in arousing him by beating him
with the butt of his spear. Juan, still groggy with sleep,
clumsily mounted and they started on their way.

They had barely started to move when they heard the
shouts of Indians. Unwittingly they had stopped on the out-
skirts of a native encampment and the moment they moved
they were discovered. Spurring their steeds, they galloped
furiously for the swamp, the Indians close at the horses'
heels, raising a terrific din.

Once in the water, the horses were protected from the
arrows, while the riders were guarded by their armor. As
luck would have it, the main encampment of the Spaniards
was not far distant, and, hearing the clatter, a group under
the leadership of Nuño Tobar came out to see what was
going on. The weary messengers were soon again among
friends. This did not end the trip for Gonçalo. He rode back
to de Soto, guiding the rescue party safely through the
swamp. Juan López stayed in the main camp, saying the general had neither commanded him to come or return; so he
would stay where he was. He undoubtedly slept.

---

[22]Garcilaso de la Vega, *La Florida* ..., 45.

The horse lore of the *conquistadores* is so closely bound up with the story of the Conquest, that one cannot be told without the other. Whether the account is about Cortés in Mexico, Pizarro in Peru, de Soto in Florida, or Coronado in the Southwest, the same is true. The men and the horses were inseparable. The affection of the men for their mounts was more like the affection of an older brother for a younger, a companionship tinged with pride. The tales of these men and of their horses will never die or grow old. Who can say there is not now a spot where the grass is always green and the water clear and cool, a place where these steeds may browse all day, waiting for the familiar call of their masters?

Mexican Color Terms for Horses

By W. A. WHATLEY

No OTHER language is so rich in hair-splitting terms for distinguishing the exact color characteristics of a horse as is Spanish. The horse played a more important part in the tempestuous national life of the medieval Spaniards and Spanish Moors than he did in the life of any other European nation; to the Castilians and the Moors, cavalry was the all-in-all of warfare. To the Spaniard transplanted to the New World, and to his mestizo sons and grandsons, confronted with boundless distances, engaging in open range ranching, and defending themselves against nomadic enemies, the horse was an hundredfold more important than he had been to the crusading Castilian.

In the busy, mobile life of the great cattle haciendas, cherished saddle horses, as well as wild range horses, often strayed and men were detailed to find them and bring them back. The need for terms by which to describe a missing horse so exactly that anyone who had his description might recognize him at sight and hold him until his owner might be communicated with tended to develop a vocabulary of colors and color markings. This vocabulary was rich in Old Spain, but the vaqueros of New Spain made it even richer. On our ranch in northern Mexico a dispute was once brought to me for settlement. It concerned the status of a sorrel horse that had recently been caught by one man and that was claimed by another. According to Mexican law, such horses become the temporary property, for use, of the man catching them, until the owner turns up; if, after legal notice and after a reasonable length of time has elapsed, no owner establishes his claim, the horse is sold at auction, the proceeds going to the municipality. The sorrel horse had been held for some time when a vaquero put in a claim to it, on the basis of having been requested three years before to look out for this particular mount. He had nothing to go by but the oral description given, but this was so detailed that there wasn't any doubt as to the identity of the horse. He was *"alazán roán cuatralbo cabiralo"*—a golden light sorrel, golden mane and tail, with four white feet and sparse-haired in mane and tail. The brand was only secondary evidence, since it had been altered beyond recognition. I awarded him to the plaintiff, and within three months the sorrel's owner was notified and he took him home.

The following terms make no pretense of constituting a comprehensive list, but they will serve to illustrate the consummate brevity and minuteness of detail to which color nomenclature has been reduced:

Alazán—sorrel.

Alazán tostado—chestnut sorrel, a color greatly esteemed.

The vaqueros have a rhyme,

Alazán tostado, primero muerto que cansado.

(The chestnut sorrel dies before he tires.)

Alazán roán—golden-maned, light sorrel.

Andaluz—yellow, with blondish mane and tail.

Aplumado—bay, dun, sorrel or black, with small white markings resembling feathers. Very rare.

Azulejo—dark blue roan.

Barroso—smudgy dun.

Bayo—dun.

Bayo azafranado—light, bright dun of saffron cast.

Bayo coyote. See *coyote*.

Bayo tigre—dun, with tiger stripes of black on the legs, often a stripe on the shoulders, generally a stripe down the back.

Blanco—white.

Canelo—blue and red roan mixed ("cinnamon-hued").

Cebruno—dark brown.

Champurrado—cholocate brown.

TEXAS.—A PARTY OF MEXICANS CROSSING THE RIO GRANDE, RETURNING FROM A HORSE-STEALING RAID IN TEXAS.
FROM A SKETCH BY JAMES GREATOREX.

Colorado—bay.

Coyote—dirty dun, with black back-stripe, black mane and tail; i.e., with *cabos negros*—black points, or ends.

Golondrino—dark brown with golden-brown flecks ("swallow colored").

Grullo—extremely dark gray, almost black; real gray, not a mixture of black and white hairs; mouse-colored, the word *grullo* meaning sand-hill crane. Does not change color with age.

Güero—albino, pinkish skin under white hair, pink eyes.

Manchado—white, with large patches containing sparse black hairs, not enough to constitute gray, but sufficient to give a discolored appearance ("soiled" or "splotched").

Melado—white, applied usually to old grays who have lost their dark hairs with age. True white; i.e., white from birth, is *blanco*.

Mojino—dark brown, almost black.

Negro—black.

Obscuro—dark bay.

Palomino—golden dun; highly esteemed in the American West, but considered of little account in Mexico.

Pinto—spotted; a general term—red on white, white on black, dun on white or vice versa; "calico."

Prieto—black.

Retinto—bright bay.

Rocillo—roan.

Rocillo azul—ordinary blue roan.

Rocillo picado—white with red roan flanks.

Rusbayo—light dun with dash of gold.

Sabino—piebald.

Tordillo—gray ("thrush-color"); iron gray.

Trigueño—from *trigo*, wheat; light brown.
Zaino—bay with light markings of any kind.

In addition to the above basic colors, the following terms denoting minor peculiarities of color and markings are common:

Cabos negros—black mane and tail.
Carablanca—blaze-face.
Casquinegro—black-hoofed.
Coliralo—sparse-tailed.
Colicorto—short-tailed.
Coludo—long-tailed.
Criniralo—sparse-maned.
Crinudo—long-maned.
Cruzado—cross-marked on forehead.
Estrello—star on forehead.
Picoblanco—white-nosed.
Rabicorto—short-tailed.
Rabón—short or bob-tailed; refers to actual mutilation, not to short hair.
Rabicano—tail and mane dark, with white hairs intermixed.
Zarco—"glass-eyed," either one or both.

White foot markings are described by convenient combinations with *albo*—white; as *cuatralbo*—four white feet; *tresalbo*—three white feet; *dosalbo*—two white feet; *manalbo*—white forefeet; *trasalbo*—white hindfeet. One white hindfoot is *patablanca*, one white forefoot *manoblanca*.

Nothing has suffered so much in verisimilitude in American fiction of the Zane Grey variety as the names of Spanish or Mexican horses. Names of animals in Spanish are generally of things or are simple adjectives denoting some peculiarity. To give an animal the name of a *cristiano* tends to be looked on with repugnance, as being in bad taste and savoring of sacrilege, since the names of persons are also the names of the saints. A horse is, first of all, likely to be named for his color —el Colorado, el Bayo, el Mojino, la Obscura, etc. But a mount that possesses some personal peculiarity which sets him apart even more than does his color may get a name that derives from it. Incidentally, only saddle and workhorses— "gentled stock"—are ever named; unbroken horses and colts and range mares never attain more than the dignity of being described.

Among the number of ponies whose acquaintance I enjoyed and who were named otherwise than for their colors, I recall the following: El Mecedor (Rocking-chair), from his easy gait; el Remo (the Oar), a horse who could only walk; el Mordisco (the Biter) ; la Duquesa (the Duchess), a mare whose extreme dignity nothing was ever able to disturb; el Arisco (Head-jerker), from his vice of fighting to avoid being bridled; el Rabeoso (Tail-switcher) ; el Plomo (Old Lead), so called because he was the last word in laziness; el Abuelo (Grandfather), one who from colthood showed the sedateness and sweet temper of old age; el Zambo (Spraddler) ; el Cacahuate (Peanut), so-called partly from his burnt sorrel color and partly from his ungainly shape; el Mesteño (the Ownerless—Maverick) ; el Cohete (Firecracker), given to running wildly, when loose, at sight; el Pajarero (Bird-shy), given to shying unexpectedly with little or no provocation; el Vaivén (Ocean-wave), a swaying pacer; el Relámpago (Lightning), a pony who could break into a dead run from a standstill, but who, incidentally, was good for nothing else; el Pando (Sway-back) ; el Desbocado (Runaway), addicted to seizing the bit and making off with his rider; el Martillo (Hammer-head) ; el Pechudo (Broad-chest); el Salvaje (the Savage), a quarrelsome beast with his mates; el Gobernador (the Governor), a huge and dignified gray who when the herd he belonged to was standing at rest always looked as if he were presiding over a legislative session; and el Misionero (the Revivalist), so-called when I got him for no reason that I could ever fathom.

Cow Horse Names, Colors and Cures

By J. Frank Dobie

I

ALL the laws, whims, associative circumstances, prosaic literalness, poetic imaginativeness and, also, poverty of invention that have through the centuries operated to fix names on places, on Pullman cars, on Southern Pacific railroad switches, on ships of the sea, on Indian warriors, on white men as respects family, Christian and nicknames, have likewise operated to give names to ranch horses. Names on a big ranch of the Plains where young white men—cut off from family life—do the work and the naming will have a different flavor and character from those on a small ranch where family life dominates. Names on a ranch in the brush country where nearly all the work is done by Mexican vaqueros will differ from those of a ranch on the coastal prairie far to the east where Negroes break the horses and ride after the cattle, or from those on a range operated by Florida crackers. Yet, if the Spanish were translated into English, no horse name on any one of these widely separated ranges would be foreign to any other. In general, the names are far more personal, spontaneous, picturesque, and expressive of both horse nature and human nature than those under which pedigreed horses—and cattle also—are registered.

The Double Circle Ranch, which at one time occupied up toward a million acres of Apache Indian reservation lands in

Arizona, has recently been dissolved for the benefit of Apache-owned livestock. While I was on it in 1927—at which date it was still expanding—I copied from its Remuda Book the names of about three hundred saddle horses. Most large ranches keep such a record of their horses. Nearly every name in that list of three hundred suggests an episode, says something about the horse, or reflects something in the nature of the namer.

Many of the horses were old, their names going back to the days of notabilities now seldom heard mentioned. I follow the spelling in the Remuda Book. Carrie Nation, Cole Oil Johnny, Bill Cody, Quanar Parker, Cole Younger, Joe Bowers, Pawnee Bill, Wild Bill, Rain in Face (changed to Casey Jones), Hop-along Cassidy ("because he had the gait" of Clarence E. Mulford's hero), Kit Carson (changed to something not printable), Nelly Grey, Sweet Alice—all tell of heroes and heroines of song and popular history. Bud Wesier was also represented. Pearl, Della, Lucinda, Daisy and Fay were doubtless named after girls on the minds of the namers.

These namers were less inclined to heroes—and to nobility of character—than veterans of the Civil War who in the sixties and seventies named their horses as well as their children after Stonewall Jackson, Robert E. Lee, and other Confederate generals. During the same period Sultan and Selim, who was a Turkish sultan, were proud names for American horses in Texas as well as over the rest of the South. Blucher, Wellington, Napoleon, and the English admirals Rodney and Nelson likewise had many namesakes on the range.

To get back to the Double Circle Remuda Book, names based on physical characteristics include Feather Legs, Tangle Legs, Bo Legs, Spraddle, Rock Crusher and Stone Breaker (horses that would pitch and pound into anything), Cave Head, Chalk Eye, Taller Eye, Marble Eye, Powder Face (his face white-splashed), Bald Eagle (hardly any mane between his ears), One Spot (on his side), Polka Dot (on his hip), White Cloud, White Man, Clabber (white), White Socks, Gray Tom, Gray Goose, Blue Jay, Freeze Out Blue, Wild Blue, Ringy Roan, Roan Sam, Red Robin, Red Rambler, Red Man, Sun Flower (a golden dun), Flaxy Ann (with flaxen mane and tail), Cream of Tartar (a palomino), Zebra Dun, Yellow Hand, Yellow Hammer, 44 Black, Black Bird, Black Kettle, Raven, Nigger Preacher, Sleepy Black, Necktie (a splotched stripe around his neck), Nubin and Pap Poose (both little ponies), Looking Glass (glossy-skinned), Two Step and Fandango (prancers), Dude (always showing off), Swift Walter, Gander and Wind Splitter (runners), Spooky (always shying), Bull Frog (a jumper), Wild Woman (shaped like a mare), Rubber Neck, Tall Bull, Gopher (built low on the ground), and Scorpion (who held his tail high). Although many of these names are derived from color, a style in nomenclature dominantly Indian makes them something more than bald adjectives.

Bumble Bee had a rapid take-off and was "a bad one." Dynamite, Bad Eggs, and Danger need no explanation. War Horse was exceptionally powerful. Mata Gente (Kills People) had a victim in the Double Circle graveyard. Explanations could be made for Maverick, Kin Savey, Tuck, Dirk, Bovine, Sugar Beet, Cat Fish, Flower Pot, Five Mile, Fliver, Nash-Quad, Wagon, Nothing, I B Dam, Lizzard, Pidgeon, Three and One, Tamale, Straight Edge, Twenty-Five Cents, Hundred Dollar Price, Eight Thirty, Poor Kid, Lemon Squeeezer, Domingo (Sunday), but the names are better without explanations.

Slicker may have shied at a slicker, or he may have pitched off a slicker tied to his saddle, or he may have pitched off a rider trying to put his slicker on. Did Jerkey chew a piece of jerked meat, or did he ram into the line on which beef was being dried?

"Many of our horses," wrote Roosevelt in *Ranch Life and the Hunting Trail*, "are named for some feat or peculiarity. Wire Fence, when being broken, ran into one of the abominations after which he is now called; Hackamore once got away and remained out for three weeks with a hackamore, or breaking-halter, on him; Macaulay contracted the habit of regularly getting rid of the huge Scotchman to whom he was entrusted; Bullberry Johnny spent the hour or two after he was first mounted in a large patch of thorny bullberry bushes, his distracted rider unable to get him to do anything but move round sidewise in a circle; Water Skip always jumps mud-puddles."

Asa Jones, who ranches in the Big Bend, knows as much about horses as any man in Texas. While I was on his ranch a number of years ago, all his hands were Mexicans and several of them were breaking *potros* (young horses). These are some of the names I copied from his Remuda Book: Venado

CHARLES M. RUSSELL IN WISTER'S *Virginian*, 1916

(Deer), Coyote, Zorrillo (Polecat, the horse being white-tailed), Cuervo (Crow, the horse being black), Hormiga (Ant), Pico Blanco (White Muzzle), Tomate (Tomato), Chapulin (Grasshopper), Campomoche (Devil's Horse), Chinati (Black Bird), Chapote (Persimmon), Nopalero (Good in Prickly Pear), Guante (Glove), Cafetero (Coffee Pot, a black), Remache (Short-Barrelled), Pelado (Hairless), Chivato (Kid), Lucero (Morning Star, Star-Faced), Tintero (Ink), Cobre (Copper, color between sorrel and dun).

The ranch on which I grew up was a small one, in the brush country of Southwest Texas; family life throve on it and Mexicans were plentiful. Horse names there reflected the mixture of life existing on the ranch. Snip and Snap, a pair of bay buggy horses, got their names out of a children's story. Old Bally (Baldy) was a dark, blaze-faced family horse, over whose death we children cried. Dandy was a Thoroughbred stallion. Maudie was named for the famous race mare, Maud S. Stray had been left, a starved, utterly played-out wreck, by some Mexican traveling across the ranch, had fattened, had been posted by my father for sale, according to law, as ownerless and had been bid in by him. Hippy had one hip knocked down—and had the best bottom of any horse I have ever known. Catarina Garza was named by a vaquero for a one-time noted Mexican revolutionist who tried to organize his *partido* on this side of the Rio Grande. Chat was bought from a Mexican horse-trader named Chato Vela. Cardenal (Red Bird) took his name from his color. Half the horses had names, some in English and some in Spanish, according to color.

Speaking of horse names in Texas during the days of the open range and of trail driving, George W. Saunders wrote:

"Slow or lazy horses were often given names such as Possum, Ox Wagon, Snail, Molasses. A pacing horse was likely to be named Sand Sifter or Trail Cleaner. Indians and gunmen furnished plenty of names. Every outfit had its Comanche. Ben Thompson, King Fisher, Mysterious Dave, Clay Allison, John Wesley Hardin and Bat Masterson were common names.

"Cattlemen were constantly selling horses to each other, and when a horse changed hands it was likely to take the name of its former owner. I have heard cowpunchers make such remarks as these: 'Catch John Blocker for Juan.' 'Dillard Fant is lame.' 'Clabe Merchant has a sore back.' 'Bill Reed broke his rope last night,' 'Mark Withers kicked the cook.' 'The dadblamed Indians stole Shanghai Pierce and George West last night'."[1]

Six Up and Down made a record that entitles his name to remembrance. Like many other names, it was derived from his brand, 69, the figure 9 in this brand being made by reversing the 6 stamp iron; thus the "up and down." As Charles M. Newman, of El Paso, recalls the history, in 1891 Ben Billingsley set out from the Newman ranch, the M F, in the Davis Mountains to the N Bar Ranch, also owned by the Newmans, on Powder River, Montana. In the remuda was a dun horse with zebra markings and the brand that gave him his name. He was as tough as rawhide, and when he was delivered, with the herd and with the rest of the remuda, to the boss of the N Bar on Powder River, he seemed ready to go on another fifteen hundred miles. Yet, so far he had not distinguished himself in any particular way. He was turned loose to winter with the other saddle horses. In the horse round-up next spring, Six Up and Down did not appear.

---

[1] "Cowboys and Cowponies," by George W. Saunders, in *The Pioneer Magazine of Texas*, San Antonio, April, 1925.

The Newmans were sending a big remuda back down the
trail to Texas and the boss wanted to put Six Up and Down
in it. Where was he? Horses drifted and thieves stole. Another
year passed. Then in the fall of 1893 Six Up and Down
showed up on his old M F stomping grounds in the Davis
Mountains. He was fat and slick, and Charlie Newman rode
him often after this, but could never get him to tell of his
experiences.

Charles A. Siringo, the "old stove-up cowpuncher" who
wrote *A Texas Cowboy*, the first cowboy autobiography
published in the world (1885), had a varied and picturesque
nomenclature for his horses. His favorite was Whiskey-peat
(or, as he sometimes spelled it, Whisky-peet). Other horses
were Gotch, Buckshot, Ranger, Comanche, Allisan (Alazán,
Sorrel), Last Chance, Creeping Moses, Damfino, Beat-and-
be-damned, Yankee-doodle, Beauregard, and Boney-part
(Bonaparte). Likewise there was Croppy. Siringo says, "They
all knew me so well by my horse, Croppy, he being milk
white and both ears being off close up to his head. He was
indeed a notable animal, as well as a long, keen, good one."

Along in the nineties, the S M S Kid, as he tells his own
story of "Old Gran'pa," in Frank Hastings' *A Ranchman's
Recollections,* had in his string, besides the heroic Sorrel Stud,
Blutcher, Alma, Polecat, Tatterslip, Bead Eye, Lousecage,
Possum, Silver Dollar and Badger.

Outlawed pitching horses are likely to have more striking
names than the ordinary run of cow horses; I have exempli-
fied their names elsewhere. While cutting horses are in a class
to themselves, their names run about like those of other ranch
horses. The following are culled from an unusually informative article, "The Spanish Horse on the Great Plains," by
L. F. Sheffy, in the *Panhandle-Plains Historical Review*, of

1933: Bob M, Ray Bob, Babe, Fox, Rebel, Sardine, Blue Dog, Monkey, Blutcher, Port, Fritz, Gray Dan, Shine Eye, Auger Eye, Diamond Eye, Three Y, Innocence, Chunk, Skeeter, Shamrock, Old Mabel, and Dough Gut.

This last name reminds me of an anecdote that Evetts Haley loves to tell. A bashful cowpuncher—in the old days most cowpunchers were bashful around women—pulled out for town one morning leading a saddle horse. About noon he came to a ranch where a governess was employed and stopped for dinner. It developed that the governess just had to go to town also, and nothing would do but that she should borrow a saddle and ride the extra horse. Maybe the cowpuncher liked the company, but he was sure afraid of it, and he had a difficult time keeping ahead of the young lady and also keeping from going in a hard trot.

Only in an oblique way was gallantry behind his dread of hard-trotting. The horse ridden by the young lady had that internal structure peculiar to a few horses that makes their entrails rumble and audibly churn when they strike a rough gait. On account of the inelegant sounds he thus made, this horse was known as Old Guts.

The governess had a hard time keeping alongside the cowpuncher, and when she got with him she had a harder time making conversation. Finally she got to praising her horse, and she wanted to know its name. The cowpuncher ignored the query and tried to steer the talk to something else.

"But such a nice horsey," the governess went on. "I want to call him by his name so he'll know how much I like him."

"He ain't got no name," the cowpoucher gulped.

"Oh, I know better than that," the governess went on. "All horses have names, and this one is so nice. Now, why are you trying to deceive me?"

This cowpuncher did not have any more imagination than a barrel of sauerkraut. He could not lie.

"Please tell me," the governess cooed.

The cowpuncher's tongue was as dry as a lime-burner's hat, but he was in a corner. He blurted out, "His name is Old Bowels."

Nobody has written of cow horses with a finer sympathy or with more ease and naturalness than Ross Santee, of Arizona, author of *Men and Horses* and *Cowboy*. *Cowboy* is the simple narrative of a kid who ran away from home on a farm in East Texas and got a job wrangling horses on an Arizona ranch. Santee used to work on the Double Circle Ranch, and much of the book is autobiographic chronicle.

"Old Wag was the leader of the remuda at the Sixes," he writes. "An old stove-up cowhorse, he didn't look like much, but he was the leader just the same. In the mornin' he was the first horse up the trail, an' he was always the first one down at night. An' none of the horses ever crowded him when he went to take a drink. If they did, Old Wag just raised his head and flattened his ears, an' they gave him plenty of room.

"There's always some fighting' horses in a bunch an' plenty of timid ones, too. Santa Claus was the worst for fightin', but he never bothered Old Wag. A little bay they called Deerfoot was scairt to death of the bunch. He was always the last horse to take a drink when the remuda watered out. Unless I watched him, he was apt to go shy on water, for he wouldn't drink with other horses around too close. . . .

"The peeler who breaks a horse is usually the man that names him. Beer-Keg an' Window-Sash was both named because of their brands. Santa Claus got his name from the

pine tree—a color splotch—on his shoulder. Kettle-Belly got
his name because of the shape he had. But Slim was a chunky
sorrel an' Shorty was a long-legged bay. Papago was an Indian
pony. An old gray that had lost his tail was called Central
Park. There was Mollie Put the Kettle On, an' a dun named
Parson that they called Old Methodist John. . . . Swallow and
Slipper had run together all their lives. Shoestring, Bloucher
and Sailor were never far from each other. Leppie would
never leave the bunch.

"The horses in a remuda are all geldings, but you'll often
find one that's named after a girl some puncher happened to
know. Pinky, the mule I rode, had been named after a red-
haired girl in town. In every remuda I've known there's
always horses named the same. There's always a Smoky, an'
Skewball, an' there's always a Zebra Dun. . . . I can think of
lots of worse company than a bunch of saddle horses."

Nobody has known the land and its people and its horses
better than New Mexico's gallant Eugene Manlove Rhodes.
Once after he had climbed with May Rhodes to the top of
a mountain for a wonderful view, he pointed to some horse
tracks on the little top-land and said: "If you want to find
horses, go to the prettiest place in reach, and there you'll
almost always find them. Horses love beauty as much as
humans do."

Maybe the horses haven't known anything about the matter, but on many occasions they have given their names to
men pretty much in the manner that men have given names
to horses.[2] In the year 1904 the ranch country around a lone
store in Yoakum County, Texas, was trying to get a post
office. One day while several cowboys were at the store, a

---

[2]Material drawn from A. T. Jackson, "Old Dobbin Still Has A Place," in *Farm and
Ranch*, November 23, 1929.

"dude drummer" blew in. He was consciously green to ranch
life and remarked that he had never seen any bronco-busting.
It happened that one of the cowboys was leading a notoriously bad horse and at the time had him tied outside with
his mount. A puncher by the name of White spoke up and
said, "I'll ride the meanest horse in the country if the crowd
will raise two and a half."

The drummer, without asking for contributions, pulled
the amount from his own pocket. One of the cowboys now
jumped in with an offer to bet White another two and a half
that he could not ride the horse without bridle or hackamore.

"I'll cover your bet and ride him without a thing except
saddle, spurs, and quirt," White said, "and I'll hit him every
time he hits the ground."

Everybody went outside the store to see the show. In a
remarkably short time White had the outlaw saddled and was
on his back. The horse sun-fished, fence-wormed and star-
hunted, but White spurred him from eye-sockets to tail-root
and stayed with him until he was pitched down.

A few days later the storekeeper received notice from
Washington that the request for a post office was being
granted and asked suggestions for a name. The name Bronco
headed the list that the storekeeper sent in. You may receive
a letter postmarked Bronco, Texas, today. Wild Horse in
Culberson County, Pony in Runnels County, twenty-seven
Mustang creeks scattered over the state, Dead Horse Canyon,
various Horse Hollows, and other such names attest to the
way in which horse hoofs have pounded horse nomenclature
into the soil.

II

According to an old saying, "A good horse is never a bad
color." Nevertheless, popular judgment on horses has through

the centuries often been based on color. If the theories and superstitions had not contradicted each other point-blank and if man were not so constituted that he, sincerely as well as hypocritically, says one thing while with consistent inconsistency he energetically does the opposite, some colors would long ago have been bred out of existence.

Take white horses, for instance. From very early times, they have been emblematic of victory. In quaint art, Saint George is represented as riding to conquest on a white horse. General Lee's Traveler was gray, but probably his color furthered the popularity of the Confederate jingle:

> Jeff Davis rode a white horse,
> Lincoln rode a mule . . .

In ancient times the white horse connoted the sacred—the "white throne of God." In *Moby Dick*—his novel of the great white whale—Herman Melville has a mighty passage associating the most famous and magnificent of all mustangs, the Pacing White Steed of the Prairies, with this idea. Mules are literally crazy about mares, and Mexican muleteers have the idea that their mules prefer a white mare over one of any other color. Consequently, the bell mare is often white. The real advantage of that color is that the leader of the mules can be seen at night. For the same reason, fighting men would not want white mounts, which would betray their presence to the enemy in the night. Yet white is the color for luck. To this day, children riding through the country keep on a lookout for white horses, and when one is seen they "pat it" by stamping the fingers of the right hand into the palm of the left, sometimes with a touch of spittle on the fingertips. Meantime a wish is made, and after one hundred white horses are patted or stamped, the wish

will come true. I grew up believing that nobody ever saw
a dead white mule, the inference being that a white mule
never dies. Of course there are white mules. But—"if it's a
fair question"—did you ever see one dead?

On the other hand, there long was and perhaps yet is in
this country a popular idea that, as respects endurance, white
is the weakest of all colors. Writing his rich and fascinating
book, *On the Border with Crook,* after a gruelling campaign
against the Sioux Indians in 1876, Captain John G. Bourke
paused to refute the superstition by noting that the "smallest
loss of horses during this exhausting march was the white
horse troop of the Fifth Cavalry."

To go on with contradictory sayings and beliefs, consider
those about white feet:

> One white foot catch him,
> Two white feet buy him,
> Three white feet watch him,
> Four white feet leave him.

> One white foot buy it,
> Two white feet try it,
> Three white feet misdoubt it,
> Four white feet do without it.

> If you have a horse with four white legs,
>   Keep him not a day;
> If you have a horse with three white legs,
>   Send him far away;
> If you have a horse with two white legs,
>   Sell him to a friend;
> If you have a horse with one white leg,
>   Keep him to the end.

The Arabs are supposed to know all about horses and horse
colors. "One very intelligent Arab sheik" told the author of
one of the best books in existence on horses and horsemen[1]

---

[1]Dodge, Theodore A., *Riders of Many Lands,* New York, 1894, 356-359.

that what he looked for first in a horse when he was considering buying, was "the color of his feet." He said:: "Four white feet are good; with a star, very good. If he has the two fore-feet and the near hind-foot white, it is good, but if it is the off hind-foot which is white, he is a bad horse — never buy him. He will cost you your life; your enemy will overtake and slay you; your son will be an orphan. Two hind-feet white and a star are good. To have the two near feet white is excellent, because then you must mount and dismount 'over the white.' Also, a dark horse with dark legs is good."

Contrary to popular idea, the Arabs seem never to have preferred paint horses. They are partial to bays, chestnut, sorrels, browns, blacks. There was not a single paint among the picked horses that Cortés originally brought to help him with the conquest of Mexico. The favor that paint horses came into in Mexico and on the Plains was due to the Indian liking for gaudy colors. If his horse was not variegated in color by nature, the Plains warrior would often paint him. Range men in America, however, have never had much use for paint horses. "I have never known a paint horse," Wyatt Earp once said, "that knew anything himself."

Whether ranch people take stock in it or not, they are all familiar with the old belief that if a horse can turn over when he wallows, it is a sign that he is a good horse. Cowboys will eagerly watch a horse just unsaddled to see if upon taking his habitual wallow, he can turn over while on his back. I have read that cowboys in the Northwest claim that a horse must make three turns in order to establish his reputation for hardihood. Again, a horse that turns over once in wallowing is worth $100; if he turns over twice, $200, and so on. An old gaucho of the Argentine told R. B. Cunning-hame Graham that if a horse succeeded in rolling over, it was a sign that he was "strong." Certainly, strong, agile, short-coupled, tough ponies are more likely to accomplish this feat. There is likely to be something to many apparently odd beliefs.

Such Arabian tenets as the following are justified: One should not keep a horse that wants to drink too often; he will be incapable of traveling long distances in the desert. Fidgety and noisy horses are worse than useless; they will arouse the enemy. The clipping of a horse's tail is prohibited; it is his protection against flies. Unless a horse is vicious or weak, he must not be castrated; otherwise he will contribute not only to keeping up the breed, but will be stronger by virtue of the fact that he is not castrated.

A mass of lore, much of it dating back to the times of Black Magic, pertaining to horse remedies flourishes even in a land populous with county agents. There may be something in funnelling the smoke of rags, up through a horn, into a horse's nostrils as a cure for distemper. The Mexican *remedio* of tying a toad on a horse's forehead to cure him of being windbroken is sheer hocus pocus. For this and certain other ailments the only sure remedy, according to hard-headed American realists, is to sell the horse. The best and most readable collection of lore of this kind ever made is Frost Woodhull's long article called "Ranch Remedios," in *Man, Bird, and Beast* (Volume VIII of the *Publications* of the Texas Folk-Lore Society, Austin, 1930). While recommending this delightful essay, I will cite the reader to another collection of horse lore of a different kind—some of the strangest beliefs and tales relating to horses that I know of — found in a chapter called "The Magician on Horse-back" in my Mexican book, *Tongues of the Monte*.

Horses in Mexico bring to mind the most popular of all Mexican dances, the jarabe. Some of the steps of this remarkable dance seem to imitate the clicking of hoofs and the pawing and prancing of spirited horses. Historians have interpreted the jarabe as a perpetuation of the imitative motions made by the native Mexicans upon first seeing the horses brought into their country by the *conquistadores*.[4]

Schwendener and Tibbals, *Legends and Dances of Old Mexico*, New York, 1934, 2.

A-Riding and A-Pitching

CHARLES M. RUSSELL IN PATTULLO'S *The Untamed*, 1911

Corazón

By George Pattullo*

A man is as good as his nerves.—Cowboy maxim.

WITH MANES STREAMING in the wind, a band of broncos fled across the grama flats, splashed through the San Pedro, and whirled sharply to the right, heading for sanctuary in the Dragoons. In the lead raced a big sorrel, his coat shimmering like polished gold where the sun touched it.

"That's Corazón," exclaimed Reb. "Head him or we'll lose the bunch."

The pursuers spread out and swept round in a wide semicircle. Corazón held to his course, a dozen yards in advance of the others, his head high. The chase slackened, died away. With a blaring neigh, the sorrel eased his furious pace, and the entire band came to a trot. Before them were the mountains, and Corazón knew their fastnesses as the street urchin knows the alleys that give him refuge; in the cañons the broncos would be safe from man. Behind was no sign of the enemy. His nose in the wind, he sniffed long, but it bore no taint. Instead, he nickered with delight, for he smelled water. They swung to the south, and in less than five minutes their hot muzzles were washed by the bubbling waters of Eternity Spring.

Corazón drew in a long breath, expanding his well-ribbed

---

*Reprinted by kind permission of the author from his book of short stories, *The Untamed*, New York, 1911.

sides, and looked up from drinking. There in front of him, fifty paces away, was a horseman. He snorted the alarm and they plunged into the tangle of sagebrush. Another rider bore down and turned them back. To right and left they darted, then wheeled and sought desperately to break through the cordon at a weak spot, and failed. Wherever they turned, a cowboy appeared as by magic. At last Corazón detected an unguarded area and flew through with the speed of light.

"Now we've got 'em," howled Reb. "Don't drive too close, but keep 'em headed for the corral."

Within a hundred yards of the gate, the sorrel halted, his ears cocked in doubt. The cowboys closed in to force the band through. Three times the broncos broke and scattered, for to their wild instincts the fences and that narrow aperture cried treachery and danger. They were gathered, with whoops and many imprecations, and once more approached the entrance.

"Drive the saddle bunch out," commanded the range boss.

Forth came the remuda of a hundred horses. The broncos shrilled greeting and mingled with them, and when the cow-ponies trotted meekly into the corral, Corazón and his band went too, though they shook and were afraid.

For five years Corazón had roamed the range—ever since he had discovered that grass was good to eat, and so had left the care of his tender-eyed mother. Because he dreaded the master of created things and fled him afar, only once during that time had he seen man at close quarters. That was when, as a youngster, he was caught and branded on the left hip. He had quickly forgotten that; until now it had ceased to be even a memory.

But now he and his companion rovers were prisoners, cooped in a corral by a contemptible trick. They crowded around and around the stout enclosure, sometimes dropping to their knees in efforts to discover an exit beneath the boards. And not twenty feet away, the dreaded axis of their circlings, sat a man on a horse, and he studied them calmly. Other men, astride the fence, were uncoiling ropes, and their manner was placid and businesslike. One opined dispassionately that "the sorrel is shore some horse."

"You're damn whistlin'," cried the buster over his shoulder, in heavy affirmation.

Corazón was the most distracted of all the band. He was in a frenzy of nervous fear, his glossy coat wet and foam-flecked. He would not stand still for a second, but prowled about the wooden barrier like a jungle creature newly prisoned in a cage. Twice he nosed the ground and crooked his forelegs in an endeavor to slide through the six inches of clear space beneath the gate, and the outfit laughed derisively.

"Here goes," announced the buster in his expressionless tones. "You-all watch out, now. Hell'll be poppin'."

At that moment Corazón took it into his head to dash at top speed through his friends, huddled in a bunch in a corner. A rope whined and coiled, and, when he burst out of the jam, the noose was around his neck, tightening so as to strangle him. Madly he ran against it, superb in the sureness of his might. Then he squalled with rage and pain and in awful terror. His legs flew from under him, and poor Corazón was jerked three feet into the air, coming down on his side with smashing force. The fall shook a grunt out of him, and he was stunned and breathless, but unhurt. He staggered to his feet, his breath straining like a bellows, for the noose cut into his neck and he would not yield to its pressure.

Facing him was the man on the bay. His mount stood with feet braced, sitting back on the rope, and he and his rider were quite collected and cool and prepared. The sorrel's eyes were starting from his head; his nostrils flared wide, gasping for the air that was denied him, and the breath sucked in his throat. It seemed as if he must drop. Suddenly the buster touched his horse lightly with the spur and slackened the rope. With a long sob Corazón drew in a life-giving draught, his gaze fixed in frightened appeal on his captor.

"Open the gate," said Mullins, without raising his voice.

He flicked the rope over Corazón's hind quarters, and essayed to drive him into the next corral, to cut him off from his fellows. The sorrel gave a gasp of dismay and lunged forward. Again he was lifted from the ground, and came down with a thud that left him shivering.

"His laig's done bust!" exclaimed the boss.

"No; he's shook up, that's all. Wait a while."

A moment later Corazón raised his head painfully; then, life and courage coming back with a rush, he lurched to his feet. Mullins waited with unabated patience. The sorrel was beginning to respect that which encircled his neck and made naught of his strength, and when the buster flicked the rope again, he ran through the small gate, and brought up before he had reached the end of his tether.

Two of the cowboys stepped down languidly from the fence, and took position in the center of the corral.

"Hi, Corazón! Go it, boy!" they yelled, and spurred by their cries, the horse started off at a trot. Reb tossed his loop — flung it carelessly, with a sinuous movement of the wrist — and when Corazón had gone a few yards, he found his forefeet ensnared. Enraged at being thus cramped, he bucked and bawled; but, before Reb could settle on the rope, he came to a standstill and sank his teeth into the strands. Once, twice, thrice he tugged, but could make no impression. Then he pitched high in air, and —

"NOW!" shrieked Reb.

They heaved with might and main, and Corazón flopped in the dust. Quick as a cat, he sprang upright and bolted; but again they downed him, and, while Reb held the head by straddling the neck, his confederate twined dexterously with a stake-rope. There lay Corazón, helpless and almost spent, trussed up like a sheep for market; they had hog-tied him.

It was the buster who put the hackamore on his head. Very deliberately he moved. Corazón sensed confidence in the touch of his fingers; they spoke a language to him, and he was soothed by the sureness of superiority they conveyed. He lay quiet. Then Reb incautiously shifted his position, and the horse heaved and raised his head, banging Mullins across the ear. The buster's senses swam, but instead of flying into a rage, he became quieter, more deliberate; in his cold eyes was a vengeful gleam, and dangerous stealth lurked in his delicate manipulation of the strands. An excruciating pain shot through the sorrel's eye: Mullins had gouged him.

"Let him up." It was the buster again, atop the bay, making the rope fast with a double half-hitch over the horn of the saddle.

Corazón arose, dazed and very sick. But his spirit was unbreakable. Again and again he strove to tear loose, rearing, falling back, plunging to the end of the rope until he was hurled off his legs to the ground. When he began to weary, Mullins encouraged him to fight, that he might toss him.

"I'll learn you what this rope means," he remarked, as the bronco scattered the dust for the ninth time, and remained there, completely done up.

In deadly fear of his slender tether, yet alert to match his strength against it once more, should opportunity offer, Corazón followed the buster quietly enough when he rode into the open. Beside a sturdy mesquite bush that grew apart from its brethren, Mullins dismounted and tied the sorrel. As a farewell he waved his arms and whooped. Of course, Corazón gathered himself and leaped—leaped to the utmost that was in him, so that the bush vibrated to its farthest root; and of course he hit the earth with a jarring thump that temporarily paralyzed him. Mullins departed to put the thrall of human will on others.

Throughout the afternoon, and time after time during the interminable night, the sorrel tried to break away, but with each sickening failure he grew more cautious. When he ran against the rope now, he did not run blindly to its limit, but half wheeled, so that when it jerked him back he invariably landed on his feet. Corazón was learning hard, but he was learning. And what agonies of pain and suspense he went through!—for years a free rover, and now to be bound thus, by what looked to be a mere thread, for he knew not what further tortures! He sweated and shivered, seeing peril in every shadow. When a coyote slunk by with tongue lapping hungrily over his teeth, the prisoner almost broke his neck in a despairing struggle to win freedom.

In the chill of the dawn they led him into a circular corral. His sleekness had departed; the barrel-like body did not look so well nourished, and there was red in the blazing eyes.

"I reckon he'll be mean," observed the buster, as though it concerned him but little.

"No-o-o. Go easy with him, Carl, and I think he'll make a good horse," the boss cautioned.

While the two men held the rope, Mullins advanced along it foot by foot, inch by inch, one hand outstretched, and talked to Corazón in a low, careless tone of affectionate banter. "So you'd like for to kill me, would you?" he inquired, grinning. All the while he held the sorrel's gaze.

Corazón stood still, legs planted wide apart, and permitted him to approach. He trembled when the fingers touched his nose; but they were firm, confident digits, the voice was reassuring, and the gentle rubbing up, up between the eyes and ears lulled his forebodings.

"Hand me the blanket," said Mullins.

He drew it softly over Corazón's back, and the bronco swerved, pawed, and kicked with beautiful precision. Whereupon they placed a rope around his neck, dropped it behind his right hind leg, then pulled that member up close to his belly; there it was held fast. On three legs now, the sorrel was impotent for harm. Mullins once more took up the blanket but this time the gentleness had flown. He slapped it over Corazón's backbone from side to side a dozen times. At each impact the horse bumped awkwardly, but, finding that he came to no hurt, he suffered it in resignation.

That much of the second lesson learned, they saddled him. Strangely enough, Corazón submitted to the operation without fuss, the only untoward symptoms being a decided upward slant to the back of the saddle and the tucking of his tail. Reb waggled his head over this exhibition.

"I don't like his standing quiet that away; it ain't natural," he vouchsafed. "Look at the crick in his back. Jim-in-ee! he'll shore pitch."

Which he did. The cinches were tightened until Corazón's

eyes almost popped from his head; then they released the bound leg and turned him loose. What was that galling his spine? Corazón took a startled peep at it, lowered his head between his knees, and began to bawl. Into the air he rocketed, his head and forelegs swinging to the left, his hind quarters weaving to the right. The jar of his contact with the ground was appalling. Into the air again, his head and forelegs to the right, his rump twisted to the left. Round and round the corral he went, blatting like an angry calf; but the thing on his back stayed where it was, gripping his body cruelly. At last he was fain to stop for breath.

"Now," said Mullins, "I reckon I'll take it out of him."

There has always been for me an overwhelming fascination in watching busters at work. They have underlying traits in common when it comes to handling the horses—the garrulous one becomes coldly watchful, the stoic moves with stern patience, the boaster soothes with soft-crooned words and confident caress. Mullins left Corazón standing in the middle of the corral, the hackamore rope strung loose on the ground, while he saw to it that his spurs were fast. We mounted the fence, not wishing to be mixed in the glorious turmoil to follow.

"I wouldn't top ol' Corazón for fifty," confessed the man on the adjoining post.

"Mullins has certainly got nerve," I conceded.

"A buster has got to have nerve." The range boss delivered himself laconically. "All nerve and no brains makes the best. But they get stove up and then—"

"And then? What then?"

"Why, don't you know?" he asked in surprise. "Every buster loses his nerve at last, and then they can't ride a pack-hoss. It must be because it's one fool man with one set of nerves up ag'in a new hoss with a new devil in him every time. They wear him down. Don't you reckon?"

The explanation sounded plausible. Mullins was listening with a faintly amused smile to Reb's account of what a lady mule had done to him; he rolled a cigarette and lighted it painstakingly. The hands that held the match were steady as eternal rock. It was maddening to see him stand there so coolly while the big sorrel, a dozen feet distant, was a-quake with dread, blowing harshly through his crimson nostrils whenever a cowboy stirred—and each of us knowing that the man was taking his life in his hands. An unlooked-for twist, a trifling disturbance of poise, and, with a horse like Corazón, it meant maiming or death. At last he threw the cigarette from him and walked slowly to the rope.

"So you're calling for me?" he inquired, gathering it up.

Corazón was snorting. By patient craft Reb acquired a grip on the sorrel's ears, and, while he hung there, bringing the head down so that the horse could not move, Mullins tested the stirrups and raised himself cautiously into the saddle.

"Let him go."

While one could count ten, Corazón stood expectant, his back bowed, his tail between his legs. The ears were laid flat on the head and the forefeet well advanced. The buster waited, the quirt hanging from two fingers of his right hand. Suddenly the sorrel ducked his head and emitted a harsh scream, leaping, with legs stiff, straight off the ground. He came down with the massive hips at an angle to the shoulders, thereby imparting a double shock; bounded high again, turned back with bewildering speed as he touched the earth; then, in a circle perhaps twenty feet in diameter, sprang time after time, his heels lashing the air. Never had such pitching been seen on the Anvil Range.

"I swan, he just misses his tail a' inch when he turns back!" roared a puncher.

Mullins sat composedly in the saddle, but he was riding as never before. He whipped the sorrel at every jump and raked him down the body from shoulder to loins, with the ripping spurs. The brute gave no signs of letting up. Through Mullins' tan of copper hue showed a slight pallor. He was exhausted. If Corazón did not give in soon, the man would be beaten. Just then the horse stopped, feet a-sprawl.

"Mullins,"—the range boss got down from the fence— "you'll kill that hoss. Between the cinches belongs to you; the head and hind quarters is the company's."

For a long minute Mullins stared at the beast's ears without replying.

"I reckon that's the rule," he acquiesced heavily. "Do you want that somebody else should ride him?"

"No-o-o. Go ahead. But, remember, between the cinches you go at him as you like—nowhere else."

The buster slapped the quirt down on Corazón's shoulder, but the bronco did not budge; then harder. With the first oath he had used, he jabbed in the spurs and lay back on the hackamore rope. Instead of bucking, Corazón reared straight up, his feet pawing like the hands of a drowning man. Before Mullins could move to step off, the sorrel flung his head round and toppled backward.

"No, he's not dead." The range boss leaned over the buster and his hands fumbled inside the shirt. "The horn got him here, but he ain't dead. Claude, saddle Streak and hit for Agua Prieta for a doctor."

When we had carried the injured man to the bunk-house, Reb spoke from troubled meditation:

"Pete, I don't believe Corazón is as bad as he acts with Mullins. I've been watching him. Mullins, he didn't—"

"You take him, then; he's yours," snapped the boss, his conscience pricking because of the reproof he had administered. If the buster had ridden him his own way, this might not have happened.

That is how the sorrel came into Reb's possession. Only one man of the outfit witnessed the taming, and he would not talk; but when Reb came to dinner from the first saddle on Corazón, his hands were torn and the nail of one finger hung loose.

"I had to take to the horn and hang on some," he admitted.

Ay, he had clung there desperately while the bronco pitched about the river-bed, whither Reb had retired for safety and to escape spectators. But at the next saddle Corazón was less violent; at the third, recovering from the stunning shocks and bruisings of the first day, he was a fiend; and then, on the following morning, he did not pitch at all. Reb rode him every day to sap the superfluous vigor in Corazón's iron frame and he taught him as well as he could the first duties of a cow-horse. Finding that his new master never punished him unless he undertook to dispute his authority, the sorrel grew tractable and began to take an interest in his tasks.

"He's done broke," announced Reb; "I'll have him bridle-wise in a week. He'll make some roping horse. Did you see him this evening? I swan—"

They scoffed good-naturedly; but Reb proceeded on the assumption that Corazón was meant to be a roping horse, and schooled him accordingly. As for the sorrel, he took to the new pastime with delight. Within a month nothing gave him keener joy than to swerve and crouch at the climax of a sprint and see a cow thrown heels over head at the end of the rope that was wrapped about his saddle-horn.

The necessity of contriving to get three meals a day took me elsewhere, and I did not see Corazón again for three years. Then, one Sunday afternoon, Big John drew me from El Paso to Juarez on the pretense of seeing a grand, an extraordinary, a most noble bull-fight, in which the dauntless Favorita would slay three fierce bulls from the renowned El Carmen ranch; in "competency" with the fearless Morenito Chico de San Bernardo; and a youth with a megaphone drew us both to a steer-roping contest instead. We agreed that bull-fighting was brutal on the Sabbath.

"I'll bet it's rotten," remarked Big John pessimistically, as we took our seats. "I could beat 'em myself."

As he scanned the list, his face brightened. Among the seventeen ropers thereon were two champions and a possible new one in Raphael Fraustro, the redoubtable vaquero from the domain of Terrazas.

"And here's Reb!" roared John—he is accustomed to converse in the tumult of the branding-pen—"I swan, he's entered from Monument."

Shortly afterwards the contestants paraded, wonderfully arrayed in silk shirts and new handkerchiefs.

"Some of them ain't been clean before in a year," was John's caustic comment. "There's Slim; I KNOW he hasn't."

They were a fine-looking body of men, and two of my neighbors complained that I trampled on their feet. The horses caught the infection of excitement from the packed stands and champed on their bits and caracoled and waltzed sideways in a manner highly unbecoming a staid cow-pony.

There was one thing that did not. So sluggish was his

gait and general bearing, in contrast to the others, that the
crowd burst into laughter. He plodded at the tail-end of
the procession, his hoofs kicking up the dust in listless spurts,
his nose on a level with his knees. I rubbed my eyes and
John said, "No, it ain't—it can't be—;" but it was. Into
that arena slouched Corazón, entered against the pick of
the horses of the Southwest; and Reb was astride him.

We watched the ropers catch and tie the steers in rapid
succession, but the much-heralded ones missed altogether,
and to John and me the performance lagged. We were waiting for Reb and Corazón.

They came at last, at the end of the list. When Corazón
ambled up the arena to enter behind the barrier, the grandstand roared a facetious welcome; the spectacle of this sad-
gaited nag preparing to capture a steer touched its risibilities.

"Listen to me," bawled a fat gentleman in a wide-brimmed
hat, close to my ear. "You listen to me! They're all fools.
That's a cow-horse. No blasted nonsense. Knows his business huh? You're damn whistlin'!"

Assuredly, Corazón knew his business. The instant he
stepped behind the line he was a changed horse. The flop-
ping ears pricked forward, his neck arched, and the great
muscles of his shoulders and thighs rippled to his dainty
prancing. He pulled and fretted on the bit, his eyes roving
about in search of the quarry; he whinnied an appeal to
be gone. Reb made ready his coil, curbing him with light
pressure.

Out from the chute sprang a steer, heading straight down
the area. Corazón was frantic. With the flash of the gun he
breasted the barrier-rope and swept down on him in twenty
strides. Reb stood high in the stirrups; the loop whirled
and sped; and, without waiting to see how it fell, but accept-

ing a catch in blind faith, the sorrel started off at a tangent.

Big John was standing up in his place, clawing insanely at the hats of his neighbors and banging them on the head with his program.

"Look at him—just look at him!" he shrieked.

The steer was tossed clear of the ground and came down on his left side. Almost before he landed, Reb was out of the saddle and speeding toward him.

"He's getting up. HE'S GETTING UP. Go to him, Reb!" howled John and I.

The steer managed to lift his head; he was struggling to his knees. I looked away, for Reb must lose. Then a hoarse shout from the multitude turned back my gaze. Corazón had felt the slack on the rope and knew what it meant. He dug his feet into the dirt and began to walk slowly forward —very slowly and carefully, for Reb's task must not be spoiled. The steer collapsed, falling prone again, but the sorrel did not stop. Once he cocked his eye, and seeing that the animal still squirmed, pulled with all his strength. The stands were rocking; they were a sea of tossing hats and gesticulating arms and flushed faces; the roar of their plaudits echoed back from the hills. And it was for Corazón, gallant Corazón.

"Dam' his eyes—dam' his ol' eyes!" Big John babbled over and over, absolutely oblivious.

Reb stooped beside the steer, his hands looping and tying with deft darting twists even as he kept pace with his dragged victim.

"I guess it's—about—a—hour," he panted.

Then he sprang clear and tossed his hands upward, facing the judge's stand. After that he walked aimlessly about, mopping his face with a handkerchief; for to him the shoutings and the shifting colors were all a foolish dream, and he was rather sick.

Right on the cry with which his master announced his task done, Corazón eased up on the rope and waited.

"Mr. Pee-ler's time," bellowed the man with the megaphone presently, "is twenty-one seconds, ty-ing the world's re-cord."

So weak that his knees trembled, Reb walked over to his horse. "Corazón," he said huskily, and slapped him once on the flank.

Nothing would do the joyous crowd then but that Reb should ride forth to be acclaimed the victor. We sat back and yelled ourselves weak with laughter, for Corazón, having done his work, refused resolutely to squander time in vain parade. The steer captured and tied, he had no further interest in the proceedings. The rascal dog-trotted reluctantly to the center of the arena in obedience to Reb, then faced the audience; but, all the time Reb was bowing his acknowledgments, Corazón sulked and slouched, and he was sulking and shuffling the dust when they went through the gate.

"Now," said John, who is very human, "we'll go help Reb spend that money."

As we jostled amid the outgoing crowd, several cowboys came alongside the grandstand rail, and Big John drew me aside to have speech with them. One rider led a spare horse and when he passed a man on foot, the latter hailed him:

"Say, Ed, give me a lift to the hotel?"

"Sure," answered Ed, proffering the reins.

The man gathered them up, his hands fluttering as if with palsy, and paused with his foot raised toward the stirrup.

"He won't pitch nor nothing, Ed?" came the quavered inquiry. "You're shore he's gentle?"

"Gentler'n a dog," returned Ed, greatly surprised.

"You ain't fooling me, now, are you, Ed?" continued the man on the ground. "He looks kind of mean."

"Give him to me!" Ed exploded. "You kin walk."

From where we stood, only the man's back was visible. "Who is that fellow?" I asked.

"Who? Him?" answered my neighbor. "Oh, his name's Mullins. They say he used to be able to ride anything with hair on it, and throw off the bridle at that. I expect that's just talk. Don't you reckon?"

—Charles M. Russell

Texas-Mexican Horse-Breaking

By Ruth Dodson

I. Domador

IN the early days when the American and the Mexican worked together on the ranches of South Texas, the Mexican took the lead, was instructor, in one phase of the range business—horsebreaking. The Mexican not only had a natural aptitude for horsemanship; he had been on the ground a hundred years, so to speak, before the American came to join him. And, too, the horses themselves—those tough and often times fiery, small Spanish horses that they rode—were a direct inheritance of the Texas-Mexican; the Americano could tell him little about these horses! That does not mean that in the early days in South Texas there were not good horsebreakers among the Americans, but it does mean that when one was found it was unlikely that he had learned the art of breaking horses from his own father or grandfather; he, likely, had learned it from some Mexican.

In those times when all the men and most of the women and children rode horseback, there was need of continual horsebreaking. This condition gave to him who was fitted for the work and who preferred doing it the opportunity to become a *domador*—a horsebreaker—by profession. The *domador* had the chance to be his own boss—at the price of two and a half dollars a head; he also had some prestige, for he was supposed to be superior in horsemanship to those

269

who would ride the horse after he had broken him.

Since every horse is as much an individual as the man who breaks him, each one is a special problem that must be dealt with according to his peculiar characteristics. A good *domador* knows this.

If old José María Cisneros, who broke horses along the Nueces River from the time he was a young man until when, at the age of eighty, he was kicked and killed by a young horse he had gentled, could have recalled every *potro* that he had broken, he probably would have found that no two had reacted in exactly the same way and that he had managed no two in exactly the same way. Yet the method of horsebreaking among Texas-Mexicans has for many generations been standardized by tradition, and the result, making allowance for the individuality of the horse, is equally uniform.

The first act in breaking a horse is to catch him. In the early days this was done by penning the *manada*, the bunch of mares, with which the young, unbroken horses ran, then roping the *potro* — the unbroken horse — that had been selected. If there were a choice, the selection would be of a *potro* about five years old. Any horse younger than this lacked the strength and endurance to do the hard work that might be required of him; older than this the horse would be harder to break and, for some reason that must have been apparent, had been avoided; in fact was something of a "cut-back." A white foot on which the hoof seemed somewhat weak would be enough to prejudice one, since white hoofs are supposed to be not so strong as black ones. It is said that when a horse has three black hoofs and one white one, if one of his hoofs "goes bad," it will likely be the white one.

As to choice of color, one sometimes has a preference. If it is a sorrel, he must remember that a sorrel horse has a thin skin; so if he is to be ridden in a brushy country, he is more likely to be scratched and cut than would be a horse with a thicker hide. But, of course, one can hardly hope to find a horse every time that suits in every respect —and horses are not to be wasted. When one, through choice, selects a *bayo-coyote*—a coyote-dun, as I hear the color called now among English-speaking people, it could hardly be that he is partial to this uninteresting color; but the *bayo-coyote* —marked with a line down his back of the color of his mane and tail—has the reputation of being a well-bottomed horse, especially a good cow-horse. Or if the choice is a *bayo-cabos-negros*, one knows that this dun with black stocking-legs, black mane and tail and a black streak down his back, is no Thoroughbred. He is a real plebeian; and being such, he is able to take the hard knocks of thirst, hunger, brush and prickly pear with more endurance than the average. Perhaps for this reason few horses have been more abused than has the *bayo-cabos-negros*. It is said of the orange-colored dun horse, *"Bayo-anaranjado, primero muerto que cansado."* If it is true that the *bayo-anaranjado*, the foundation of the palomino, is "dead before he is tired," the inference is that the endurance is that of the spirit. And he is a showy horse, if that is what is wanted. But when the consideration is that of a white, paint, or other conspicuously colored *potro*, one might be reminded of the saying: *"Caballos blancos, como pendejos, se conozen de lejos."*—"White horses, like fools, are known from afar." "Why ride a horse that could be so easily recognized?" one might ask.

Whether the *domador* is entirely alone or whether there is available help sitting on the corral fence makes a difference as to how he ropes the *potro*. But to be alone would be a rare situation because there are, usually, spectators who are glad to witness the handling of a *potro* for the first time and glad to lend a hand.

In that case the *potro* is roped around the neck. The gate is opened long enough for the *manada* to run out, and the young horse is separated from his clan for the first time. Terror possesses him. He is at one end of the rope matching his strength against one who is expert at handling his kind. He rears and plunges. He might fall broadside, only to jump up and try again. He snorts and nickers wildly to the distant *manada*. It is useless; the thirty-foot rope holds him within its radius. He stands, finally, quivering with fright. The *domador* slowly approaches him, hand over hand, along the rope. The *potro* attempts to back away until he is almost on his haunches. But the *domador* holds him firmly, reaches and fits the *tapojo*—the blind, over his eyes. The blind may be, as I saw in at least one case, only a red bandanna handkerchief; more often it is a strip of soft leather with buckskin strings attached to tie it on with, or it may be a fancy article made of canvas and cross-stitched in red, yellow, and green—the work of sweetheart or wife. To the *potro* it is all the same; he is in darkness.

Then the *jáquima*—corrupted into *hackamore*—is handed to the *domador* by the self-appointed helper. He fits it on the head of the *potro*. This halter has a strong rope attached to the back of the noose that goes around the *potro's* nose. The entire article is made of rope and is constructed for strength—and it needs to be.

Now the *tapojo* is raised from the *potro's* eyes and the *domador* gives him rope. The gate is opened and he dashes through it; but the man, digging the heels of his boots into the ground and dragging to the end of the rope, holds him down. Then, where there is plenty of room, the *potro* will not only be allowed, he will be encouraged, to exert himself all that he will. He will pitch. He will attempt to run, but the rope still holds him. He keeps on trying, stopping only to get his wind occasionally, until he and the *domador* both are pretty tired out. So that is enough exercise for this time.

Then by giving slack on the rope in the desired direction, by scaring him, by whipping him with a rope, or by waving

A LECTURN ON RIDING BAD HORSES.

When you go to ride a bad horse, first get your horse by the bridle and pull his head to one side as far as you can and stick your fore fingers in his eyes as deep as you can and if the horse pitches sit as limber as you can and twist your toes around in your saddle stirrup and you will find that it will be much easier on you aud always handle stubborn horses rough and use limber bits and make him go your way and not his.

A page from *An Old Time Cowboy*, by LONDON BROWN, WHO LEARNED TO SET TYPE SO THAT HE COULD PRINT HIS STORY—A PAMPHLET ISSUED AT NOCONA, TEXAS, ABOUT 1892. COURTESY OF EARL VANDALE, AMARILLO a saddle blanket at him, the *domador* urges the *potro* to move to a certain nearby tree. At the tree the rope is thrown over a limb and tied with enough slack to give the *potro* further chances to learn the restrictions of the rope but with not enough slack that he might get tangled at the trunk of the tree.

Now is the time for a cup of coffee with reminiscences of cases of horsebreaking as the subject of conversation. And it is the time when the *potro* may be named. But about the only name that is indicated at this stage is that suggested by the color of the horse. Since that requires little imagination, the naming is usually left until later. Still, Dorado —golden bay; Zaino—solid dark bay; Alazán—sorrel, are among the euphonious color-names that are often used. Media-Cara—Half-Face—was a bay horse with half of his face white. He, as the Mexicans say, brought his name with him when he was born. Lagrimas—Tears—was hard to break and of little account after he was broken. But, El Criminal —The Criminal—excites the imagination. He pawed a pet lamb to death while he was a *potro*.

While the *potro* is tied to the tree, the *domador* need not necessarily remain idle. He may have five or six horses, in different stages of being broken, tied to different trees or logs. But he is not to get too ambitious and take more horses to break than he can attend to properly. Old José María Cisneros, whom I have already mentioned and who was a noted horsebreaker, told me the day before he was killed, a few years ago, that when he was a young man there were times when he was breaking as many as twenty horses at one time. "Yes," the still spry old wife added, "and we used to go to all the dances on some horse that he was breaking." She boasted: "I would tell José María to put his hand over the horse's eye so that he couldn't see me and to let me have the stirrup. I would get up behind him, and here we would go to the dance!" I was amused by the mental picture of the couple on their way to the dance riding tandem on a frisky, half-broken, young horse. Doña Aurelia, I knew, enjoyed the reputation of having been quite a belle in her day, and, she assured me, she had been *"muy bailadora"*—much of a dancer. José María, I felt sure, cared less for the dancing than he did for the opportunity to do some horsebreaking on the way to and from the dance. This extending his work into the night was probably what made it possible for him to break as many as twenty horses at one time.

The next day or perhaps the day after, the *domador* decides to saddle and ride the *potro* that has been tied to the tree. It has been told by old-timers that when Neville Dobie —an uncle of J. Frank Dobie—was a young man working for his uncle, Sterling Dobie, who had a large horse ranch in Live Oak County, and was going to break a horse, he would tie him to a tree and then time the saddling by the coming along of someone whom he could invite to ride the *potro*. If after a reasonable length of time no one appeared, then Neville himself would do the riding. And, it is said that he was a good rider and a good horsebreaker.

Before being saddled, the *potro* is blindfolded and, if he is inclined to kick, his right hind foot is tied up with a loop that can be released easily. While the saddle blanket is spread on his back and the saddle put on and the girth tightened, the *potro* will squirm and hump his back, but that is all that he is able to do. Then the loop is released from his foot, the *tapojo* is pushed off his eyes, and the *domador* stands back and slackens the rope. The *potro* stands perfectly still for a moment; then, all at once, he goes into action.

Few objects stir the imagination more than a riderless, saddled horse. The Mexicans say: *"Nunca hay caballo ensillado que á alguno no se le ofrece viaje."*—"There is never a saddled horse that doesn't offer a journey to someone." But the suggestion is not always so pleasant. More often the sight of the riderless horse suggests sadness, if not actual tragedy. The following story is of an event that happened so near to my childhood recollections that hearing it talked of left a lasting impression.

Juan Burmudez, a native of Goliad, was our neighbor and a horse raiser at the time the range was free. In a band of horses that ran some distance away from his home were several *potros* that he wanted broken. He hired Felipe Pacheco, a traditionally good *domador,* to break them for him. Felipe camped near where the horses ranged and proceeded to break the *potros.* His method would, necessarily, be somewhat different from the usual, since he had no one to help him. He would run onto the *potro,* forefoot him, throw him and tie him down; then he would blindfold him and put the *jáquima* on while he was tied down. After that the *potro* could be handled in the customary way.

One day a vaquero came across Juan's *manada* and saw a saddled *potro* in it. The young horse was exhausted and his sides were so swollen that the girth was buried into the flesh. It was evident that he had been saddled several days. Search was made and Felipe was found, dead, under a mesquite tree, where he had been dragged off the running horse.

And then there was that mysterious, saddled, but not riderless, horse that Mexicans on the old Kentuck Ranch, in Live Oak County, used to tell about. Sometimes, at night, they said, a big black horse would charge out of an old unused rock building on the place, one that had been built many years before for a wool house. The squeaking of the new saddle could be plainly heard, they said, and the phantom horse was tightly reined by an invisible rider. No one seemed to know the story back of the apparition, but the fact that the rider, whoever he might have been, rode a *black* horse would suggest that he had been involved in some dark adventure. And of all places for a horseman to have taken up residence, in a wool-house!

Still, the spectacle of the *potro* with his first saddle does not excite the imagination of the onlooker to any great extent. On the immediate ground there is no association of ideas between the empty saddle and an absent rider. The *potro* is too ungainly, too violent, too new to suggest anything but action.

The grip of the saddle, the squeaking of leather, the flapping of stirrups, all fill the *potro* with panic. He pitches. He may, in desperate extreme of fright, throw himself back, at the risk of breaking the saddle, or he may simply lie down, too confused and frightened to know what else to do. When a *potro* lies down, the Mexicans, generally, say that he is high tempered, that he is angry; but an old vaquero, who is my brother and who has broken many horses, says that this is not the case. He says that a horse that is very nervous and highstrung will, sometimes, through fright, resort to lying down instead of pitching, and that while this is a most difficult type to handle, the patience required to help the *potro* overcome this reaction is well expended, for the qualities that cause the trouble, rightly directed, help to make a good horse, especially a good roping horse. He emphasizes that the *potro* should not be whipped.

After the *potro* has had the chance to get the feel of the saddle, the *domador* goes up to him and pulls the *tapojo* down over his eyes and, perhaps, again ties up his hind foot. It is natural for a horse to try to protect himself by kicking whatever he is afraid of. When his kicking is restrained, he will give up the idea of attempting it. Then the rope attached to the noose on the *jáquima* is looped and tied into a pair of reins—there will be enough of the rope left over to handle the horse with from the ground. This rope end is usually coiled and tied to the horn of the saddle while the rider is on the horse. But an old horsebreaker, Hilario Chapa, who had been a mustanger in his young days, always carried this, loosely coiled, in his hand and used it instead of a quirt. If he should be thrown, which was most unlikely, he could hold to the rope and thus prevent his horse from running off. Perhaps he adopted this method in the days when he rode mustangs, for to have a horse escape with the saddle was then really serious.

If the *domador* is still young enough to get a thrill out of *jinetiando*—broncobusting—he will do the riding. But there may be some young fellow standing by who would like to try his skill as a *jinete*. The *domador* will generally let him. For the actual riding of a horse, the mere staying on or being thrown, is the least part of the work of the *domador*. His reputation does not rest on his being a good *jinete;* that was in the beginning of his career. Now, as he grows older, he tries to save himself as much as he can from jolts and possible falls. He may already be taking doses of tea made of the inside bark of the *huisache*, the remedy for *golpes viejos*—old knocks—suffered in the course of being knocked about by wild horses.

Sometimes an old Mexican man, groaning with the stiffness of age and the pains of rheumatism, will explain that his trouble is the result of his having been so *golpeado*— so beaten up—by his work when he was younger. The old man feels that he need not explain that his work was not that of a cotton picker, a grubber, a posthole digger, and above all things, not that of a shepherd. He expects one to know, without being told, that he is carrying the honorable scars incidental to the work of a horseman.

The *potro* is mounted. The loop is released from his foot and the *jinete* reaches over and raises the blind off his eyes. Then he grasps the rope reins firmly, braces himself, and tries to stay on. Everyone encourages him by yelling, *"No te aflojes!"*—"Don't turn loose." If the *jinete* should lose his hat, a yell of derision goes up. When a rider loses his hat, it is a sign that he is losing his balance and that he may not be long in following his hat. If he is thrown, unless he is hurt, he would be embarrassed not to try again; he feels that this is a challenge that he must meet. The *potro* has thrown down the gauntlet, so to speak, and a real combat is on. But if the *jinete* should hesitate in the least, should show the slightest fear of the horse, some wag might call out to bring the *yerbanis*—an herb used in treating those sick from the effect of having been badly frightened. Few *jinetes* could stand this indirect ridicule. But the *potro* will be ridden. There is a saying: "There never was a horse that couldn't be rode; nor a rider that couldn't be throwed."

Not all *jinetes* ride alike. Some wear spurs and do most of their holding on with them; again, there are good *jinetes* who never put on a pair of spurs; they hold on by clinching the legs tightly against the horse, and ride more on a balance. The balance and rhythm maintained by the rider are important, especially when he doesn't wear spurs. One might wonder why the fanning of the *potro's* shoulders with a quirt or even with the hat of the *jinete* could help. It seems that the only reason for this fanning is to help maintain a balance—just as a tightrope walker carries a cane while walking the rope.

However a *jinete* rides, each horse may have his own idea of how to get rid of him. They say that one of the worst kinds is a *potro* that runs; particularly is this so if he is hard to circle. When he starts off by running, the best thing the *jinete* can do is to spur him and make him pitch; this will keep him somewhat located. For even when the *jinete* manages to stay on—and it is not so easy to stay on a wild horse in a dead run, one that takes prickly pear and brush in his stride—he may, by the time the run is over, find himself so far from where he started that he will have difficulty getting back.

After the first ride, the *potro* (but we will no longer call him a *potro*; he is now a *quebrantado*—a partly-broken) will be unsaddled and again tied to the tree.

The *domador* will ride the horse at least twice a day, morning and afternoon. In a few days he will be riding him bareback to water and to stake him. The more he is handled, the sooner he will be gentled. But a horse should never be gentled according to the saying: *Con sacate nada y agua poquita sale un caballo muy mansito.*—"With no grass and little water results a very gentle horse." A poor *domador* sometimes starves his horse for grass and water in order to make him weak and easier to handle, but such a one stands low in his profession. It is said of him that he breaks the spirit of the horse. A good *domador* may well boast that, always, when he returns a horse to the owner, he is *entero* —whole—is as sound as he was when he took him to break.

In the early days horses were fed by staking them out to grass. Horses that were not gentle were preferably staked to a log or some other drag, for if they were tied to something fixed, they were likely to break the rope or to injure themselves. And, too, the log could be shifted from place to place to better grass. At a dirt tank near the ranch house where I grew up was a large mesquite tree known as the "stake tree." How many horses, first and last, wild and gentle, had been staked to that tree! There it stood alone in a grassy flat; now, if it still stands, it is buried in a thicket of brush and trees. When a tree or log was not near, a horse could be staked to the ground. A hole a few inches deep was dug in the ground with a pocket knife; then a large knot or a bunch of grass was tied in the end of the rope and buried in the hole, and the dirt trampled down on it. The wildest horse couldn't pull it out—and there was no danger of the horse's getting tangled in the rope. Again, there were stake-pins to be driven into the ground on the prairie.

After the horse has been ridden (with the *jáquima*) until he can be handled with less force, the *jáquima* is exchanged for a much lighter halter called a *bozalillo*. It used to be that some artistic skill was often put into the making of the *bozalillo*. If made of thin hemp rope, it might be decorated with tassels of the untwisted rope or of colored yarns; but the nicest nose-bands were made of hair rope, beautifully intertwined in different colors, and decorated with tassels and intricate woven knots of the hair.

The most important training of a young horse comes by way of the *bozalillo*. The horse himself may be given credit

for a beautiful color, a good gait, a gentle disposition, the
ability to endure hard usage, but the horse's rein always
reflects on the man who trained or failed to train him to a
quick and easy response to the rein. There are riders who
would not attempt to break a horse; yet they will take a
horse that is newly broken, and, through riding him, continually improve his rein. The ability to do this is always
spoken of with admiration—the mark of a real horseman.
On the other hand, a rider might take a young horse already
started with a good rein and, through the wrong method,
ruin his rein; this happens more often when a green hand
is afraid of a horse. It is said that when one is afraid of a
horse he should never ride him, because such a rider ruins
the horse.

While the *domador* is working with the *quebrantado*, he
holds him from the left side to put the *bozalillo* on him;
he saddles him from the left side, and he mounts him from
the same side. Before long the horse learns that while the
rider is on the ground, he can move only to the left and
around the rider. When a horse learns to do this, the *domador*
says that he is *pidiendo el vaquero*—"inviting the rider."
This constant turning to the left gives a better rein in turning to that side. But a good *domador* always sees that the
horse gets plenty of turning to the right while he is being
ridden. If a horse ever gets "cold-jawed," it is usually on
the right side. But no matter how one tries to keep the rein
of a horse well balanced, the rider himself will sometimes
favor one side, without knowing that he is doing so. This,
it is said, is noticed by others after a left-handed rider has
used a horse for some time.

So the *domador* gives much attention to handling the
quebrantado with the *bozalillo*—to giving him a good rein.

Then he puts the bridle on; sometimes he may do this a little prematurely, if, as they say, the horse *busca el freno*—"hunts for the bridle." This hunting for the bridle, anticipating it, they claim, is indicated by the horse's champing an imaginary bit. The *bozalillo* is left on with the bridle until the horse is used to the feel of the bit in his mouth; then it is taken off and the bridle used alone.

By this time about a month has gone by, and if everything has gone along all right, the *domador* leads the young horse back to his owner and collects his two and a half dollars. But is the horse now gentle enough for anyone to ride? That depends on the horse—some horses are never thoroughly gentle; and it also depends on the rider—some people never learn to ride.

II. ARRENDADOR

To have had the opportunity to practice his profession in South Texas, the *arrendador* must needs have been in a locality where men were often on horseback in the interest of sport or pleasure. His services were not required in the work of training horses for general use; that was and is the work of the *domador*—the horsebreaker. The *arrendador's* work was to teach a horse obedience to the reins, the word being cognate to *rienda* (bridle rein), *arrendar* (to teach a horse to be bridlewise), etc.

The *arrendador* was, generally, a Mexican man no longer young. After having spent many years breaking and training horses, he had become expert in reining them and had come gradually to specialize in this, the highest branch of the art of horse training. Any horse given into the hands of the *arrendador* had been at least partly broken but had not yet been bridled. The horse selected for special training would show exceptional promise and be of excellent appearance. Consequently, if the training resulted in failure, the failure reflected on the *arrendador*, not on the horse. The *arrendador* was supposed to know horses too well to put forth effort on one not capable of responding intelligently.

The initial training was with a *bozalillo*—a noose, often finely plaited of hair or rawhide and decorated—held in place by a light headstall. When the horse could be whirled, first to the right and then to the left, with only the slightest pull on the reins of the *bozalillo;* when he could be put into a run and then stopped in his tracks, with only a slight tightening of the reins, then he was ready for the bridle. The *bozalillo* was used in conjunction with the bridle, each with a separate pair of reins, until the horse was rein perfect; then it was discarded and the bridle used alone. By this time the horse was so well trained that the bridle was brought into only the slightest use. Never was there enough force used on it to cause the bit to cut the horse's mouth or even to cause him to open his mouth on the bit; such action on the part of the horse would reflect discredit on his *arrendador*.

To accomplish this training, much patience and much, much practice were required. But there was always plenty of time, for the *arrendador* required something like eighteen months in which to give a finished rein to any horse that he considered worthy of his time and efforts. And the price, perhaps, was around twenty-five dollars.

Among the legends that surround the work of the *arrendador*, this one was told by an old Mexican man, Tiburcio, who lived in Nueces County fifty years ago. He vouched for the truth of the story, because he was present at the climax, he said.

It happened in Mexico, where he had a *compadre* who was an especially good *arrendador;* he was *"como pocos."* This *compadre* had an only son who, he proudly hoped, would in time develop into an *arrendador* as good as he himself was. With this in mind he went to great pains to instruct the boy in the art of reining a horse. He hoped to impart to him the knowledge of a good foundation for the profession he was expected to follow. He did not expect, however, to live to see his son equal him in skill, for that, he felt, would come only—if, indeed, ever—through more years of experience than he had in which to live.

But the son proved so apt that by the time he had reached young manhood the father decided to try him out—to see just how good he really was. He selected a superb young horse and turned him over to the boy. He charged him to give the horse the very best rein that he possibly could, since he wanted him for his own use, he said. And he cautioned him that he need not expect any help from him, that he was to do the work entirely alone. The son realized that he was being tested. He took the horse and spent the necessary time in training him, all the while being entirely ignored by the father.

Finally, and it so happened that our old Tiburcio, so he said, was standing talking to his *compadre* when the boy rode up and announced to his father that he was ready to deliver the horse to him. *"Bueno,"* the old man said, *"pasea-lo."* Obeying the command, the boy put the horse through his paces for inspection, and the old man appeared to be satisfied. But he must try the horse himself before he would pronounce final judgment.

When the boy got down, he stood for a moment rubbing the forehead of the horse, caressing him it would seem, before handing the reins to his father. Tiburcio noticed this, but attached no importance to it at the time. The old man got on the horse and settled himself in the saddle. The horse started off quietly, and then, without any warning whatever, took the bit between his teeth and ran away. After a startled moment the old *arrendador* pulled back with all his might, but the horse had forgotten the meaning of the reins. Never, in all his life, had the *arrendador* had such an experience. Finally, by sawing and pulling in the crudest manner, he succeeded in circling the "cold-jawed" brute and bringing him back to where his *compadre* and his—apparently—crestfallen son awaited him—the horse with his eyes flashing and his mouth wide open on the bit, Tiburcio said, and his *compadre* "*chiando de coraje*" sputtering with anger.

The old man threw himself off the excited horse and tossed the reins to his son. "There," he exclaimed, "is your horse. I was mistaken; you are no horseman. Pity that I didn't put you to herding goats in the first place; you are fit for nothing but a shepherd." The father scolded while the son stood, holding his hat under his arm and, again, passing his hand over the forehead of the horse.

When the father had exhausted himself of his tirade, the boy, timidly, asked him to try the horse again. For surely he must have done something to the horse, that had grown quiet by this time, to cause him to react in such a way. Who? He who had spent his life working with horses? He who was an *arrendador* the like of which his son would never be? And, no! he wouldn't ride the horse again. But the boy still pleaded. Well, then he would. But this time he would show the horse that he was being ridden by a *caballero* instead of by a *pastor*.

The old man mounted once again. The horse started off

quietly, as before. But the *arrendador* was ready for him, alert. He indicated a sudden turn to the right; the horse turned, perfectly amenable to the reins. Then, as quick a turn to the left, and he responded as easily. A touch of the spurs, and he dashed forward in a run; then a hint of the reins and he stopped in his tracks. "Well," thought the old man, "almost as good as if I had given him the rein."

He put the horse to test after test and he came out of each one with credit to his *arrendador*. Then the old man made the final test. He got down, pulled three hairs out of the horse's tail, then cut the reins and spliced them with these three hairs. He mounted the horse again, and with only the strength of three hairs to manage him with, put him through the tests as before. He might have done it with one hair, Tiburcio thought—the horse was so well-reined, so near perfection.

He wheeled the horse and came back to his *compadre* and his slyly-smiling son in a dead run; he stopped suddenly, and the lines that the feet of the horse made were "from here to there"—and Tiburcio indicated a generous distance that the horse slid in his abrupt stop. The father beamed, "But, son, the horse is perfection—is almost as if I had given him the rein. But," and his face clouded, "how did it come to pass? What made him act as he did in the beginning?"

"Well, I'll tell you, *papacito*," the boy bragged. "*Yo, lo que se hacer, se deshacer.* What I can do, I can undo. I not only can rein a horse; I can also unrein him." He was already better than the old man.

"Yes," Tiburcio nodded, "there are people like that—*diableros*, devil-workers. *Muchacho sinverguenza!*" (Boy without shame.)

III. CORRER EL GALLO

The delicate, refined art of the *arrendador*—like various other arts—belonged in the realm of luxury. The rider, no matter what his skill as a vaquero—a hand working with cows—might be, became, when mounted on this super-reined horse, a knight-errant for the time being. He was ready to go courting, if so inclined; he was prepared to offer or to accept challenges on horsemanship, or to enter any equestrian game demanding skill and affording entertainment.

Chief of these games in the early days was that of *correr-el-gallo*, which was played on the Día de San Juan (June 24). On this day someone by the name of Juan would arrange a celebration in honor of his Saint's Day, and of his own birthday. Regardless of whether he had been born on that particular day or whether he had been born on one of the several other days dedicated to some San Juan, he always considered June 24, the feast day of John the Baptist, as his natal day.

So he would select a rooster of the game variety or other light breed and have him much decorated with ribbons, or in any other way that his fancy dictated. Those who were to engage in the game with him would be grouped, on their well-reined horses, off to one side. Juan, mounted on his best horse and holding the rooster by its legs high in his right hand, would pass the group in a dead run. At a "grito" by the umpire, the participants would charge after him. There were rules governing the game, but the object was to take the rooster away from Juan. When one succeeded in doing this, then he became the object of the chase; and so on, until the rooster, or that part that represented the rooster, was carried across the goal. Only the head of the rooster was the trophy, and that was usually all that the victor could show, for the fowl had been, literally, torn to pieces in the contest.

Since the best way to avoid the pursuers or the best way to capture the prize was by being able to make quick turns or sudden stops, the rein of the horses involved was of more importance than their speed.

This game was not without considerable danger. At a San Juan celebration that was held near the old town of Banquete, Nueces County, some time in the eighties, an accident occurred that the old-timers tell of. Among those who entered the game of *correr-el-gallo* were two brothers, Ed and Cap Perkins. These young men were of a family of outstanding horsemen. In the struggle that took place, the brothers ran together in a head-on collision; horses and riders fell in a heap. Cap Perkins was killed outright, and so was the horse of Ed Perkins. This tragedy had much to do, it was said, with causing the game of *correr-el-gallo* to become unpopular in Nueces County.

From the standpoint of the rooster, the game always resulted in annihilation. As my mother used to tell, the first Día San Juan after she came to the ranch in Nueces County, as a bride, in 1869, the Mexicans on the ranch and their friends from the surrounding country arranged a celebration. One of the vaqueros on the ranch by the name of Juan prepared to enter the *correr-el-gallo*. My mother, not being informed on the entire nature of the entertainment, gladly consented to decorate the rooster for him. He brought the rooster to her and also yards and yards of ribbon of every color that he could get at the nearest store. My mother said that she fitted a piece of muslin neatly around the body of the rooster, and on this foundation sewed the streamers of ribbon.

Having decorated the rooster, she, naturally, wanted to see the sport of running him. She saw it and the sight remained an unpleasant memory. The start, she said, was a colorful spectacle—Juan in the lead with the rooster held high and the ribbons flying. Then came the onset of the young vaqueros; horses and riders had grown expert through their work of running longhorn cattle and constant practicing of equestrian feats when not engaged in work. The gay silk handkerchiefs; the decorated Mexican sombreros with hanging colored chinstraps; the red and green sashes; and the glimmer of silver on saddle, bridle, spurs and pistol handles—all lent brilliance in the June day sunshine. The local *platero* (silversmith) converted many of the silver dollars that were plentiful in those days into whatever ornament the customer might fancy; this included the traditional spread-eagle browband that Doña Martina Torres used on her silver-plated bridle.

Everyone moved at full speed on agile Spanish horses, each of a different color. Then came a horrified squawk from the rooster as he was snatched none too gently away from Juan. From then on it was not a pleasant sight, especially if one were in sympathy with the rooster. Even after the goal had been obtained, the running, the wheeling, the reckless dashing and stopping did not cease as long as there was a fragment of rooster or a piece of ribbon to contest.

Pitching Horses and Panthers

By J. Frank Dobie

I HAD quit going barefooted before I heard the word *bucking*, and I was old enough to vote before I realized that it was not strictly a literary locution, like "bucolic" and "beatific." The difference between bucking and pitching is merely geographic: the farther south you sweat, the higher they pitch, and the father north you freeze, the harder they buck. As one old peeler remarked, "Wherever there's broncs, there's likely to be promptitude." A special diction pertaining to the subject is as extensive as it is vivid and vigorous. This diction popped out of a big, free, fresh, lusty country where cries like "Sock the spurs to him," "Bathe his butt with yer quirt," and "Let 'er buck," vivified the air around camp and corral. It expressed the nature of men who called any horse that had been saddled a time or two "broke," and who had no use for a horse "without a little life to him." It has been amply treated of by Ramon F. Adams in his *Cowboy Lingo;* it highly seasons the meat in the chapter on "Breaking Horses" in the revised edition of Philip Ashton Rollins' *The Cowboy.*

"Any mustang," Rollins quotes one longhorned patriot as saying, "that outgrows a hankering to elevate is guilty of treason to the grand old State of Texas." Texas has been given credit for a great many lively things, and the bronc "with a belly full of bed springs" is one of them. It is said that horses do not pitch—or buck—in Europe or Asia. Cer-

291

tainly, one cannot imagine a "gut twister" of the mustang breed as having afforded the basis for the ancient Greek fable explaining the original subjugation of the horse. "A horse, annoyed by the invasion of a stag into its pasturage, asked a man to help it punish the poacher. The man promised to do this if the horse would allow him to bestride it, javelin

Will James in *Cowboys North and South*

in hand. The horse agreed, the stag was frightened away, and the horse found that he was now a slave to the man."

Pitching is supposed to be an equine institution of the Americas, and plenty of theories have been advanced to explain its origin. The commonest theory is that the Spanish horses of the Americas were preyed on by panthers—which is a fact—and learned how to "unwind" while trying to pitch off panthers that had leaped on their backs. Then the colts of these panther-throwers inherited the peculiar calisthenics generated by their ancestors and practiced them to unseat men. This folk idea is a contradiction to the law that acquired characteristics or habits are not hereditary. Yet if an animal never acquired anything new, how could evolution ever proceed? The panther idea is thus elaborated by an Englishman who cowboyed in Paraguay:

"We got on to the subject of why American and South American range-bred horses buck. Byro's early experience had been gained in Hungary, where cattle are worked by horsemen, and mighty good ones at that. We agreed that in both England and Hungary no horse knows how to buck like an American, North and South. Horses in Europe can be, and often are, hard to tame and wild to ride, but they seem never to get their heads right down between their legs or to double up like a jackknife with a spring in it. Why should this be? After long discussion, we decided that it must be on account of the mountain lions, or pumas, which are common to most sparsely settled parts of the two Americas. The puma, sometimes called the friend of man in South America, is very fond of horse-flesh. In certain parts of the Cordilleras it is impossible to let horses run free, bunches of brood mares especially. Some ranchers always let a few mules run with the mares, as mules will fight pumas, and also are crazy over little foals, probably on account of their own sterility. Certain it is that most mules have the mother-complex strongly developed. Some ranchers tie little collars of dogskin around the foals' necks, as pumas are supposed to be afraid of the smell of dog, but I do not believe that this is at all a certain remedy. We decided that the explosive quality of the range-bred horses' bucking is the result of generations of experience with mountain lions. The puma, when attacking a colt, generally jumps from slightly behind, gets one arm over the withers and the other over the nose, usually breaking the horse's neck. I have seen horses with deeply scored withers and claw-marks over the nose, and can quite believe that the only way a horse could get free from such an encumbrance would be by bucking. Hence the difference between European horses and American."[1]

Some pitching horses have made reputations through their performances in professional rodeos; others, in the days before rodeo managers grabbed their kind up, became famous over restricted ranching areas; but no bad horse has ever become widely and enduringly famous like certain bad men or like the fictional Black Beauty, the semi-historical, semi-legendary Pacing White Stallion, or, through racing prowess, like Man o' War. Phillip Ashton Rollins alludes to "a mythical bronco named Armageddon that ate nothing but gunpowder and cholla cactus, and, having bucked itself completely out of its skin, continued to pitch until nothing of it remained beyond its ears and memory." I think that Mr. Rollins is entirely responsible for the memory. There was Pecos Bill's Widow-Maker, who performed quite a feat in pitching Pecos Bill's bride over the lower horn of the moon, but this is a Pecos Bill story and not a horse story.

---

[1]Craig, C. W. T., *Paraguayan Interlude*, New York, 1935, 48-49.

Probably the two best known outlaw horses of America are the Zebra Dun and the Strawberry Roan. The endurance of their reputations is largely due to the cowboy songs taking their names that have been popularized by Jack Thorp, John A. Lomax, and others. "The Zebra Dun" begins with the advent in camp of a mouthy stranger who used big words and "talked about foreign kings and queens." Finally, after he had showed how green he was, he wanted to borrow a nice, fat, gentle horse to ride on to the 7 D ranch. With glee the boss roped him out the horse nobody could ride.

> Old Dunny was a rocky outlaw that had grown so awful wild
> He could paw the white out of the moon every jump for a mile.
>
> When the stranger hit the saddle, Old Dunny quit the earth
> And traveled right straight up for all that he was worth,
> A-pitching and a-squealing, a-having wall-eyed fits,
> His hind feet perpendicular, his front ones in the bits.
>
> We could see the tops of the mountains under Dunny every jump,
> But the stranger he was growed there, just like the camel's hump;
> The stranger sat upon him and curled his black mustache,
> Just like a summer boarder waiting for his hash.

The admiring cowboys learned a lesson in sizing up strangers right then; the boss allowed this was the kind of hand he had been looking for "since the year one." There isn't anywhere a more vivid or picturesque description of a pitching horse's activities than the verses of "The Strawberry Roan" afford.

There used to be some debate over whether the horse of the song should be called Z Bar Dun, on account of his brand, or Zebra Dun, on account of the stripes down his back and legs. John Custer, an old trail driver, living in San Antonio, told me that while he was on a ranch north of Big Spring,

Texas, about 1880, a "slim feller wearing a little hat" and otherwise looking like a tenderfoot came into camp, asked for a job, and was given an outlaw horse branded Z Bar L to ride. The apparent greenhorn "rode that horse to a fare-you-well." Then some of the boys made up the song about him, sung today under the title of "The Zebra Dun."

With varying circumstances the story celebrated in the song has been widely distributed. The best version of it that I know—told, however, without any reference to a song—is recounted by William French[2], who ran the noted W S Ranch in western New Mexico. The horse was a man-fighting outlaw, about six years old, named Bullet. The man was an elderly stranger who had drifted into the ranch the night before and had, on account of his looks and manners, been dubbed "The Granger."

"Bullet was now alone, and he careened around the enclosure, stopping every now and again to snort defiance, and as soon as the riders came back they looked at him, especially those who did not pretend to be riders. Others thought it advisable to throw him back in the bunch 'til they had more time on their hands. Everyone had forgotten about the old gentleman on the fence. He was still chewing tobacco and apparently not taking much interest in the proceedings.

"Some one was about to open the gate when he held up his hand and asked what was the matter with the bay. He was told that he was a pretty bad *caballo* and they thought of tying a saddle on him and leaving him saddled up for a day before attempting to ride him. His only remark was to spit the quid out of his mouth, slip down off the fence, give a hitch to his old pants and say: 'Hell! I'll ride him.'

[2]French, William, *Some Recollections of a Western Ranchman*, London, 1927, 210-215.

"It took a minute or so for the observation to sink in, and then it was received with an ironical cheer. At first nobody thought he was serious, but when he borrowed a pair of spurs from Fred and proceeded to buckle them on, it began to dawn on us that he really meant to ride him.

"Some caustic remarks were addressed to him in regard to his will and his choice as to the mode of burial, but of these he took no notice, merely indicating with his hand to go ahead and get the saddle on. The proud Bullet was fore-footed, and busted so hard that it broke his front teeth. Then it took all hands to hold him while he was hobbled fore and aft with the usual slip knot. A hackamore and blind was placed on his head and a saddle securely fixed before he was allowed on his feet.

"When he got up, although blindfolded, he still looked defiant, the more so on account of the blood from his broken teeth. He did all that a horse can do to get rid of the saddle, but with men holding on to a rope from either side he gradually quieted down. Taking advantage of the pause, the old man crawled on to his back, the blind was removed from his eyes, and we all ran to climb the fence and witness his demise.

"For a moment or two Bullet stood still with surprise, and then realizing that something was on his back, he turned himself loose. He pitched as only a Western bronco can pitch, with his head almost between his hind legs and his back arched. He sprang into the air fully five or six feet, reversing his position in the process and keeping it up in quick succession, till it looked as if his rider's head must have been shaken loose from his body. We all looked for both man and horse to come down in a heap, but they maintained their respective positions.

"When Bullet found he couldn't unseat him, he fairly screamed with rage and went round and round the enclosure, alternately pitching and plunging, for fully ten minutes, when, finding it necessary to slacken his efforts in order to regain breath, he broke into a trot and eventually came to a halt. This gave his rider a chance to settle himself more firmly in his seat and prove to the maddened beast that he was his master.

"The old fellow drove the spurs into him, and taking off his old hat, which had been pressed down on his ears, he slapped him with it in the face. This not having the desired effect, he reached down to the ground and, seizing a handful of sand, rubbed it in his steaming nostrils. Bullet was not prepared to stand much of that kind of work, and after making a futile effort to kick him like a cow, threw down his head and commenced his pitching. He went through the same performance for another ten minutes and with the same result, this time coming to a stand with a regular scream.

"At first we had looked on with astonishment and incredulity depicted on our faces, but when we realized that the old fellow really could ride, the cheering that we gave him made the whole place ring. When they came to a halt after the second round, the old fellow himself was glad to take a breather, but he made no attempt to dismount, merely remarking: 'He sure is a daisy.'

"Then it was suggested that he should take him outside, and every one who had a horse saddled there got ready to accompany him, prophesying that by the time they got back Bullet could be thrown into the regular *remuda*. The gates were thrown open, and, seeing a chance for liberty, he went through them like a shot, proving that he had been correctly named. He was joined on the outside by all the boys who were mounted, and they went off 'hell for leather,' as if the devil was behind them.

"I followed on foot, determined to see all I could, but they had not gone more than fifty or sixty yards when Bullet, to show he was still in the ring, threw down his head and renewed his pitching. This time he had the whole world before him and his efforts, if possible, exceeded anything he had done in the corral. The yipping and yelling went on for a minute or two and the old man seemed comfortable, but all of a sudden I saw him sway in his seat and slip round to one side under the animal's feet.

"The saddle had turned, and it looked as if the infuriated animal must trample him to death. I ran up as fast as I could and all the boys had pulled up and were forming a circle round him. He was equal to the occasion, however, for on going over he had managed to get hold of the nose-band of the hackamore and was holding on for grim death with a hand on each side of the animal's jaws. In this way he managed to keep his head and body off the ground while his feet were still in the stirrups with the spurs hooked into the broad hair cincha and over the animal's back.

"The infuriated brute, being unable to bite him, was endeavoring to rake him off with his front feet. How long the struggle might have gone on it was impossible to say, but for the minute or two that it lasted it looked as if it could have only one end, and that we would be compelled after all to consign the old gentleman to a decent grave. He couldn't have held on much longer, when Fred, with great presence of mind, rode up as close as he could to the plunging brute and, seizing a favorable moment, pulled out his gun and shot him through the head just under the ear.

"He dropped in a heap like a bundle of clothes, and, to our great relief, the old man rolled out from under. He was not in the least flurried. His first care was to shake his foot loose from the cincha, after which he helped himself to a chew of tobacco, got on his feet, looked at Bullet for some time without comment or remark of any kind. It was apparent he was quite dead, and, seeming satisfied, he pushed him with his foot, said he was 'a likely kind of a hoss,' and proceeded to undo the cincha.

"We all congratulated him on his escape, but he didn't seem to notice it—just said it was a pity to have to kill him—and we all pitched in and rolled him over to free the saddle. That was the end of poor Bullet.

"His late rider shouldered the saddle and blankets and we all marched back to the corral. He was offered his choice of the mounts on the ranch, but he wasn't interested, and after he had sat long enough on the fence to recover his breath he went back to the house, and that was the last that I saw of him. I never learnt his name, nor where he went, nor where he came from."

Milton composed grand poetry out of a roll call of fallen angels. The names—ironic, sardonic, satiric, metaphoric—of bad horses that have in this century made reputations in riding contests over the country compose a kind of poem, unrhymed and unmetered, also. Chant a selection of them aloud: Steamboat, Flying Devil, Undertaker's Pet, Angel, Angel Maker, Gizzard Popper, Gut Buster, Cholera Morbus, Leprosy, Appendicitis, Ulcerated Tooth, Gangrene, Annihilation, Sudden Death, Gentle Lizzie, Long Tom, No Name, Grave Digger, Corkscrew, Shooting Star, Hotfoot, U Tell 'em, Skyrocket, Crooked River, Powder River, Hesitation, Windmill, Nutcracker, Sunnybrook, Wiggles, Dimples,

Tickle Toes, Fire Alarm, Scrap Iron, Spanish Fly, C. O. D.,
Guess What, Disaster, Last Chance, Stop Light, Destiny,
Rocking Chair, Whirlwind, Gin Fizz, Midnight, Five Min-
utes to Midnight, Damfiknow, Black Thunder, Black Pow-
der, Red Pepper, Yellow Fever, Blue Monday, Parson Brown,
Booger Red, Hammerhead, Saint Peter's Agent, He'll Do,
Hightower, War Bonnet, Hell to Set, Gas Tank, Tombstone,
Billy the Kid, Dynamite—balladized by Phil Le Noir—and
lovable Jack Thorp's Sky-High:

> "You've all heard of pitchin' horses
> From Steamboat down the line,
> Old Barometer, en Step Fast,
> En a mare they called Divine,
>
> Old Prickly Pear, en Pizen,
> Lop Ears, en Stingaree—
> They all wuz Shetland ponies
> 'Sides this horse from Santy Fee."

Two accounts of bucking horses that follow may be taken
as representative of many such that have been told over and
over around camp fires on the range but that are going into
oblivion. A horse that proves himself to be a genuine outlaw
on a ranch nowadays is picked up by rodeo managers.

(1)

"By way of relaxation Blanco busted four broncos for us,
and on a bet of two dollars tackled one of the worst outlaws
in this section. How a man of his age could stand the jarring
he got has always been a puzzle to me. The name of the horse
was Muldoon, bestowed on him, I suppose, from his knack of
falling on people and crushing the life out of them. But he
met something as tough as he was when Blanco stepped into
the ring. Muldoon's method was to stand perfectly still while

being saddled and bridled, but the second a man got seated he would rear straight in the air and throw himself backward, or he would buck up to the side of a corral and then hurl himself against it.

"He tried all these tricks, but in vain. Blanco, for a wonder, was absolutely silent, but I knew he was boiling within. This could be seen by the way he dug his spurs into the brute to make him get up after he had thrown himself. The end was tragic and looked like suicide. The horse, after a few rounds of furious bucking, got fairly exhausted, and was covered with dust, sweat, and blood. He had just made one of his backward lunges, and Blanco was on the ground. With a squeal of rage Muldoon stood upon his hind legs, made a couple of vicious drives with his fore feet at his tormentor, who had not had time to mount him, and fell back. He never moved again. His neck had been broken."[3]

(2)

"We passed through the Pawnee Agency, arrived at the Bar X Ranch with the horses in good shape, and turned them over to Bob Lemons, the foreman. The ranch had just changed hands and the men were getting ready for the spring round-ups. The cowpunchers were selecting their horses. These horses had been fed some corn all winter, and were slick and fat and full of ginger. They had not been ridden all winter, and some of them were sure to make the boys pull leather. There was a big, hog-backed, dun-colored horse that had glass eyes, and a stripe down his back. He was an outlaw. Many of the boys picked this horse, but after Lemons told them what he was they selected something else. A cow-

---

[3]Steedman, Charles J., *Bucking the Sagebrush*, New York, 1904, 218-219.

puncher, who lived at the Pawnee Agency, said, 'Bob, I'll ride that horse.'

"Lemons said, 'If you do, you do it at your own risk.'

"The boy said, 'I can ride him.'

"The horse was rode, and say! he fought like a tiger. They had to hogtie and blindfold him in order to put the saddle on. They let him up, and, fellows, he sure could make the stirrups crack together over his back. He just squealed and bucked. Lemons held the horse and the cowpuncher tried to mount him, but he whirled around, never still. Finally the boy got his left foot in the stirrup and his hand on the horn of the saddle. He pulled the bronc's head around, and as he whirled, he swung into the saddle, and Bob Lemons pulled the blind away. That bronc went up in the air like he was shot out of a cannon, and when he hit the ground you could not see daylight under him. He pitched straight and then went to bawling and bucking with the grapevine twist. The puncher lost his right stirrup and hooked his right spur in the cinch, and was sure riding.

"We were sitting up on the corral fence and the bronc came straight for it. We fell off like turtles off a log. Just then the bronc whirled and bucked down along the corral, the boy staying with him. The bronc quit pitching and started to run towards the creek, and it looked as if he were going over a high bluff, the cowpuncher all the time quirting hell out of him. He ran for a mile or so and the cowpuncher rode him back to the corral, a subdued horse for the time being, but not yet broken. The blood was running out of the rider's mouth. The horse had bucked so hard that some small blood vessel in the boy's head had broken. He got all right, and he broke the big dun outlaw.'"[4]

'Barnard, Evan G., A Rider of the Cherokee Strip, New York, 1936, 71-72.

Ballad of Manuel Rodriguez

By FRANK GOODWYN

IT HAS been several years now since I heard a vaquero on on the King Ranch sing a long string of *versos* concerning another vaquero who got pitched off by a horse and took to cotton-picking. The incident took place at La Parra, headquarters of the Kenedy Ranch, comprising Kenedy County. I can recall only nine *versos*—but they tell the story. All of a *corrido* that you can put on paper, anyhow, is the skeleton. The timbre of the singer's voice, the feeling, the tempo, the enthusiasm—the flesh and blood of a vigorous folk ballad— are out there in a cow camp serenaded by coyotes; the essential elements refuse to get into type.

FROM SWEET AND KNOX, *On a Mexican Mustang*, 1892

Subió Manuel Roderiguez
En la puerta del corral;
No había otro en la corrida
Que le ganaba en jinetiar.

Manuel Roderiguez climbed
Up on the gate of the pen;
There was no man in the camp
Who could beat him riding.

Estaba el caballo monjino
Lo ensilló Manuel Roderiguez
En la orilla del corral;
Por orden del caporal.

The mouse-colored horse
Stood in the edge of the pen;
Manuel Roderiguez saddled him
According to the foreman's orders.

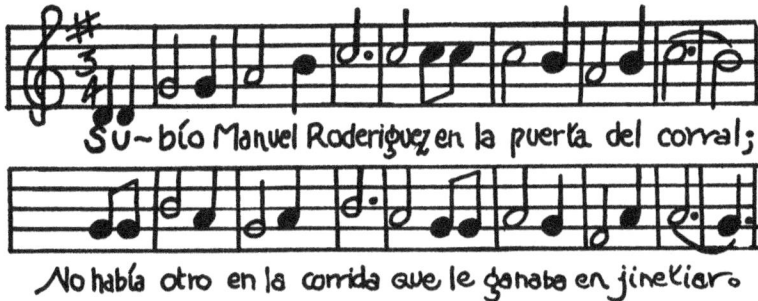

Lo subió Manuel Roderiguez
Y la silla se ladió;
Al salir para la plaza
El caballo le tumbó.

Manuel Roderiguez mounted
And the saddle went sidewise;
On coming out into the big pen
The horse threw him off.

Decía Manuel Roderiguez
Con el sombrero en la frente,
No dolio tanto el porazo
Pero me vió toda esta gente.

Manuel Roderiguez said,
With his hat on his forehead,
"It wasn't the fall that hurt
But that all these people saw me."

Subió Luís Librez
En la puerta del corral;
Todos le tenían confiansa
Y también el caporal.

Luís Librez climbed
Up on the gate of the pen;
Everybody had confidence in him
—Even the foreman.

Decía Manuel Roderiguez
Sacudiendo se el talon,
Ya me voy para Mercedes
A las piscas de algodón

Manuel Roderiguez said,
While dusting off his heel,
"I'm going to Mercedes
To pick cotton."

Decia Luís Librez,
Se agachaba y se sonrilla,
No tengan miedo, muchachos;
Yo se defender mi silla.

Luís Librez said—
He bowed and smiled—
"Don't be afraid, boys;
I know how to defend my saddle."

Decía Manuel Roderiguez
Sacudiendo se el sombrero,
Ya no vuelvo pá La Parra
Al trabajo de vaquero.

Estaba el caballo monjino
En la orilla del corral.
Lo esilló Luís Librez
Por orden del caporal.

Manuel Roderiguez said
While dusting off his hat,
"I'll never come back to La Parra
To work as a vaquero."

The mouse-colored horse
Stood in the edge of the pen.
Luís Librez saddled him
According to the foreman's orders.

A Man and His Horse

CARSON AND HIS FAVORITE HORSE, "APACHE."

FROM MASON'S *Romance and Tragedy of Pioneer Life*, 1884

He Knew His Master's Voice

By G. C. ROBINSON

RIDING in the lead of his *caballado,* the horse drover had just come down from the treeless country west of the Nueces River into the more hilly land bordering the level valley. His drove of horses, some three or four hundred head, were strung back along the road for a quarter of a mile; riding on either side were Mexican vaqueros, and one rode at the rear of the herd.

The drover cast frequent glances backward, apparently at his drove, but in reality he was watching a lone horseman approaching at a swift gallop. He had first noted this horseman when the latter was more than a mile away; yet he had not once slackened speed until he neared the herd. There, after apparently a brief conversation with a Mexican, he turned out of the road and in a moment resumed his swift ride alongside the advancing herd.

To the drover it seemed apparent that the purpose of the lone rider was to overtake him; and this caused him to note the appearance of the man as he drew nearer. It was second nature, in that lonesome land, to be wary and on guard; for it was during that disturbed and lawless period which succeeded the Civil War.

The stranger wore a large Mexican sombrero; yet as he drew near the keen eye of the drover saw that he was an American.

"Good morning," the stranger greeted in a pleasant voice as he drew rein. The drover returned the greeting. Then followed a mutual introduction, and though they had not met before, the drover knew that the other was a ranchman living on Lagarto Creek, distant some thirty miles, whose ranch he had passed on one of his trips to the Rio Grande. The ranchman had heard of the drover from many persons. Yet neither of them now mentioned his knowledge of the other.

Meantime the drover noted the appearance of the ranchman. He wore a beard, as was customary, and both hair and beard were dark brown; his skin was bronzed by sun and wind. His nose was strongly aquiline, and his eyes were sky-blue, strongly contrasting with his beard and hair. When he removed his sombrero to adjust it, he exposed an unusually high and broad forehead.

"Your horse is wet; you must have ridden hard for quite a distance," ventured the drover.

"Yes," was the frank reply, "I have been riding to overtake you. Yesterday I received a message from a friend of mine that my cavalry horse was in a drove traveling up the road that would cross at San Patricio. I lost no time on the way to overtake the drove. I saw my horse in your drove as I rode by."

This was spoken in a pleasant and matter-of-fact tone in no way offensive to the drover.

"Are you sure that it is your horse?" he asked. "I bought all these horses down on the Rio Grande."

"Yes, it is my horse," affirmed the ranchman. "No doubt you bought the horse. Most of your bunch have Mexican brands on them. This horse was stolen about four years ago when a regiment of Mexicans discharged from the Federal army passed through on their way to Mexico. The mate to this horse was taken at the same time, and last year a man rode him up to my gate."

The ranchman then continued to establish his claim: "I rode this horse four years in the Confederate cavalry. He is the best known horse in all the country around here. A hundred men in the country know him."

He then called the names of a dozen men who knew the horse. Most of these the drover knew, and he had heard of all the others, for he had been about a great deal among the scattered ranches.

"Well, show me the horse you claim, and we will see about it," finally consented the drover, hoping that he would not lose the animal.

The two then turned aside and let the horses pass by. Well towards the lead of the drove the ranchman pointed out a medium-sized bright bay. This horse was in prime condition, bore no saddle marks, nor other evidence of having been ridden, though he had an ideal "saddle back." He had a body longer than that of the usual horse of his height, but any good horseman would have chosen him for the best horse in the drove.

"Man, that is a wild horse," declared the drover, much elated. "There is some mistake somewhere. You never rode that horse any four years in the cavalry, nor anywhere else. The rattle of saber and carbine would scare him to death. No, I'll be damned if I will give him up to any man who claims him for a gentle horse, for he is as wild as a mustang. I bought him cheap for that reason."

The manner of the drover was triumphant, and the tone of his voice was bantering, but it was apparently lost in its effect upon the ranchman, whose features became a shade more grim as he replied: "Gentle or wild, he is my horse. That is my father's brand on him and I put it there, though another letter has been burned over it to make it look more like a Mexican brand. We will put the drove in the big pen near San Patricio, rope him out and see how wild he is."

For a moment the drover hesitated. This man with his even and pleasant voice had made no bluster, and his demand was a reasonable one. This man, notwithstanding his quiet manner, would brook no injustice. He had made no threat, but it was plain that he had come to take his own. The drover felt confident that he would win out on his assertion about the horse.

"Well, it is a whole lot of trouble just to show you that what I have said about the horse is true, but I will do as you say in order that you will be satisfied about it. You will see that this horse is really wild."

The two then rode along together, talking about other matters, neither of them referring again to the horse. The drover, however, wondered why the other said no more about the bay. Could he be as sure as he appeared to be?

In due time they reached the pen and corraled the drove. The Mexicans put up the bars at the gate, and at the drover's word a Mexican dismounted, took his lariat and went among the horses to rope the bay. Upon seeing the man with the lariat, the bay crowded deep among the other horses, but soon the Mexican had maneuvered him into a corner with other horses crowded around. These others began to run out, and finally the bay broke cover to join his companions, giving the man a chance with his lariat.

A true throw and a quick jerk drew the noose around the bay's neck just behind the ears. Already under way, the bay redoubled his speed at the touch of the lariat, whereupon the captor prepared to throw him. Catching the larait under his left hip, at the split second when the line was coming taut, the Mexican heaved backward with a mighty jerk, giving slack to the lariat when the force of the jerk had been spent. But the bay, though turned by the jerk, righted with the slack instead of falling sidewise, and went on, dragging his captor, who now sat upon his doubled left leg with the right braced forward. The bay soon felt his wind being shut off by the closing noose, and faced about, charging past the man, getting the advantage of two lengths of the lariat. The captor came up and the same tactics were repeated with the same results. In the beginning of the struggle the other horses had

CHARLES M. RUSSELL IN WISTER's *Virginian*, 1916

fled to the farthest side of the pen, leaving a clear field for horse and man. After several dashes, the bay toned down and stood still. His captor arose and tried to approach by taking in the taut lariat hand over hand, but after the Mexican had made two or three steps, the bay forthwith bolted.

"Well, I told you he was a wild horse, and now you see it for yourself," bantered the drover. But the ranchman was approaching the scene of the struggle, and if he heard the other, he paid no heed. Just as the ranchman came near the Mexican, the horse yielded to a pull on the lariat and came a step or two forward. The Mexican turned to the ranchman and said: "*Este caballo es muy diabolo.*" ("This horse is very mean.")

"Rat!" called the ranchman in a loud but pleasant voice.

The bay stepped forward again, raised his head high in the air and pointed his ears toward the speaker "Rat! Come here," called the ranchman. At this the bay ran forward, making a detour around his captor, and ran almost against the ranchman before stopping. The ranchman spoke to the horse, put his hand on its mane and removed the lariat from its neck.

The Mexican stood perfectly still, looking at the two, and he saw a glitter in the eyes of the horse and in the eyes of the man.

The ranchman, keeping his hand on the mane of the bay, turned to face the drover. He saw an expression of deep admiration lighting up the drover's countenance as he shouted in a hearty voice: "He is your horse. Take him."

The master, his hand still on the bay's mane, started toward the gate; the two kept step as they went, the bay spurning the ground with his feet and still holding a lofty head, chafing at the slow speed of the man. The Mexican, at the direction of the drover, hastily removed the bars from the gate. At the gate, the ranchman and the drover had a few kindly words and shook hands in farewell. As the two passed through the gate the bay lowered on his haunches and drew the air audibly through his contracting and dilating nostrils, his sharp ears working forward and backward, and he eyed the Mexicans on either side, as though daring them even to attempt to touch him.

Still keeping step, they went to the tired mount of the ranchman, and while the others stood watching he changed his saddle to the bay, adjusting saddle and blanket with extreme care. The bay was all a tremble to go; yet he stood while his master mounted; then he started in a long, easy, striding walk with the other horse leading behind.

The ranchman watched the two until a bend in the road hid them behind the mesquite and huisache. The step of the bay had reminded him of cavalry on parade, and then he thought of his remark about the rattle of the saber and the carbine.

"Well, I have heard of such horses. Now I have *seen one.*"

He might as well have been talking to himself, since none of his hearers understood English. But the Mexican who had roped the bay knew just what had happened, and thought that the remark of the drover was something about the horse. Turning to the other he said: "*Señor, aquel mesteño sabe ingles.*"

"No," the drover replied in Spanish, "it is not that the horse *understands English,* but he knows his master's voice, and he will tolerate no other."

A Horse Never Forgets

I. Cristiano, a Sentinel Horse

By W. H. Hudson[*]

A GAUCHO of my acquaintance, when I lived on the pampas and was a very young man, owned a favorite riding horse which he had named Cristiano. To the gaucho "Christian" is simply another word for white man: he gave it that name because one of its eyes was a pale blue-gray almost white—a color sometimes seen in the eyes of a white man, but

[*]Reprinted by permission of E. P. Dutton and Company, New York, from *The Book of a Naturalist*, by W. H. Hudson, New York, 1919, 119-122.

E. W. THISTLETHWAITE IN *Hoofs and Horns*

never in an Indian. The other eye was normal, though of a much lighter brown than usual. Cristiano, however, could see equally well out of both eyes, nor was the blue eye on one side correlated with deafness, as in a white cat. His sense of hearing was quite remarkable. His color was a fine deep fawn, with black mane and tail, and altogether he was a handsome and a good, strong, sound animal; his owner was so much attached to him that he would seldom ride any other horse, and as a rule he had him saddled every day.

Now if it had only been the blue eye I should probably have forgotten Cristiano, as I made no notes about him, but I remember him vividly to this day on account of something arresting in his psychology: he was an example of the powerful effect of the conditions he had been reared in and of the persistence of habits acquired at an early period after they have ceased to be of any significance in the creature's life. Every time I was in my gaucho friend's company, when his favorite Cristiano, along with other saddle horses, was standing at the *palenque*, or row of posts set up before the door of a native rancho for visitors to fasten their horses to, my attention would be attracted to his singular behavior. His master always tied him to the *palenque* with a long *cabresto*, or lariat, to give him plenty of space to move his head and whole body about quite freely. And that was just what he was always doing. A more restless horse I had never seen. His head was always raised as high as he could raise it—like an ostrich, the gauchos would say—his gaze fixed excitedly on some far object; then presently he would wheel round and stare in another direction, pointing his ears forward to listen intently to some faint, far sound which had touched his sense. The sounds that excited him most were as a rule the alarm cries of lapwings, and the objects he gazed fixedly at with a great show of apprehension would usually turn out to be a horseman on the horizon; but the sounds and sights would for some time be inaudible and invisible to us on account of their distance. Occasionally, when the bird's alarm cries grew loud and the distant rider was found to be approaching, his excitement would increase until it would discharge itself in a resounding snort—the warning or alarm note of the wild horse.

One day I remarked to my gaucho friend that his blue-eyed Cristiano amused me more than any other horse I knew. He was just like a child, and when tired of the monotony of standing tethered to the *palenque* he would start playing sentinel. He would imagine it was war-time or that an invasion of Indians was expected, and every cry of a lapwing or other alarm-giving bird, or the sight of a horseman in the distance would cause him to give warning. But the other horses would not join in the game; they let him keep watch and wheel about this way and that, spying or pretending to spy something, and blowing his loud trumpet, without taking any notice. They simply dozed with heads down, occasionally switching off the flies with their tails or stamping a hoof to get them off their legs, or rubbing their tongues over the bits to make a rattling sound with the little iron rollers on the bridle-bar.

He laughed and said I was mistaken, that Cristiano was not amusing himself with a game he had invented. He was born wild and belonged to a district not many leagues away but where there was an extensive marshy area impracticable for hunting on horseback. Here a band of wild horses, a small remnant of an immense troop that had formerly existed in that part, had been able to keep their freedom down to recent years. As they were frequently hunted in dry seasons when the ground was not so bad, they had become exceedingly alert and cunning, and the sight of men on horseback would send them flying to the most inaccessible places in the marshes, where it was impossible to follow them. Eventually plans were laid and the troop driven from their stronghold out into the open country, where the ground was firm, and most of them were captured. Cristiano was one of them, a colt about four or five months old, and my friend took possession of him, attracted by his blue eye and fine fawn color. In quite a short time the colt became perfectly tame, and when broken turned out an exceptionally good riding-horse. But though so young when captured, the wild alert habit was never dropped. He could never be still; when out grazing with other horses or when standing tied to the *palenque,* he was perpetually on the watch, and the cry of a plover, the sound of galloping hoofs, the sight of a horseman, would startle him and cause him to trumpet his alarm.

It strikes me as rather curious that in spite of Cristiano's evident agitation at certain sounds and sights, it never went to the length of a panic; he never attempted to break loose and run away. He behaved just as if the plover's cry or the sound of hoofs, or the sight of mounted men had produced an illusion—that he was once more a wild, hunted horse—yet he never acted as though it was an illusion. It was apparently nothing more than a memory and a habit.

II. Sorrell Top, Booger-Hunter
By Lincoln A. Lang*

Of a different stamp was Sorrel Top, my star mount, easily the best horse I ever straddled. With racing and mustang

---

*Reprinted by permission of J. P. Lippincott Company, Philadelphia, from *Ranching With Roosevelt,* by Lincoln A. Lang, Philadelphia, 1926, 293-296.

stock in his ancestry, the combination had been a particularly good one. Blended in him to an unusual degree were speed and endurance, together with a disposition that could hardly have been improved upon. I broke him mainly myself, experiencing but little trouble, except that at the outset he could and did outshy anything I ever rode. Like a bundle of steel springs, a live rubber ball, he was apt to side-bound from under you at any instant if you did not look carefully to your seat.

Alongside of the road, near the ranch, stood an old stump. For some reason he had taken a special aversion to this, shying from it forcefully every time I rode him past it. But realizing that he was much too sensitive to stand beating, I adopted the plan of merely riding him back and forth past it until he quit shying for the time.

One evening, after he had become fairly well broken, while riding him past the stump, my attention having, for the moment, been taken by something, he all but jumped from under me.

"All right, old boy. Bet you don't do it tomorrow night," I said, as, regaining my seat by a narrow margin, I suddenly made up my mind what I was going to do.

As it happened, I had business at a ranch down in the Cave Hill country, some fifty-odd miles to the southeastward. It had been my intention to start the following day, making a two-day trip of it. Now I changed my plans.

It was midsummer. Before sunrise the following morning I was on my way, riding the culprit with the fixed intention of making the round trip that day. Most likely I would have to lie out that night, but if my mount held out, I was certain he would see nothing the matter with that stump when we passed it on the way in.

Gleefully he hit the road away from the barn. As we passed the stump, he made his usual side-jump, perhaps by way of impressing upon me that he was all right and in need of exercise.

"Fine," I said. "But just wait until tonight."

Through the Bad Lands we threaded our way, across the divide and out on to the rolling slope country beyond. Frequently I was seeing bands of range horses. Clearly my mount was overflowing with enthusiasm. So I would let him take some of it out in detouring to look the stock over. But there seemed to be no dampening his ardor. Like a live rubber ball, gleefully he bounced along, bringing me to my destination with all colors flying, along about 11:00 A. M.

Two hours later I started back. From anything I could see to the contrary my mount was regarding the sixty-odd miles we had already covered as mere exercise. Apparently going as strong as ever, he was unquestionably enjoying himself. For myself, I was all right so far. But by the time we made the top of the divide, along in the evening, I was surely feeling the trip. Frequently I had ridden well over a hundred miles in a single day, on round-ups, it is true, but always with several changes of mounts. A very different thing, the changes acting to rest one up.

The remaining twenty-five miles my mount covered apparently without difficulty; sobered up a little, but still going strong. Perhaps he understood what I had told him the previous evening and was out to show me. Be that as it may, in passing that blamed old stump he side-jumped just about as far and suddenly as usual, all but getting me, for I was about in.

And so I was obliged to admit myself beaten at my own game. But, at least, I now knew the kind of timber Sorrel

Top was built of. If anybody ever got him away from me thereafter it would be no fault of mine.

III.   Teaching a Horse Trust and Distrust

By Willis J. Powell*

Whilst your horse is eating, let another person come in to him with a stick sharpened at the end. Let him prick his nose with it, to irritate him; but slightly, drawing back at the same time. Let him repeat the same an instant afterward, and every time the horse begins to eat again. Come to him yourself, and caress him and talk to him. Go out again, and cause another person to come in with the sharpened stick; but not the same one that came in at first. Let him fret him in the same manner as the other did. Call him out and go in yourself; handle the horse gently, and talk to him. Call in a third, and a fourth, and perform the same; always retiring suddenly from the horse, as if they were afraid of him, every time he leers at them, or endeavors to bite them. These lessons, repeated a few days, will inspire your horse with so much distrust against every person but yourself, and a certain confidence in his own strength, that he will not suffer anyone but yourself to come near him.

If you would not wish to have a person, for example, wearing a white hat, come nigh your horse, put on a white hat, go into the stable where your horse is, and take a whip in your hand: go up to him, and give him a few good lashes with it. Retire and change your hat for one of another color: leave your whip, come in again without it; stroke your horse, pat him, talk to him and feed him. Go out again, and put on your white hat: come in and whip him soundly. Then

*Extracted from Powell, Willis J., *Tachyhippodamia*, New Orleans, 1838, 51-33.

retire, put on another hat, and come in and handle him gently. Repeat the same for a few days, and your horse would as lief see the devil as a man with a white hat, and will not let such a one come near him; and thus, it will happen with any other clothing.

I will relate a little incident that took place in Mexico, a few years before I left there. One of my friends had a horse extremely gentle, and of such an easy, agreeable gait, that he took the greatest care of him, and held him at a great price. A well-fed, big and lusty friar was a friend to our neighbor: one who liked the good things of this world, as well as he liked to ride out to the small towns, bordering upon the City of Mexico, and take a dinner with the bonny lasses and countrymen inhabiting those villages. He used to ask my friend to loan him his horse, to take these excursions just around the capital; and, as his requests were granted with so good a grace, he in a short time went so far as to ask the loan of this favorite animal to go to Cuernavaca, a distance of eighteen leagues, or fifty miles. As this happened pretty often, our friend complained to me one day at the indiscretion of the friar.

I asked him if he could procure me a friar's dress, for a few days, and leave his horse with me for the same time. He did so. I dressed myself in the friar's dress, and went in where the horse was. I took a good whip in my hand, and made him do penance for no other sin but that of too much gentleness. On going out, I took off the friar's dress, and went in again in my own dress, and handled him gently. I repeated the operation a few days, at the end of which time I took the horse back to his master, and told him he might lend him to the friar whenever he pleased. A day or two after, he came to my store. "Your remedy," said he, "has had a marvelous effect. Our monk has just left my house, perfectly persuaded that my horse is possessed with the devil. For, when the holy personage came up to take him by the bridle to get on him, he was so frightened and wheeled round so quick, and flew away from him with so much terror, that one would have said he took him for the destroying angel." The friar crossed himself many times, hurried away with all haste to his convent to sprinkle himself abundantly with holy water, and never asked my friend for his horse again.

Anti-Indian Horse

By James K. Greer

A T THIS stage of training, Blue was to be ridden only occasionally and a few minutes at a time about the lots. He
was too young, his training was not complete, and he was
not to be considered ready for hard service until he was four
years old. Thoroughly gentled and broken to ride, Blue was
on the point of becoming a "one-man horse." Although he
was high-spirited and possessed a temper, he was now trained
to allow my mother and me to catch, bridle and saddle, and
ride him. This took time, but it was accomplished by such
simple means as allowing only us to feed and pet him. If
anyone else tried to feed him and he offered to eat, he was
to be frightened by a stranger concealed in the hay. Of
course his trusted ones were not on hand when this happened.
Neighbors and one of our boys (a slave) were pressed into
service to teach the horse that others would be unkind to
him if he allowed them to catch and mount him. Whips and
spurs and loud shouts were among the means used to secure
this end.

The chief desire of all of us was to have Blue afraid of
Indians. This part of his training proved surprisingly easy,
due, no doubt, to the odor of Indians and to the fact that
all our horses were restless when Indians were around. Tonkawa Indian acquaintances of my father's, from the Fort Bel-

---

[1]Reprinted by permission of the author from *Bois d'Arc to Barb'd Wire*, Dallas, Texas,
1936.

knap reservation, were used in the training of Blue. He was naturally nervous when approached by these Indians and would snort and race around the corral. One day we allowed them to lasso Blue and instructed them to mildly abuse him. It took only a few lessons to make him difficult to be lassoed by Indians; he became artful at dodging, and he finally arrived at the point where he would whinny a loud alarm even on the appearance of an Indian.

In the meantime, Blue was trained to come to either of us upon hearing a certain peculiar but simple whistle, although he was always careful to verify the source of sound by sight as well as by his ear. This not uncommon artifice was first practiced in the corral and then out on the range. At night and in the daytime, when he was alone or with the *caballada*, the Negroes were ordered to ride out and shoot guns about him. In short Blue was being trained for possible emergencies as no other horse in our part of the country had ever been trained. Not only was the animal to be of potential aid to my father in his regular round of duties, but, if occasion arose, he was expected to prove the difference between life and death in case Mother or I had to ride to some of the neighbors to appeal for help against an Indian attack or to give warning of the enemy's presence in the community.

When he was four years old, Blue was sixteen hands high, clean-limbed, deep-chested, short-bodied, with small head, large eyes, and long black mane and tail. Solid in color, except for a small white star on his forehead, full of vigor and well gaited, the horse was soon a favorite of Father's. There was little question as to his speed and endurance, and if in an emergency he proved to be as intelligent as he seemed, he would be a prize indeed.

To test out his speed and endurance he was raced against

a relay of two or three horses. It was only three miles from our house to a spring near present-day Walnut Springs (in Bosque County)—a favorite starting place for horse races. Blue was run the three miles from Walnut Springs to our ranch again and again. I would ride out with my Father, and he would place me on a high hill, some three-quarters of a mile from the house, where I could witness much of the race and gallop in to see the finish. On one occasion Father decided to make a test with a somewhat realistic finish. Five or six Tonkawa bucks out on a hunt had camped near our house. Father knew one of them very well, having talked to him at the reservation and given him food and tobacco more than once. He explained briefly to these Indians that he thought he had a good horse and wanted to see if his opinion was well founded. Would they assist him? They acceded to his request, looking upon the event as quite a lark, no doubt.

It was agreed that three Tonkawas would secrete themselves near the spring, while the others would hide themselves beside the road about half-way between the spring and the house. They had guns, and Father gave them some extra ammunition, as they were to shoot into the air and give their war whoops at the proper moment. At the appointed time, Father rode up to the spring. There was a war whoop, and out from the brush rushed the three Indians. Blue sprang into a run. In a very few seconds he was gaining on the pursuers, who were firing their guns, whooping, and earnestly trying to overtake the blue horse. Not many minutes were required to leave these Indians well behind, and Blue was allowed to slow up. Just at this time the second group of Indians came around the side of the hill where they had posted themselves.

The shots, the piercing yells, and the evident earnestness

of his master in wanting to get away from the Indians stimulated Blue to do his best to reach home in a hurry. Spurs were unnecessary. As the rider leaned forward, Blue lengthened his stride. But the ponies of the pursuers were fresh; moreover, the Indians had not been over one hundred and fifty yards away when they made the alarm, and now they were quartering to head off the flying rider. So Blue ran like a quarter-horse at the finish. His mane and tail were streaming, while the rush of the wind pushed the front of the brim of Father's hat flat against his head. How that horse did run! It was like the dash of a trained sprinter against an ordinary runner. He just floated away. The house was reached with the nearest Indian several hundred yards behind. While some of the Plains Indians had good horses and there was an occasional warrior who rode a horse which could have stayed close to Blue, it was evident that the average Indian's mount would not be able to overtake Blue or stay close enough to him to permit a dangerous running shot. We were very well satisfied with our pet's performance that day.

In 1857 there was a raid in the edge of our community. A neighbor brought the alarming message that the Indians had come, evidently looking for horses. The assembly place for the settlers to take their trail was some distance to the west. The messenger borrowed a fresh horse and rode on while Father made hasty preparations to depart for the designated rendezvous. As he ate a hurried supper, he told Mother that he had decided to ride Blue.

It was nearly sundown when he started, and he rode half the distance before he stopped to get a little sleep and to rest his horse. He wanted Blue to be fresh and free from any sprained ligaments caused by a possible misstep, and he knew that the settlers would not take the trail after night.

About two or three hours passed before the sleeper was disturbed. At times a man who is asleep will subconsciously become aware that something is amiss but will fail to respond promptly. For some seconds, noises were clamoring to be recognized by the sleeper before realization of his surroundings came. Blue was stamping the ground and walking about at the end of his rope. Obviously, whatever had disturbed the horse was not dangerously close, or he probably would have betrayed the fact by pawing the earth rapidly or even snorting. Now his master spoke to him in an undertone, but the voice carried, and Blue stopped and stood quietly. His ears pointed in the direction of whatever it was that had alarmed him.

It would be fatal to stay rolled in the blanket if Indians were near and if they should see the horse, guess the situation, and charge. Father quickly rolled up his blanket and crawled to the horse. Blue was quiet but quivering; the telltale ears remained pointed forward. No prowling wolf or mountain lion had caused this behavior! Indians were coming and were near. There was only one thing to do at the moment; stay quiet and perhaps escape detection. A moving figure would likely be seen by some pair of eyes of a war party.

In two or three minutes the horse's alarm was verified. Passing to one side, but near enough to be counted, rode eight figures, one behind the other, their bodies bobbing from high stirrups. They rode at a running walk and would have been identified as Indians in even a weaker light than that which the moon was still giving forth. Apparently they were intent on some destination and hardly expected early pursuit; certainly they did not suspect the presence of an uncomfortable witness as they rode silently, with heads down, seemingly

glancing neither to the right nor to the left. This fact probably accounted for Blue's not being observed.

When the riders had passed and Blue's quivering had ceased,
my Father lay down again for a short rest before daylight,
when his ride was to be resumed. This time, however, he
held the end of the horse's rope in his hand. But there was
no other disturbance.

Blue's behavior on this trip only served to increase the
affection which we already had for him. So on the occasion
of my Father's next ride to investigate the operations of the
Indians, which was near Stephenville, Blue was left at home.
There were other good horses, although they were not so
fleet nor so well trained, and Father deemed it inadvisable
on this trip to make himself a mark of special envy on
account of his mount. Many warriors would risk their lives
trying to secure an unusually good horse. A well-mounted
rider, therefore, was sometimes the object of an especial
attack in prairie or plains country fighting, and the Indian's

"On the prairie's rolling plain"

CHARLES M. RUSSELL IN COBURN'S *Rhymes*

desire for the possession of his steed increased his chances of death.

Blue would be a special protection for the family because of his habit of sounding alarm when an Indian approached. To increase his value as a protector and also partially to provide protection for him, we decided to tie him to a post of the little front porch. All settlers knew by experience, or by truthful reports from their neighbors, that the Comanches were the most devoted horse lovers of the Southwest. Some of the Tonkawas had told my father that the Comanches thought the Great Spirit had created horses especially for them.

Blue was tied at the house for three nights before anything happened. During the first night I had lain awake, determined to protect the horse. I lost several hours' sleep and nothing occurred. The second night was a repetition of the first, so that by the third night I was very drowsy and fell asleep soon after supper. Some hours later I was awakened by two or three barks of our dogs. I looked out through a small hole in the wall near my head. But as I could see that Blue was still there I fell back on my pillow, immediately deciding that the invasion of some animal had aroused the dogs.

My head hardly settled on the pillow before there was a piercing whistle from Blue, followed by the sound of one of his fore feet striking the porch as he pawed. I sprang from the bed, seized my rifle lying on the floor alongside, and rushed over to a window to look out. Blue was pulling back on his rope and had turned to one side and was snorting loudly. I could see only one of our hounds, which was walking toward the gate of the picket fence of the yard. The horse also was looking at the dog, although I could not understand why, as the dog was nearly through the gate and about twenty steps from Blue.

At this instant an explosion which seemed near my head caused me to spring back and straighten up from my peeping. My ears were ringing, and I was not sure but that I had been shot. Then I realized that I was unhurt and the only armed person in the house as Mother and the other children came running to my side.

"Ken, what is it? Are you hurt?" Mother cried.

"No, Mother," I replied, "that was a gun fired outside."

Then I ducked to my window for another look and saw what I thought was my dog floundering about in the open gateway. Another glance showed that it wasn't a dog but an Indian, badly hurt, who was trying to crawl through the gate. While I watched, he lurched to his hands and knees and crawled through the gate before I could raise my gun to my shoulder. It suddenly dawned on us that the gun had been fired from the kitchen behind the house and some yards away. One of the Negroes, ordered by my father to sleep on guard there, had been aroused by Blue and had taken a pot shot at the Indian horse thief. This fact was known immediately when Mother turned to him and asked, "Was that you, Elijah?" And the answer came, "Yes, Missus, dat was me."

Mother insisted that I wait several minutes before going to the back door and asking Elijah to bring his gun and come with me to look for the wounded Indian. Elijah whistled for the dogs to go with us before he dared to venture out. I was satisfied, however, since Blue had quieted down, that any Indians who had been lurking about had gone. This proved to be true. The Indian was neither on the outside of the fence nor in sight.

Next morning his blood was found on the gravel near the house and on the outside of the gate. A few yards away traces showed where he had been picked up and carried by his comrades to a waiting horse. Whether they had only been after Blue or whether they first wanted to secure him and then attack the house, we did not know. That well-placed shot of Elijah's evidently upset their plans, whatever they were, because they rode away without stealing any stock, which fact was unusual. It may have been that they thought their presence in the community was known, and that the stock and the house were being guarded.

One naturally wonders why the dogs had not attacked the intruders or continued to give the alarm. The explanation is simple: the dogs had not been trained and were easily decoyed from the yard by the Indians trying to steal Blue.

Yet there came a time when we almost wished that Blue did not so hate and fear Indians. One night in 1858 when my father had ridden over to the lower Indian reservation, only to be gone for a night or two, he neglected to tell me to place Blue in the corral with some of the saddle horses there or to tie him up at the house. There had been no rumors of Indian signs in the community recently; so Blue was being allowed some extra freedom and grazing privileges in the little horse pasture about a mile from the house.

I rode down to see if Blue and the other stock were undisturbed. Not a horse was in sight! A few looks around told the story.

The horse pasture did not contain more than ten acres and was constructed with the idea of having a place to pen the horses near the house. At this time we had only a portion of our herd in it, the others being over on the Paluxy River hidden from the Indians.

A light shower of rain had fallen and plenty of signs were discernible to explain what had happened to Blue and his companions. The other horses, about forty in number, had been rounded up and driven out of the gate and away, although it was evident that this had not been an easy task for the raiders. Perhaps the example of Blue and their fear of the strangers, together with the fact that it was an unusual time to be driven from their pasture, caused the horses to be difficult to handle. Nevertheless, they had been herded to the gate in the stake-and-rider fence and driven off. Not so with Blue, although we were almost to wish that he had been stolen with the others, as there might have been some chance for him to escape, or we might have trailed the herd and recovered him.

Blue was lying in the middle of the pasture—dead—filled with arrows so that he looked like a horse pin cushion. He had been dead for several hours. His ordinarily glossy hair was covered with dried perspiration and his hoofs were filled with damp earth and grass. The fairly close-cropped grass and his shoes, which were different from those of the other saddlers, enabled us to read the story of his encounter with the Indians. He had broken through the Indians' ranks time and again, only to be pursued to the fence, where he would wheel and race back toward the center of the pasture. We had seen to it that the fence was high and strongly built to keep wild horses out and to prevent any of ours from jumping. Blue, a trained jumper, knew the futility of trying a fence of that type. After several attempts at driving him, the thieves had attempted to rope him. Finally, they had tired him sufficiently to throw a couple of lariats on him. Then he had broken one of the lariats in a mad charge, but the other one was sufficient to check him somewhat, as he was growing tired. Almost exhausted, wild with fear and desperate, Blue charged the rider and horse from which came the second lariat.

The result of his efforts to smash this persecutor was easy to trace at the edge of a horse wallow near the center of the pasture. There the grass was worn away and the imprint of the fall of the horse and rider was plain. But the rider who was bowled over evidently decided that this experience was the last straw, or perhaps he had to save himself from the infuriated Blue. So he reached for his bow and arrows. Any one of two or three arrows would have been sufficient to bring down the horse, if he were not instantly killed, but "Mr. Lo" vented his anger by loosing what must have been half the stock of his quiver. Blue was facing toward the wallow, and all indications were that he had knocked horse and rider down and had faced about for another charge to finish the work he had started.

The remnant of one lariat was still about Blue's neck, while a burn made by the second lariat was plain. There were also the tracks where an Indian had walked to the dead horse and removed the second lariat. Blue would not be driven, he would not allow himself to be lassoed and led, and he undoubtedly had shown magnificent fight. No doubt the Indians lost some time in trying to secure Blue. They must have seen, even by moonlight, that he was the best horse of the herd. Perhaps some brave or the leader of the raiders wanted him for a buffalo-mount or a war-horse.

———————

Accounts of other Anti-Indian horses follow:

(1)

Mr. Maberry had a beautiful blue-roan that the Indians sought on every raid. He had his right ear split twice and his left ear split once, showing that he had been taken by the Indians three times. They would ride him down after so long and turn him out with their other ponies, but Blue would escape at the first opportunity and sooner or later appear on his old range, so poor that he could hardly walk. With rest and the lush grass he would soon be fat and sleek again. Finally, after he had been stolen a fourth time and had again made his way home, the Mayberrys found him dead one morning with an arrow through his heart. It was supposed that the Indians, unable to catch him again, had killed him for spite.[1]

(2)

In 1875 we settled on the West Prong of the Medina River. Indian raids were not uncommon, and we had to be on the alert at all times. We lived in a one-room log house without any windows and only one door. At night the door had to be barred. Sometimes the Indians would make circles around the house. During long dry spells, we had to go about three miles to water. One day I hitched up the wagon and drove my wife, with our baby, to the waterhole to wash clothes. We had just got a fire going under the pot when my team, still hitched to the wagon, became excited. Looking around, I saw on a bluff not more than a hundred yards away, a bunch of silent Indians gazing at us. The horses were getting more and more excited.

---

[1]Brown, John Earl, *Yesteryears of Texas*, San Antonio, 1896, 43-44.

I did not want to say anything about the matter to my wife. I just picked up my rifle with one hand and, while holding the horses with the other, told my wife to get the clothes back in the wagon quickly, as the horses would not stand much longer. She wanted to know why. I told her I didn't know, unless they just wanted to run away. She put the clothes in and climbed in with the baby. The Indians were still standing there watching us. I raised my gun in their direction and let the horses go. They headed straight for home, and were not long in getting there. My wife did not say a word all the way home. She couldn't in that jolting. When the horses got to the house, they stopped and my wife said, "Sam, why in the name of God did you let those horses run all the way home?" I then told her about the Indians. My team were the only horses left on that side of the Medina during this raid by the Indians.[2]

(3)

One night in 1868 W. T. Taylor of Parker County heard a commotion out in his horse lot. Running forth in his night clothes, he, guided by sounds only, began to shoot with his long-barreled gun. The next morning he found evidence that one bullet at least had found its way in the dark, for on the ground were a buffalo robe, a bow, a quiver with arrows in it, and a tomahawk. On the grass and leaves near them were blood marks. The noise that Taylor heard was made by the Indians tearing down the rail fence—and despite the fusillade they had driven away all the horses. Some of them returned next day, however, among them a mare called Old Puss. She lived to be twenty-five years old, and every time

---

[2]"Samuel H. Sutton, Frontiersman," by Mrs. F. V. Tankersley, in *Frontier Times*, August, 1940, Vol. 17, 430-431.

the Taylor family hung the Indian robe out to sun, Old
Puss and the other horses that had been taken from the pen
that night would raise a quick snort and stampede.[3]

[3]Afton Wynn, Austin, Texas.

Canelo, A True War Horse

By HELEN MICHAELIS

THIS is as the story was told to me by General Esteban Falcón of San Buenaventura, Coahuila, Mexico. He owned Canelo, said to have been a palomino, though his name, descriptive of a common color, means *cinnamon*. Canelo was a gelding and was by an Arabian stallion and out of a Mexican mare, having been bred on the famous Cloete Ranch in Coahuila. While he was yet a *potro* (unbroken horse), Esteban traded for him and, hence, had the training of him.

About 1914, when Pancho Villa was powerful, Canelo was

—GUTZON BORGLUM

339

six years old. He was pretty, big and stylish. He was the
fastest horse of his day. He was a one-man horse and only
his master rode him. He could jump a five-wire fence and
make a broad jump of fifteen feet or more. He could sense
an enemy six leagues (over fifteen miles) away. In camp
he was never tied or hobbled. At night he grazed always
near his master. He was Esteban's bodyguard, and if the
enemy was approaching by night, Canelo awakened his
master by nipping him and pawing the ground.

One night in the time of the Revolution, Canelo was in a
house with Esteban and his army. Villa and some of his men,
or some of his followers, were expected at any time, but less
so on this particular night. About two o'clock Canelo started
kicking the door and whinnying. Esteban thought he wanted
maiz (corn) and called his *mozo*. When the *mozo* offered
Canelo a morral of corn, he merely pawed it from his hand.
Then he wheeled and kicked in the door. Not until then did
Esteban realize that Canelo was warning him of the enemy's
approach. The General and his three hundred men hurriedly
arose and saddled their horses and stationed themselves on
the top of a near-by hill to await the enemy. There were
six hundred of them, all of whom were killed.

Canelo had no fear of a gun or of its report, but it made
him furious if someone pointed his finger or a stick at him.
Then he became so angry that his eyes turned red, and if
he could reach the offending person would tear him to pieces.
Once a boy who carried water poked his finger at him.
Canelo's eyes turned red and he tried to get to the boy, but
he was tied with a strong rope. The General told the boy not
to tease his horse. He warned him that Canelo was not
often tied and would never forget or forgive the offense.
The water carrier was an ignorant boy and did not heed

his General's warning. One day he poked a stick at Canelo as he passed him. The powerful horse lunged and broke his stake rope and caught the boy by the nape of the neck. He bit him severely, pawed him until his ribs caved in and then broke his back. Esteban arrived just in time to save the boy's life.

Another time a soldier teased Canelo, but he did a better job of this man. He grabbed him by the neck and handled him as a fox-terrier handles a rat. He broke the soldier's neck and then dropped him. When he was sure the man was dead, he turned and went to his master and laid his head over his shoulder.

Canelo was a horse that knew no fear and when he was needed to shield his master from flying bullets, he willingly placed his big, golden-colored body between the enemy and the General. Standing or flat on his side, Canelo was ample protection for Esteban because the horse was loved and well known throughout the country and no one wanted to kill or even shoot him.

Once Esteban and two other men were riding abreast down a street in San Buenaventura. The other horses were shot and killed and their riders wounded, but Canelo was spared and Esteban escaped with a broken arm. During the years Canelo carried Esteban the horse never was wounded, but while mounted on him Esteban received seven shots in the back and one leg and one arm wound.

Esteban was offered ten thousand pesos for Canelo at a time when two pesos equaled one dollar, but the horse was not for sale. He lent him to a general friend one time, and Pancho Villa stole him. Esteban later heard that Canelo had been crippled but no other word about his loved horse ever came to him.

"In the nineties a flashy Mexican named Gregorio Cortez operated throughout the territory including Gonzales and DeWitt counties, Texas, and west to Laredo, and probably into Mexico. At one time he owned a horse that would gallop backward ahead of an attacking party, while his owner, mounted upon him, defended himself with a pistol in each hand. I saw him practicing this stunt often, near Union, in Wilson County."—Patterson, C. L., *Sensational Texas Manhunt*, San Antonio, 1939, 5.

Horse Sense

By ALBERTO GUAJARDO

I. LISTÓN AND THE LIPAN INDIANS

THE Lipanes, after being harried out of Texas, made their last stand in their old raiding grounds of northern Coahuila and northeastern Chihuahua. No man knew them better than the vaquero, Isabel Rubio. He could out-Indian any Indian of the frontiers. In riding over the vast, empty country where he made his home, his manner upon approaching a crest was to dismount, leave his hat with his horse, stick a handful of green brush—the kind growing where he had stopped—under his belt, and thus camouflaged, creep up for a searching view of the country beyond. Taking advantage of the lay of the land and of his mastery of desert camouflages, he could traverse the plains in open day. Unseen, he could watch Indians for hours at a time. Sometimes, with the skin of a deer or of a coyote placed on his shoulders, he would sneak up close to them on all-fours, certain of not attracting attention.

He had a *señu—* a sign—that he often left in a spirit of irony to let the Lipanes know who had tricked them. It was a piece of red ribbon. His favorite horse, a true partner to the man, was named Listón (Ribbon).

Once Rubio, mounted on Listón, followed a band of Lipanes that had stolen horses from the Hàcienda de San Francisco. On an evening he located their camp beside a waterhole in a dry arroyo and observed how all the horses, both those stolen and those ridden by the raiders, were hobbled. That night, Listón aiding him, he got the horses all together, drove them off some distance, left Listón to keep them, returned to a spot near the camp, and howled like a *lobo* and then gobbled like a turkey, to mock the Lipanes. They, fearing an attack, sought in vain to secure their horses. They hid away until daylight, when they found the tracks of their vanished *caballada*. Following the tracks, they came upon a bit of red ribbon. They followed on. Toward the end of the day they saw some of their own scattered horses. Rubio had cut them out of his bunch, keeping only the stolen horses he had come to recover.

He was not malicious. Once he watched Lipanes snaring antelope, gutted one that a warrior had killed and left, and was tying it on Listón, behind the saddle, when the warrior returned. Rubio shot and broke the neck of the Lipan's horse. Another time he surprised a Lipan butchering a deer and had to shoot him in the hand with a pistol in order to disarm him. Then he bound up the wound, gave the man water to drink from the gourd canteen he always carried, gave him a beautiful hunting knife, and at parting, presented him with a red ribbon—as a talisman and a token of friendship. This Indian, called thenceforth Mano Chueca (Crooked Hand), had a chance in time to show his friendship, and showed it.

At nightfall of one summer day Rubio unsaddled in a grassy spot about two leagues (six miles) away from the Ranchería del Nacimiento, on the Río de Sabinas. He was as much at home in one place as another, so it was far outdoors. Some time before dawn he noticed in the bright starlight that Listón was continuously raising his head and look-

ing in the direction of the Ranchería del Nacimiento. The
ranch on which he worked was in another direction and he
had no intention of going to the Nacimiento. But the
horse's actions made him curious. He untied the stake rope
and led Listón some steps away from where the saddle was
lying. Then he stopped and went to looking also in the
direction that Listón was now watching more intently than
formerly. His own eyesight, good as it was, could not carry
very far in the night. He pretended intense interest, caressed
the animal, and from time to time asked, "Listón, what
do you see? What peculiarity have you sensed?" He had this
habit of talking to his horse as if the horse understood.

Listón grazed a few mouthfuls of grass, then showed more
alarm. He came to Rubio and rubbed his nose on his arm,
made as if to shove him toward the saddle, seeming to say,
"Why are we waiting here? Let's go."

Rubio knew that something was up, though he could not
sense what. Now dawn was about to come. In that country
the horizon begins to light up about three o'clock on a
summer morning. Rubio shook his blanket and raised his
saddle. Listón stepped nearer to have it placed on his back.
Soon he was mounted. Listón understood that he must travel
as quietly as possible, must pick a cow trail to follow, avoid-
ing brush, passage through which makes noise. They went on
for a good while, the light of dawn lingering long before
actually appearing. Occasionally Rubio would stop and
loosen the reins. Each time Listón would shake his head with
alertness, snort as low as a whisper, and look toward the
Nacimiento.

If there was danger ahead, why was the horse so eager to
approach it? Before crossing the last line of hills overlooking
the valley of the Sabinas, Rubio halted, about a league

still from the Nacimiento. He sniffed the air for the smell
of a fire—an odor that he could detect a long way off from
its origin. He could smell nothing. He could hear nothing.

The light grew strong enough that he could make out the
dark line of timber along the river. Now a fan of sun rays
was coming out of the east and the shadows were leaving
the plains to hide in the canyons. The splendor of the coming
light and the colors in the sky made Rubio glad. He kept on
gazing, searching for details—in the spread-out plains, along
the timber, over the sides of the hills beyond.

At last he distinguished a compact line of horsemen
moving parallel to the river, toward the ranchería. Now he
knew what Listón had known for hours. The Lipan Indians
had risen to attack.

Tightening his girth and drawing his rifle from its scab-
bard, Rubio prepared to ride. His route lay so that he could
maneuver to keep the ranch houses and certain trees between
himself and the Indians, who could not possibly have seen
him, and who, though they were nearer the houses than he
was, were moving slowly, secure in the knowledge that the
terrain would keep them hidden from view until they were
almost upon the ranchería, when they would, no doubt,
attack with lightning speed. Listón carried Rubio so swiftly
that a counter-attack was raised and carried out successfully
almost before the Lipanes were aware of having been discovered.

II. The Back-Trailer

Some few horses have such a passion for following their
own tracks back to camp or ranch that they will go out of
their way back-trailing, rather than cut straight across. If
the tracks are fresh, the horse will hardly put his nose to

the ground once on a stretch of several miles. It is hard to say at times whether he is trailing by sight or by smell, but if the trail is cold and dim, he smells it like a dog, taking especial account of any droppings. Upon returning home from a region that is strange to him, a horse likes to follow the way he came.

Back in the Indian days, during my boyhood, Don Miguel M. Peña, who ranched above Múzuiz, Coahuila, owned more than three thousand head of horses. At times when they were being worked, the colts branded, *potros* cut out for breaking, new *manadas* of mares made up for certain stallions, etc., all the rancheros over a big country joined in the running. They came partly to get horsestock of their own that had strayed off and partly to admire the superb manner in which Don Miguel could control and direct herds of *ladinos*— horses wild, crafty and bent on never being brought into a pen. Also he had a sense of direction surpassed by no coyote or eagle.

Every man went armed against the Indians, but Don Miguel never carried anything but an old pistol that, so I believe, had not once been cleaned or oiled or had the shells changed in it since the time it came into his possession. He was forever losing it and then, maybe not for two or three days, going back to it. Only at the corral, after the run was over, would he miss it. Then after a volcano of words he might say: "Let me see, let me see. Oh, I remember now. Probably I lost it in that mountain where the *canelo* mare made her break. I will go to it in the morning."

Yes, he would go to it. He, many other horsemen, and five hundred head of racing range horses had all made tracks. But the next morning after we had all ridden some distance in the direction we had come from the day before, Don

Miguel would suddenly stop and exclaim, "Here is my horse's track! Please allow me to go ahead now and back-trail." Everybody would fall back, all marveling. Don Miguel would ride slowly, giving his horse free reins. Eventually he would stop and, pointing over into some grass, say to me, "Boy, get down and hand me the pistol."

One day when I was alone with that old man, so skilled in handling horses, and he was in a good humor, I said, "Listen, Don Miguel. To do all the things that you do, it is necessary that you have a faculty unknown by others. What it is?"

"Listen, boy," he answered. "I am not the one with the abilities. It is the horse. Always train your horse when he is young to back-track. He will take you to anything lost off him not more than two days past. Please do not tell anyone what I have told you."

I believe that Don Miguel sometimes dropped his pistol on purpose in some place he could return to readily. At the same time, he had his mounts so trained that one of them could thread his own trail even in a maze of hundreds of other horse tracks.

III. La Mula Gavilana

In 1883 while I was a trooper in the Sixth Auxiliary Cavalry, Colonel Advícula Valdés ordered me to carry a message from our camp at the Paso del Moro on the Río Bravo del Norte to Múzquiz, Coahuila, more than a hundred leagues away. At this time there was hardly a habitation in the whole country to be traversed, nor was there any direct road or trail. I was obliged to traverse some of the roughest mountains and deepest canyons of all northern Mexico. Most of the country was strange to me, though I was familiar with that kind of country. As I was young, the guides of military education loaded me full, before I set out, of rules relating to deverse slopes, the "nose" formed by the confluence of two streams, and the like—all of which meant as little to me as classical music still means. I had a compass that was valuable in orienting me after I had twisted forty ways getting down into a canyon and more ways than that getting upon the other side.

And I had Gavilana, a little Spanish mule as wise as the Biblical serpent. It took us ten or twelve days to get to Múzquiz, and then, almost immediately, I set out to return to the Paso del Moro. Before long I noticed that Gavilana was constantly stepping in her own tracks, made days before. After days of travel and after topping out from the Cañon de Cíbolo, I could see clearly the contours of the far-away hills guarding the pass leading to the military camp. I headed straight for it, but at once Gavilana set her head on making for a point far above, to the left. I kept pulling her back to the course I knew was right, and she kept pulling away from it to take the course she had selected.

The exercise of such stubbornness was tiring both to mule and to me, and finally I slackened the reins, leaving her to pick her own way until she should discover her mistake. There were no trails to follow. Gavilana, in order to keep her direction, had to cross various deep gullies, cañon-heads, but after making any necessary swerve, she always bent back to her arrow-like course. Finally, after we had climbed to the crest of a range of hills, I stopped to let her rest a little. I loosened the cinch, took off the briddle, and while she jerked grass into her mouth, examined the country through my field glasses. I could see very plainly the cuts made by canyons coming into the Río Grande from the Texas side, and I calculated that if we kept going in the direction Gavilana insisted on, we would strike the river at least a league above the Paso del Moro. Like a head-strong brute, Gavilana was grazing on in that direction, often raising her head to look intently, as I examined the land. Presently I made out some animals, which I judged to be horses, about a mile away. The sight confused me, for I knew that our cavalry horses were the only ones in the region and they had no business so far from camp. Then I saw the sorrel bell-mare of the *remuda*, her colt playing around her. Just at this instant Gavilana threw up her head and tail both and cut loose with a vibrating bray, long and powerful, that ended in a kind of a squeal.

At once I bridled her, gave her an approving pat, and let her travel. The new camp proved to be quite near the horses. When Colonel Valdés came in, he asked if I had found the note left hidden in a tin can on some ashes at the old camp site. I replied that Gavilana would not let me come that way.

"My boy," he said, "you have done well to take your mule's advice. To discover the why of things, it will be well many times to follow the way your mule wishes to go." And multiplied examples during more than fifty years of experience since that time have taught me that the animals of the range have certain stores of intelligence often hidden from the pompous "lords of all creation." Many say that the source of all their knowledge is in the nose. Some of it, yes, but I do not think all is. Yet I do not understand.

Death Comes at a Trot

By Riley Aiken

"GIL PEREZ at your service," said the little man with a straight back and bow legs. "Ah, so my friend Miguel Contreras of Patos sends you to me. Come in, *señor*. Seat yourself. You speak Spanish like a Mexican. West Texas? *Que casualidad;* I have broken horses there."

"In addition to making your acquaintance, horses are the reason for my visit," I said.

There were some minutes given to a rodeo of conventionalities during which time I shifted the weight of conversation to him.

"Like you, *señor*, I love horses. I never forget them, and when they die it gives me a desire to weep. *Sí señor*, most of my friends, horses and men alike, are now gone, and there is little I can do to console myself except at times to recall

—Ross Santee

the good old days. And did you ever notice, *señor,* how hard it is to be happy in the memory of the dead when they were better to you than you to them? I recall—"

"At last," thought I. "Here comes the *cuento.*"

"I recall," he continued, "a little horse I used to ride while working at the Piedra Blanca. His name was Chepito. No man or woman has ever understood me as did he. Though man and horse, we worked together like brothers, were happy and sad, hungry and tired together. One day, however, it was Gil Perez and not Chepito who did not remember to do the right thing in the right way, and the poor little brown horse—well, he lost his life. You see, *señor,* I staked him one night in a grove of palmillas, and he, tangling himself in the rope, broke a leg.

"Another was a large bay. We called him *El Diablo.* How this horse liked to pitch! But don't imagine for that it was make believe. He meant every stiff-legged blast of it. He and I had a great time, for when once I learned to stick with him I would mount, run my thumbs along his neck to his ears and scream like a panther, and then I would begin a job of clawing leather you should have seen. The very memory of him makes my bones ache from the base of my skull to my ankles.

"But it was Gil Perez again who was thoughtless, and while showing off before the *señoritas* in Músquiz on a Sunday afternoon, I ran El Diablo over a log, and his neck was broken.

"Once while taking a herd of cattle from Santo Domingo to the border at Del Rio, we had camped near an old placer mine. The next morning the remuda was herded into an angle formed by two deep pits and a slag heap. Most of the men had gotten their mounts and were gone when the cook called me. You see I had been on guard that night.

" 'What horse do you want, Gil?' he asked. 'While you eat, I'll saddle him for you.'

" 'Oh,' I said, 'choose him yourself. Anything will do.'

"After breakfast I went to the improvised corral and behold there stood a horse I had never seen before. He was a *grullo*, with black hoofs, black mane and tail, and a fringe of black on each ear. When he saw me, he lowered his head, pointed his ears toward me, and breathed an uneasy warning. I reached for the reins. He snorted, sprang into the air and barely missed me with his left hoof. *¡Que sorpresa!* He had none of the marks of a *ladino*. His nose was straight, ears large, neck short and slender, and his eyes were as mild as those of a doe.

"But he wheeled and kicked, broke the reins, and headed for the shafts. He slipped on the loose slag and fell. His right hip was broken and we killed him. Whenever I recall the *grullo*, I feel death cheated me out of a good horse."

There was a pause.

"You surely know some *cuentos* and *historias*," I said, "like for instance the devil changing into a horse, or Pinto Verde, the famous mount of Don Cacahuate, or the favorite horse of Benito Canales, Pancho Villa or the Marquez de Aguayo."

"No, *señor*, I recall no particular story," he replied.

"Once in Piedras Negras," I prompted further, "a stanza from the poems of the Negrito Poeta was quoted to me. The officer reminded me in this stanza that death like a *caballo* might come at a trot. Did you ever hear of Godmother Death riding a horse?"

"*A sí, ¿cómo no?*" he said. "My friend Daniel Cantú and other *vaqueros* from a *costeña* ranch on the Gulf of Mexico in Tamaulipas were camped one night on an island. His private mount was a large broken-eared gray called Gacho. Since this horse refused to run with a remuda, they belled him before he was driven with the bunch into the mesquite south of camp for the night.

"After the *muchachos* had had their *frijoles, tortillas,* meat, and *café,* they leaned against their bedding, smoked, and listened to the roaring of the surf about a kilometer to the east. Presently stories were told, a song or two was sung and all lay down for the night. Daniel couldn't sleep. He was afraid the gray *gacho* would slip by the camp and try to swim the bay to mainland.

"He had lain for some time in a half doze listening to the bell and the surf and watching a black cloud coming in from the Gulf when he became aware of the fact that Gacho had quit the remuda and was on his way to the pass. He arose from his bed, crept to a bush by the trail and waited in order to turn him back.

"But there was something strange about the bell. No horse without a rider or driver ever gave it such an even and purposeful rhythm.

" '*Pues ¿qué tendrá?*' thought Daniel. 'Could someone be riding him?'

"But behold twelve fighting men in silver armour and riding white horses came into view. A full moon was shining from directly above. The storm cloud out over the Gulf was cut at quick intervals by lightning, and the thunder was lost in the roar of the surf.

"On they came at a slow, even trot. Daniel, his heart in his throat, dropped to the ground behind the bush and watched. Now they were even with the camp. They passed in pairs and were followed by a priest in black, riding a black mule.

" 'How strange,' thought Daniel. 'They are from a thousand years ago, from a land of yesteryear. But, look! What is this?'

"Two skeletons carrying a corpse on a litter followed the knights and next came a woman dressed in white. It was La Madrina Muerte—yes, the Godmother. The fact that she rode Gacho seemed to have little meaning for Daniel until—until he awoke—awoke and sat up in bed.

"It was a dream. Yet, was it a dream? The bell had been south with the remuda; now it was north and it tinkled a slow, even saddle trot. He listened until the sound of it mingled sadly with the surf, then went to sleep again."

"Did he find his horse next morning?" I asked.

"No, *señor;* Daniel says there is no doubt that the Madrina took him away."

Horse Heroes

GRISWOLD TYNG IN HAWKES' *Patches*

Canebrake and the Carpetbaggers

By Frank Bryan

I

THE Reconstruction era has been generally recorded in history as "tragic." Historians are notoriously short of humor. The early settlers of East Texas were not. It takes spice to make a pudding remembered. The visiting Carpetbaggers gave spice to life in the Piney Woods. Certain of the natives of the Piney Woods, it used to be said, could smell a live Carpetbagger five miles away, and then their bristles would begin to rise like those of any good dog passing within five miles of Dogfight Crossing on Tanyard.

With all the ex-soldiers disfranchised, formal law was in the hands of foreigners, appointees sent out from Washington to subdue a hostile land. The prosecutor in Cass County was a young lawyer from Illinois, who, having decided to install the Illinois system in Texas, always in formal address referred to himself as "The State's Attorney." The judge, too, was from somewhere north, a practical politician, sucking blood where he could find it.

The High Sheriff was an arrogant crusader at heart. Wearing two cap-and-ball revolvers at belt line in the most approved gunman style, he rode the rounds like a conquering hero of old, followed close behind by a bodyguard of four deputized freed-men, also armed with two guns each. Each day this romantic, armed band rode forth through the pleasant Piney Woods. It was in search for villains who oppressed the poor. It administered the law on the spot, when and where, in the opinion of the Most High Sheriff and his sable brother officers, its dignity stood in need of being administered. They were "The Law," and both black and white were proud of their recent rise to such a high station in society.

And then one day this armed band came, in a shaded road through the pineland, face to face with Old Man Douglas on one of his semi-weekly trips to inspect his stock in Cane-brake pasture.

Old Man Douglas had reached the three-score-and-ten mark long before the War began. He was of Scotch ancestry. He had come to Texas by the Tennessee route, he being a Cumberland Presbyterian of the "Hardshell" school. Frugal, saving, and the owner of a bit of rugged hill land, and a broad width of dense cane in the river bottom for winter pasture, he believed that man's allotted path through life should consist of a stern devotion to hard work during week days, and an equally stern devotion to the worship of the Lord on Sundays. He believed that any and all forms of personal vanity were a sin to be sternly scorned. The breeding of fine horses for buggy and saddle animals was, he fervently believed, a curse to the land. Horses, like men, were put here for a purpose, to serve man at hard labor and thus add to the yield of the land.

But even in the breeding of work animals, Old Man Douglas believed in the virtue of good blood and the follow-ing of tradition in family life. His one pride and joy was a powerful bay stallion named Canebrake. He was so named because of his tremendous size and power; he could tread through the dense head-high cane of the brakes of the bottomlands as easily as an ordinary horse can tread through a field of Johnson grass.

Canebrake was a registered Clydesdale. His ancestors had stopped the despised Norman chargers on many a bloody field; like many of the useful things of life, his kind had been produced to meet the needs of war. His ancestors had fathered the modern tanks; they had the size and weight it took to bear an armored knight, plus the weight of protecting metal, hurtling headlong into battle. During the rise of the Christian era, they had become the most powerful single fighting units the western world had ever known.

Standing nearby seventeen hands high, with the proud, short-arched neck of his kind, as thick at the top as that of a blooded bull, Canebrake carried his massive, flat-hipped body with all the sureness of the giant chargers of old. Canebrake admitted only one conquering hand, that of the old man on his back. He was intolerant and held himself with an immensely superior air when in the presence of other men or of beasts of his own kind.

When not mounted on Canebrake Old Man Douglas was a thin, frail old man, slightly gaunt of shoulder. His hawk-nosed face was made severely long by a thin spray of whitish whiskers. His normally faded blue shirt, open at the neck, and tight-fitting jeans pants, shrunk by many washings, added to the wither of age. On foot he leaned heavily on a cane, whittled from a length of second-growth hickory sapling.

But, mounted on Canebrake, Old Man Douglas gave a sense of virile manhood at its fullest. His frail shoulders squared; his eyes took on, or borrowed from Canebrake, a commanding sureness. He carried his cane with a lighter grasp, more like a riding crop.

Old Man Douglas was riding Canebrake to inspect the stock in the pasture and check up on the calves that had been born, when he met the High Sheriff and his armed party. The road was narrow and brush-lined. The shade of giant trees gave the whole a jungle-like denseness. There was barely room for the armed party to pass the lone old man, even if they formed in a single file. Now he stopped Canebrake to give them a chance to pass. Canebrake stood mountain firm, his alert, commanding eyes looking over and beyond the lesser animals, both horses and men, before him. From the lift and fixedness of his stare, Old Man Dougles seemed to see something even farther away.

The High Sheriff's gelding had stopped short of its own account. Angry spurs forced it to face the great stallion. The armed escort bunched up close behind, as restless and

—GUTZON BORGLUM

curious as their suddenly-alert mounts. The High Sheriff, who did the law enforce, demanded that the old man ride out into the brush and let him and his party parade by. It was beneath the dignity of his high position for him to turn his party into the brush and let a Southern farmer go by. It was also impossible for him to force his gelding to within ten feet of the intolerant stallion.

Being a two-gun man by choice, when the old man and the stallion stood as firm as the rock of Gibraltar under his verbal commands, the High Sheriff announced that he would shoot his way by. The law was not to be monkeyed with.

When the High Sheriff reached for a gun, Old Man Douglas gave Canebrake a slack rein and a light tap with the cane.

Canebrake knew no danger. He only knew that he had been given a free rein and had been impatiently hit with a walking stick. Before his proud, haughty eyes, he saw only scum barring his path. The very thought lifted his anger to a fighting pitch. With eyes suddenly bulging with angry fire, he bared his great teeth and charged the first horse in his path. He piled the High Sheriff and his mount back into his frantic, rearing escort, and simply hurled his giant body through the tangled mass. In the melee, the High Sheriff was unhorsed and struck dead.

The case came up in court. Old Man Douglas was on trial for murdering a Federal officer. It was a serious offense.

To preserve the peace and dignity of the law, a company of soldiers was imported and strung around the weather-beaten, clapboard courthouse in the middle of the sandy square. Each public-spirited citizen who desired to enter and see Carpetbag justice done was searched for weapons as he passed the line. The warmish air was tight. There was no talk in the groups about the store fronts and hitching racks. Mostly the loitering men just stood and stared.

But there was a steady stream that filed through and filled the bare board benches in the primitive courtroom. The great majority were spare men, slightly hooked of nose and straight of beard, Cumberland Presbyterians who had migrated to Texas from the Tennessee hill country. Of these, the majority had fought with Forrest and Lee. They were so grim that their blue eyes glowed like clean gunmetal in bright sunlight.

The prisoner at the bar—behind a battered table—sat slumped in his chair, spare whiskers against caved chest, an old, old man on trial for his life. The prosecutor was young, eager to carry to its bitter end the letter of the law. The first witness was a perspiring Negro, a member of the armed escort. He told no story. The prosecutor did all his thinking for him. His questions on direct examination were of a leading character. They could be answered by either a yes or a no.

"Now didn't you see this murderer lift a wooden club and deliberately strike down and kill your superior officer on his orderly round of duty?"

"Yes, suh!"

"Would you know this murderer if you saw him again?"

"Yes, suh!"

"Isn't that the man right there?" He pointed an accusing finger at Old Man Douglas.

A deathly hush settled over the courtroom. One man present afterward remembered hearing a rooster crow somewhere, and a distant dog bark, so keenly alert were the minds and ears.

Then there was a new sound. It made the blood run cold. It was a repeated *"click-click!"* as of pistols being cocked. It arose from all over the room, where stern men leaned forward, eyes ablazing like live coals.

Actually, there were no pistols in the room. The men were thumbing the blades of open pocket knives, which sprang back with a click that sounded like an exploding fire-cracker, so tense was the silent room.

New sweat sprouted on the witness's brow. His eyes grew great and round. "No, suh!" he emphatically declared. "That ain't him. That's Mister Douglas. Knowed him all mah life. He sho' is a fine man."

The prosecutor stood with open mouth. He had just seen his carefully-rehearsed case collapse in utter stillness, like a dead tree before an approaching storm. He needed to think. He took time to mop his brow.

Old Man Douglas arose slowly to his feet. For a moment, he might have been mounted on Canebrake, so fierce did his eyes shine, so lightly did he heft his cane. He belonged to the school that believes that in truth, and in truth only, is there right.

"Nigger!" he accused, "you lie. Now if you don't tell this court the truth, and nothing but the truth, by the grace of God, I'm going to come over and thresh you to within an inch of your life."

The witness was visibly relieved. This was talk which he understood. "Yes, suh, Mister Douglas. I wants to tell 'em the truth all the time. This sheriff man, he say to you: 'You long-wiskered—I sho' do hate to use his words before all you white folks—he say, 'you long-whiskered bastard, you don't get out of my way, I'll blow yo dam brains out.'

Them's his very words. And you don't pay him no mind. You just let ole Canebrake have his head. He do a squat-lope an' then he sho' do get his-self mad at them hosses in his way. He rolls his eyes big, and takes a bite of that sheriff man's hoss, rite be-hind his saddle.

"That hoss squall lack a panther. I gets me all mixed up wid hosses an' hoss feet. Then you an' Canebrake is gone. My hoss is gone. This sheriff man he done bumped his haid on Canebrake's foot. An' he sho' is daid."

A new light glittered in the young prosecutor's eyes. Old Man Douglas had saved his case for him. He smiled broadly and let the old man continue to hold the floor.

"Now that the truth has been told," Old Man Douglas said, "I can see no further need for my presence here." He gathered up his battered hat, turned toward the door.

"I protest!" the prosecutor shouted.

Again there was silence. Again there was that sinster sound, the click-click of thumbed knife blades.

The judge swept the room with a searching gaze. He blinked his eyes before the grim purpose behind the stares he met, hate to the point of instant death. Sweat broke over his forehead. The judge was a practical politician. There is grave doubt as to whether he had ever read of the principles of law as laid down by Solon. But he had the breadth of vision—it was there in the courtroom before him—to see eye-to-eye with Solon when he laid down that broad principle: Laws are made to fit the needs of a people; the customs of a people should never be changed to fit the letter of a law. The judge took Solon's advice.

"Objection overruled," he sternly declared. "Case dismissed for want of evidence."

II

East Texas in the early days was a land of individuals. Most landowners had registered horses, cows, hogs and even bird dogs. Each of these was known by name to the whole community. Men took pride in the horseflesh they rode and not the trappings with which their mount was loaded down, as in the cow country and in the movies of today. Simplicity left only the horse to be remembered. There were no silver mountings on briddles. The saddles were of the tiny, "Virginia," "postage-stamp," or "muley" kind, common to the English fox hunt of today, whereas, in West Texas, horses were "mounts" and a man's most treasured possession was his saddle.

The men in East Texas belonged to the breed prefigured by General Wade Hampton, of South Carolina. He was as noted as a hunter as he was magnificent as a cavalry leader. He had a remarkable memory for faces and names. He might forget a man sometimes, but it is claimed that, once having had a good look at a horse, he never forgot it. During the Civil War, it is asserted, he knew not only every private but every horse in his command. If he met a trooper riding a strange horse, he would stop him and ask for an explanation.

In East Texas, men prided themselves upon riding animals that would leap, like shot from a catapult, the instant rein was slackened. To wear spurs lowered the prestige of the horse you rode. I saw my first riding spur at the age of ten, when we moved to the Indian Territory, where men rode runty, Choctaw ponies, worth five dollars apiece, and owned splendid silver-mounted spurs to prod them into action.

But even in the Indian Territory in the early days, a

modern western movie hero would have been looked upon as of a very low order. Spurs were never worn inside a house; not even a country store. Spurs and guns were removed and left over saddle horns by all gentlemen when they dismounted. To enter a private home with spurs on was considered an intentional insult.

During the days when the Jefferson Road was the principal trade route of East Texas, horse discipline was concomitant with man's. The pioneers were a sternly self-disciplined people to begin with, for being pioneers in a primitive land forces discipline upon those who live.

In West Texas, if a horse became crippled, other mounts were to be plentifully had. Along the Jefferson Road, the average man was a one-horse man. That is, he could afford only one good saddle animal, but every member of a family old enough to ride had to have a horse of his own. A person's horse was largely his own personal care. It was his one constant companion. He rode somewhere almost every day. For this reason, his enduring thought was of his horse and its well-being.

A horse had to have corn three times each day, winter, spring and summer. Green grass was a luxury for idle times, but corn was the staff of life. No man dared let his horse go for a couple of days without corn, for on the next day he might want to ride to a town thirty miles away and back in a few hours. Sixty miles between sun and sun was not a hard night for a blooded horse that had been used regularly and was bottomed with corn fed to him three times each day.

The horse was ridden hard regularly, fed regularly; he was curried and rubbed down three times each day, even if there was nothing at hand but a corn cob, which is better than most curry-combs anyway; his hoofs were rubbed with linseed oil, and twice daily the frogs of his feet were searched for a chance gravel or piece of angular rock. A man was judged by the horse he rode. A careless, slovenly man could not ride a sound horse, not for long. But when a man started with good blood and treated it right, gave it constant care, he could ride it all day, every day, and have it look out on the world with high head and searching eyes each and every morning when taken from the stable. And if it was a real horse, he could expect it to reach back with bared teeth and raise a two-inch blood blister beneath the seat of his pants every time he carelessly pinched horse flesh while tightening a saddle girt.

Some men took great pride in riding stallions no other man could mount. The veterans of the Cass County company liked to tell of one such horse which broke up a Union charge on an outpost one cold morning a few days before the Battle of Nashville. The outpost was a part of Hood's cavalry screen. Thomas was feeling it out by hitting at designated points with detachments of a hundred or more mounted men that had been ordered to break through the screen and discover the location of the larger bodies behind.

On this particular cold night, the owner of the stallion had been on picket duty all night. Under a screening tree by a glade, he had sat on the stallion all night, not daring to move more than to rub hands beneath thighs to keep fingers from freezing stiff. When relieved just before dawn, he rode the short quarter of a mile back to the outpost position, curried and resaddled his horse, fed it on a blanket and then lay down for a before-breakfast nap by the embers of last night's fire. He had barely stretched out weary bones before he fell into the dead sleep that only soldiers just off sentry duty know.

Barely had he fallen into sound slumber before a Union troop, a full company strong, hurled itself headlong in a column of fours, through the picket line, flashing sabers held high and mounts racing at full speed. On catching sight of the small knot of horses by the fire, the column swung and came in on a flank, madly determined to destroy the detail. To offer resistance was useless. All but the sleeping sentry mounted and fled. He went unnoticed amid the scatter of hurriedly discarded blankets.

But his splendid, high-headed, snorting black stallion was not so lucky. The commanding officer of the Union detachment, being mounted on one of Thomas' hurriedly-collected plow horses, saw just what he had long been looking for, a cavalryman's dream of a perfect horse, and swung the column toward it. He thought to quickly dismount, snatch the bridle tied to the saddle, place bits in mouth and mount and ride on. He dismounted and slashed the halter rope with a saber stroke. Two orderlies were down to help with the bridle. The whole troop was standing high in saddles, bringing plunging mounts to a stop.

No sooner was the rope cut, and strange men were around him, than Black Prince went into action on his own hook. He bit a hunk out of the captain's sleeve, pawed the two orderlies into the day's casualty list, and then declared a personal war of his own on all horses present. With angry eyes wide and white, teeth bared like a snarling lion's, he bit, pawed, reared and struck, charging this way and that, shooting his terrible teeth out like an angry goose, but taking a bite of screaming horse with every thrust. Black Prince didn't know how to retreat. He had fought in many hand-to-hand battles with guns roaring and sabers flashing. He only knew to fight as long as there was an alien horse near. He covered all the ground he stood on and constantly enlarged the circle.

The terrible frightened screams of the bitten geldings threw all of the Union mounts into a rearing, plunging panic. Soldiers dropped sabers and struggled with the one and only pressing problem, getting their mounts out and away and under control. The lone Confederate, who shucked out from under a blanket in the thickest of the fray and came plunging toward the angry stallion, went completely unnoticed. He took the saddle at one leap and Black Prince was under control. With the Union detachment plunging into the brush in every direction, like hell beating tanbark, escape was easy. Black Prince responded to the press of knee better than to the pull of bridle anyway. There were soldiers who swore that he, even unbridled, responded to the commands, "Halt!" and "Right-about-face," and took his place at the head of the column when reinforcements galloped up.

No one thought this Confederate soldier a brave man because he plunged into the widening circle and mounted his fighting stallion. That was like going to the rescue of a member of his own family.

Among the men of the Piney Woods of northeastern Texas, a man was considered only a half-man until he was mounted. Then he was judged largely by the mettle of the horse he rode. They had horses worthy of their own breed. In blood both men and horses reached back to the same land, had traveled the same road. In a century long past they had stood together, like Old Man Douglas and Canebrake, warding the hated Norman conquerors from their land.

The breed had settled Virginia, ridden west into Kentucky and Tennessee, come on down through Arkansas and built homes in the Piney Woods along the great road that led to

Jefferson. Whether riding, camped or homesteading, the breed, like splendid stallions, always, with lifted heads, had their eyes on the horizon beyond. Their guiding passion was for land and its fruits and freedom. Their one abiding ambition was to own an uncramped spread of land, to be able to stand on it and feel that it was their very own. The old settled down on their lands, their titles in fee simple. The young rode on, west and west. They left the woods behind them and in the broad, endless plains of the vast region known as West Texas found the answer to ancient Anglo-Saxon prayers. There they could sit an alert mount on the crest of a hill and with unimpeded vista contemplate their own land.

Old Gran'pa

By Frank S. Hastings*

IT WAS early in June, 1906. Those were the days of Hynes Ranch buggies and "broom tails." Throckmorton Ranch was a full day's drive away. An unexpected turn in events made it necessary for me to make the drive by night. I stopped at headquarters and asked Mage, the foreman, to meet me in Stamford at 7:00 P. M. I told him we would drive Beauty and Black Dolly, two spanking mares he had bought for me. They could take their ten miles an hour steadily for hours, and I threw them in as a special bait to tempt Mage against any local duty he might urge.

Mage stood six feet five inches in his socks, every inch of it cowman and horseman. He came to the ranches at thirteen years of age—a much misunderstood kid. But he had grown into a manhood of sweetness and strength, which had surrounded him with the love and respect of every man, woman, and child in the country. Mage was a dead-game sport, a rider whose skill and daring are still traditions in the big-pasture country. His stories and personal reminiscences, told with rare

---

*Back in the Age of Horse Culture, a man riding west might meet a man riding east, neither knowing the other, and right there, away out on the range, forty miles from nowhere, or in the middle of some lane leading to a village hidden by woods, match a horse race. A large percentage of the men who took an interest in horses and in horse racing were willing to "back their judgment." Every big ranch had a horse that its cowboys believed in; some little ranches and stock-farms were extremely little because their owners had put faith in the wrong horses.

"Old Gran'pa," through gracious permission of Mrs. Frank S. Hastings and of the publishers, *The Breeder's Gazette*, is reprinted from *A Ranchman's Recollections*, by Frank S. Hastings, Chicago, 1921.

humor and dramatic force, made a journey with him a real entertainment. I always sparred for an opening to get him going when we made drives together.

At seven o'clock he was on hand to the minute, talking to the mares as though they were human. We were off—"heads up and tails over the dashboard." As we swung into the main thoroughfare, the people on the street turned round to watch Mage handle the mares. They were having their little fun before settling to the steady, distance-killing gait, and they were a pair to look at. Beauty a deep chestnut, both wilful and beautiful, and Black Dolly, with her sleek sable coat, still at the giddy age. Mage had the stage driver's trick of coming into town or going out in style. The mares knew his voice and hand, and the light that shone in his eyes told where his heart was. For two hours we chatted or were silent by spells, as is the habit on long drives.

W. R. LEIGH in *The Western Pony*

The moon came up in soft fullness—one of those southern moons like the ripeness of love, a perfect heart full. The cool night air was stirring caressingly, and we were both under the spell. The mares had steadied down to normal. We were crossing a prairie near Rice Springs, once a famous round-up ground in the open range days. Mage raised his six-feet-five in the buggy, looked all around, and as he sat down, said: "This here's the place. Here's where me and Old Gran'pa won our first ditty."

The moon had risen high enough to flood a great flat until we could see for a mile or more. I saw just a beautiful expanse of curly mesquite grass, blending its vivid green with the soft silver moonlight, but Mage saw great crowds lined on either side of a straight half-mile track; two riders; the one on a midnight black and the other on a speed-mad sorrel, in deadly contest for supremacy. The stillness of the night—which to me was the calm benediction of peace and rest—was broken for him by wild cheers as a boy and a sorrel horse crossed the line, victors. His face was tense, his eyes shone with the fire of strain and excitement, and then slowly he came back to the stillness and to the moonlight, and to me.

I waited a minute, and asked, "What was it, Mage?"

He did not answer until we had crossed the flat. Then, with a little short laugh, peculiar to him before telling a story, he began: "As fur as thet's consarn, it was this away—."

But here let me tell some true things I knew about Old Gran'pa. He was a famous cow pony, originally known as Sorrel Stud. Mage broke him as a three-year-old, and had ridden him some eighteen years. The last few years of that time Stud had come to be known as Old Gran'pa. He was still alive, but had been turned out under good keep, winter and summer, to end his days in peace. He was very fast, and was considered

among the top cutting horses of his time. Mage's worship of
this horse is only typical of every cowboy's love for his pet
horse. But to his story:

"It was this away. We hed fenced some, but allus hed lots
o' strays on the open range, an' Shorty Owen [who, by the
way, stood six feet six inches] tole me early in the spring he
would send me out to gather strays when the big round-ups
begun, an' 'lowed I best be gettin' my plunder rounded up.
That was 'fore you come, but you know he was the SMS
range boss, an' mighty nigh raised me. He tuk to me the day
I hit the ranch. 'Kid,' he says, 'you ain't never hed no chanct,
an' I'm a-goin' to giv' you one.'

"Shorty taught me to ride—hobbled my feet under a three-
year-ole steer onct, an' turned him a-loose. We hed it roun'
an' roun' with the whole outfit hollerin', 'Stay with 'im, kid!'
I stayed all right, but when he pitched into a bunch o'
mesquites, I sure would 'a' left 'im if these here preachers is
right 'bout 'free moral agency,' but them hobbles helt me
back, and I stayed fer the benediction. Since thet time I never
seed a hoss I was scairt to climb on.

"Shorty cut Sorrel Stud out to me when he was a bronc,
an' said, 'Break him right, kid; I think you got a cow hoss if
he ain't spoilt in the breakin'. An' I done it without ever
hittin' him a lick. As fur as thet's consarn, I never hit him
but onct, an' thet was the time him an' me both failed, only
Shorty said we didn't fail; we jes' went to the las' ditch. But
thet's another story.

"I wisht you could a-seed Sorrel Stud in his prime. He was
a hoss! I thought 'bout it today when you hed yore arms round
his neck an' was a-talkin' to him 'bout me, an' I wondered
if anybody 'cept me could understan' thet Sorrel Stud an' Ole
Gran'pa was the same hoss. But when I got up an' thumbed

him an' made him pitch me off jest to show you what a twenty-
year-old hoss could do, did you see the fire come back into
them eyes, an' them ears lay back? Hones' to God, Frank, he
was a hoss!

"I know I was jest a tough kid when I come, but a-tween
Shorty Owen an' maybe a little doin' right fer right's sake,
I tried to live an hones' life. But they's two things me an' St.
Peter may hev to chew 'bout a little at the gate. You know
what a fool I am 'bout tomatoes? Well, onct I stole a dozen
cans from the chuck wagon and hid 'em out in the cedar
brakes. But the boys at the wagon hed me so plum scart 'bout
Injuns thet I never did git to them tomatoes. Well, Ole
Gran'pa is jest as plum a fool 'bout oats as I be 'bout tomatoes.
I'll admit I stole this here outfit's oats fer him ten years, till
the high boss was out onct from New York and seed Ole
Gran'pa go to a prairie fire. Of course I was up, an' he sed he
guessed he could pay fer Gran'pa's oats the rest o' his days.
Joe was mighty perticular 'bout company oats. We hed to
haul 'em sixty miles, but I think he slipped a mess to White
Pet onct in a while hisself. I used to wait 'til the boys hed hit
their hot rolls, then I'd slip out to the corner o' the hoss pasture, an' Ole Gran'pa was allus waitin' fur me an' he'd never
leave a stray oat to give us away.

"They called me 'the S M S Kid.' I was 'bout sixteen. I
could ride some an' I allus hed a little money back from my
wages. So when Shorty Owen tole me I was a-goin', I used
thet an' all I made up to the goin' time fer an outfit. I hed
a good season saddle, a Gallup; but I bought a bridle with
plenty o' doo-dads on it. Then you know my Injun likin' fer
color. I bought a yaller swet blanket, an' a top red Navajo
blanket fer Gran'pa. He kinda leaned to color too. I set up
all night with Swartz an' made him finish a pair o' top-

stitched boots, an' I hed enuff left fer new duckin' pants, red flannel shirt, an' a plaid fer change, shop-made bit an' spurs, both inlaid, a yaller silk handkerchief, a new hot roll, an' a twelve-doller beaver John B. Then Shorty Owen cut out my mount. In course I hed Sorrel Stud; he was six years old, right in his prime, an' I kep' him shinin'. Then there war nine more, all good ones—Blutcher, Alma, Polecat, Tatterslip, Bead Eye, Louscage, Possum, Silver Dollar, an' Badger, three of 'em from Shorty's own mount.

" 'Kid,' says Shorty, 'you got as good as the best o' 'em. I wants fer you to mind thet on this here work you're representin' this here outfit. Keep yore head, an' come back with it up. But I'd bet my life on you, an' this here outfit is trailin' you to the las' ditch.' "

Mage's voice was getting low here, and he swallowed on the last words, paused for a moment, then with that laugh of his continued: "Well, I'm stringin' 'em out a mile here, when I ought to have 'em bunched. Thet was a great summer. I worked in the big outfit with men an' hosses thet knowed how to turn a cow, an' the captain o' the round-up got to puttin' me an' Stud into the thick o' it purty reg'ler.

"It allus seemed thet when I rode Stud, Split Miller rode a little hoss called Midnight, an' he sure was a hoss; black as midnight, 'cept fer a white star in the forehead, short-coupled an' quicker then forked lightnin'. He would cut with the bridle off, an' fast? He was a cyclone. Every night 'roun' the camp-fire Split kep' pitchin' a load into me 'bout the Stud. Onct it was, 'Well, Kid, I seed you hed the little scrub out watchin' Midnight work.' Or, 'Say, Kid, I believe if you hed somethin' to ride you'd be a hand.' I swelled up some, but I remembered what Shorty Owens sed, 'Keep yore head an' come back with it up.' An' Split wusn't mean. He jest loved to josh. Two or three times the captain said, 'Split, let the Kid alone.' But he'd shoot one at me as he rode by in the work, and was allus badgerin' me fer a race.

"Then I kinda fell into watchin' Midnight run somethin'; an' I'd start Stud in the same direction to pace him. An' I come alive; the Stud was full as fast. I jest naturally supposed thet Midnight could beat anything, but I kep' a-tryin' an' my eyes kep' a-openin'. One night Split got mighty raw, an' finally says, 'Kid, I'll jest give you twenty dollers to run a half-mile race, standin' start, saddle agin' saddle.' An' then I fergot Shorty's instructions an' los' my head.

" 'Split,' I ses, 'you been pickin' on me ever sinct I come to this here work. Me an' Stud don't need no twenty dollers to run you. An even break's good enuff fer us, saddle fer saddle, bridle fer bridle, blanket fer blanket, spur fer spur.'

" 'Good enuf, Kid,' sez Split. 'Got enything else — eny money?'

" 'No,' I sez, ' ain't got no money, but I got sum damned good rags and a new hot roll.'

"Then the captain o' the round-up tuk a hand. But my blood wus up, an' they put cash allowance on all my plunder, an' I bet it 'gainst money. They give me twelve dollars fer my Swartz boots, eight dollars fer my John B., five dollars fer my cordaroy coat, four dollars fer my shirts, an' two dollars fer my duckin's. It war Wednesday, an' the race was to be pulled off Saturday evenin', straight half-mile, standin' start at the pop o' a gun. The captain tuk the thing in charge an' sed he'd lick eny damned puncher thet tried to run a sandy on the kid.

"It was all settled, but by the time I hed crawled into my hot roll thet night I 'membered the talk Shorty Owen give me. Stud was kinda mine, but he war a company hoss, arter all, to work on an' not fer racin', an' I sure was in a jackpot fer losin' my head. Well, the nex' day I tuk Stud off to practice fer a standin' start. You know how I say 'Now!' when I'm workin' on a hoss and jest as I want him to do somethin'. Well, Stud he'd been trained thet away, with jest a little touch o' the spur, an' I figured to say 'Now!' as the gun popped an' touch him thet away, an' he got the idee.

"Thet night I tuk him to the track an' put him over it four or five times. An' onct when we was restin' a-tween heats I says to him, 'Stud, if me an' you loses this here race, looks like we'd hev to steal off home in the night an' both o' us mighty nigh naked.' Everybody knocked off work Saturday. You know how even in them days word gits 'bout by the grapevine. Well, by noon they was ridin' an' drivin' in from all directions. The wimin' folks brought pies and cakes. The cusey cooked up two sacks o' flour an' we hed to kill two beeves. Everybody et at the chuck wagon an' it was some picnic.

"I tol' the fellers not to bet on me an' Stud, but they was plenty o' money on both sides. An' a girl with black eyes an' hair jest as purty as a bran' new red wagon, sez, 'Kid, if you win I'm a-goin' to knit you some hot-roll socks.' An' Ole Pop Sellers sez, 'Better look at them feet an' begin figgurin' on yarn, 'cause the Kid's a-goin' to win.' But Split hed a girl, too, an' she up an' sez, 'If the Kid's depending on them there socks to keep warm, he's mighty apt to git frost-bit this winter.' Well, you know the josh thet goes 'round when a big bunch o' cow people git together. An' they was a plenty, until I was plumb flustrated. When the time cum, a starter on a good hoss was to see thet we got off fair an' then ride with us as sort o' pace-maker an' try an' see the finish. But his hoss wasn't in Midnight's an' Stud's class.

"Split he seemed to figure thet Midnight didn't need no

trainin', he hed run so meny races an' never been beat. So all Split did was saddle Midnight an' stan' 'round an' josh. But me an' Stud was addled, an' I warmed him up a bit, talkin' to him all the time. I was worrited 'bout urgin' him in a tight place. I hed played with my spurs on him, but he never hed been spurred in his life 'cept a signal touch to turn or jump. I allus carried a quirt on the horn o' my saddle, but 'cept to tap him in a frenly way or in work he hed never knowed its use. What was I a-goin' to do in a pinch? I knowed he would use his limit under my word, but what if he didn't? Did I hev to hit him? If I owned this here ranch I'd hev give it all to be out o' the race an' not look like a quitter.

"Well, the time was cum. Stud he'd been frettin' an' I was stewin,' but when we toed the line sumthin' funny happened: We both seemed to settle down an' was as cam as this here night. I jest hed time to give him one pat an' say, 'God A'mighty, Stud, I'm glad I got you,' when the starter hollered, 'Git ready!' An' the gun popped! I yelled, 'Now!' at the same time, an' we was off.

"Midnight was a mite the quickest, but Stud caught his neck in the third jump, an' I helt him there. I wanted Midnight to lead, but kep' pushin' him. We didn't change a yard in the fust quarter, an' Split yelled, 'Kid, yer holdin' out well, but I got to tell you farewell.' An' he hit Midnight a crack with his quirt. Stud heard it singin' through the air an' jumped like he was hit hisself. In thirty yards we was nose an' nose; ten more, a nose ahead. Then I knowed we hed to go fer it. I was ridin' high over his neck, spurs ready, my quirt helt high, an' I kep' talkin' to him an' saying, 'Good boy, Stud!' The crowd was a-yellin' like demons. We was in the last eighth, nose an' nose, an' I let out one o' them Injun yells, an', 'Now, Stud! Now!'

"It seemed like he'd been waitin' fer it. I could feel his heart beatin' faster. There was a quiver wint through him like a man nervin' hisself fer some big shock. An' I could see him gainin'—slow, but gainin.' The crowd hed stopt yellin'. It come sudden. They was so still you could hear 'em breathe. I I guess we must a-been three feet ahead, with a hundred yards to go. Split was a-cussin' an' spurrin', an' whippin'. I didn't hev no mind to yell in all thet stillness. I was ready to spur, ready to whip, an' my heart was a-bleedin'. I don't think now thet I could a-done it to win, an' I jest whispered, 'Now, Stud! Now! Now!'

"I thought he was a-runnin' a-fore, but he shot out like a cry o' joy when a los' child is foun'; an' we crossed the line a length an' a half ahead. I seed the black-eyed girl with her arms 'round Pop Sellers' neck an' a-jumpin up an' down. Pop was jumpin' too, like a yearlin', an' the crowd was doin' an Injun dance generally. Stud didn't seem to sense the race was over, an' was still hittin' the breeze. I checked him in slow, pattin' him on the neck, an' talkin' to him like a crazy man, 'til he stood still, all a-quiver, his nostrils red as fire an' eyes still blazin'. Then I clum down an' throwed my arms 'roun' his neck and sez, 'God A'mighty, Stud, I didn't hev to hit you.' Stud's eyes seemed to softin, an' he laid his head down over my shoulder. I was cryin' like a baby, huggin' him hard. The boys was ridin' to us an' Stud raised his head an' whinnied. I guess it was jest the other hosses comin', but I thought he sed, 'Didn't we raise hell with em?' An' I sez, 'You bet we did, Stud, but it was you done it.'

"News travels fast, an' long 'fore I got in with my strays, they knowed all 'bout it at headquarters. I kep' thinkin' 'bout what Shorty sed, 'Come back with your hed up,' but I hed mine down when he met me at the corral. I knowed we hadn't no hosses to race fer money. He looked kinda hard at my extra saddled hoss an' roll o'plunder an sez, 'Kid, this ain't no racin' stable. This here is a cow outfit, an' our best hosses is fer cuttin', not racin'.' I didn't say a word, jest unsaddled, an' started fer the dog-house, when I heard him comin'.

"He caught up with me, grabbed me by both shoulders an' turned me 'roun'. I saw a great big tear stealin' down his cheek, an' he sez, 'God A'mighty, Kid, I wisht you was my boy!' Then he turned away quick an' was gone, while I set down on the groun' an' blubbered in my ole fool way thet I hev never got over. When pay day come, Shorty handed me my wage check, which had growed some, an' sed, 'Kid, when a boy does a man's work he gits a man's pay. You begin doin' a man's work when you went to gather them strays, and you come back the same way.'

"Then he started to go on, but turned an' sed, 'Say, Kid, if I owned this here S M S Ranch, hosses an' cattle, I'd a-give the whole damned outfit to a-seed you an' Stud come over thet line.' "

Peepy-Jenny

By John A. Lomax

Blaze, the mother of the heroine of this story, was a pure-bred Kentucky mare. Her brother herded a large bunch of wild mustang fillies up and down the lovely valleys of Bosque County. But for him they would have run over the hills and far away. Blaze was a gentle bay of medium size, with an elongated white triangle in the middle of her forehead as her one distinctive mark.

One night she added to her family of children a little daughter. The fence enclosing our horse lot was made of cedar pickets—small, pointed saplings set into the ground side by side and fastened together at the top by two continuous wires that laced the pickets together. During the night the small colt, staggering about the lot, found a hole in the fence where a picket had been broken off. Through the hole the colt blundered away from her mother. Blaze, in terror at being separated from her infant, attempted to jump the fence. She faltered and fell across the cruelly sharp pickets. The next morning we found her body pierced through with these cedar spears, almost an entire panel of fence soaked with her blood. Not once had the little orphan nuzzled her mother for food.

But my mother—with a bottle fitted with a white rag for a nipple—a bottle filled with milk several times a day—saved the life of the baby colt. She was a quiet youngster. Not for many months did she once nicker. Perhaps she was feeling the loss of her mother. Every two or three hours she would wake from her sleepy brooding, come to the picket fence and peek through a crack toward the kitchen door out of which her milk came.

"There's that colt, hungry again," my mother would say, and out she would go with a fresh bottle of milk. Already we had named her Jenny. From her habit of peeping through the fence the name grew to Peeping Jenny; that name came to be finally shortened to Peepy-Jenny, a name that stuck for her life of more than thirty years.

A little browner than her mother, Peepy-Jenny became otherwise the image of Blaze. A household pet, she also became a household pest. She learned to open every gate on the place and could deftly let down any rail fence that stood in her way. Whenever in later years she or any of her family got hungry, she could open the door that led to the feed room. I used to watch her pull out the pin that held down the latch, lift the latch with her teeth, and then swiftly push open the door. At last we had to buy a Yale lock on which she almost broke her teeth.

From three years old on, early in the spring Peepy-Jenny would annually find a new colt out in the pasture. Truly we

--CHARLES M. RUSSELL

children called them "woods colts." We kept all her progeny. They were almost like members of the family. It was a blot on the family escutcheon for anyone to speak of selling a child of Peepy-Jenny's. To strengthen these ties, each one of my numerous brothers and sisters claimed one of Peepy-Jenny's colts. When we were all supplied, Peepy-Jenny generously and obligingly began to furnish mule colts, which grew into brawny draft animals for the farm work.

Out on the range, neighbors began to speak of Peepy-Jenny surrounded by her progeny as the Lomax herd of horses (and mules). I cannot recall all the names, for each horse and cow, even some of the chickens and ducks on our place, bore names. I remember Princess, Fan, Jack, Jenny, Selim, Brownie, the Little Yellow Mule, and Pacing Jim. Selim belonged to me, a sturdy, bright bay pony. I always rode him to Sunday school, spelling-matches and play-parties. He used to walk close behind me when I walked home with my sweetheart from church.

When I was in my early 'teens, I hauled heavy loads of wood from our upper farm to Meridian, six miles away. The trip over a rough, rutty road took two or three hours. I always drove Peepy-Jenny as one of the span, though she really deserved freedom from all work. But I wanted company on the lonely drive. So I'd swing the big gate wide open as I drove away and out would come every descendant of Peepy-Jenny, from her last baby colt to the big, stately work mules. They made a brave show. Prancing, bucking, squealing, the bunch would dash ahead and over the next hill. In a moment, back they would come as if frightened, run around the wagon in widening circles, all stop as if in terror, and then off again. My customers would tell me that when they saw that cavalcade came streaming down Main Street, they knew that

Johnny Lomax was somewhere back up the road, hauling to town another load of firewood. As I tumbled out the logs in some backyard, the entire bunch of curious young steeds would explore back alleys and stare at passers-by just like a group of country children on an infrequent visit to a city. Peepy-Jenny's low, anxious neigh during these forays would keep her youngest-born close to her side.

By the time the procession was headed for home, their edge worn off, the revelers would lag behind. A lightened wagon enabled me to drive faster. After crossing a hill, I would speed my driving and put two or three hills between myself and the jaded crew. Peepy-Jenny would miss her baby and give a piercing call. Far back, all of her children, suddenly awake to the loss of their parent, would reply in various keys from the high treble of the youngest colts to the deep bass of the braying mules. Then I would soon hear the thud of flying hoofs, a wild orgy of sound, and again I would be surrounded by the entire bunch. It was fun for them and fun for me. If they had been able to laugh, they would have laughed with me as I laughed at them.

One day I started across the pasture, with a sack on my shoulder, to pick cotton in the bottom field. I came on Peepy-Jenny with her crowd grazing around her. I stopped to pet Princess, her youngest child. The colt kept following me as I started to go on, begging for more rubbing under the chin. Finally I pulled my cotton sack over its head and neck and tied the strings. The colt, unable to see, stood motionless. I walked aside—and waited to see what would happen. Peepy-Jenny was busy hunting green tufts of grass. Presently she looked at her offspring. She started at the strange object. An awful monster stood where a moment before had been her child. She raised her head in alarm. Then she nickered softly, for at least half of that body looked familiar. At the sound of its mother's call, the colt walked gingerly and very slowly towards her, lifting its feet high. Peepy-Jenny stood her ground, though as the colt came nearer, she, trembling, sat backward on her haunches almost flat on the ground. At last, when the terrifying white face pushed itself a few inches from her own, she gave a scream of terror, wheeled, and dashed away. Then followed as wild a scene as ever happened in anybody's pasture.

The cry of their mother brought quick attention from each and every son and daughter. The sight that met their gaze froze them with terror. They stood as if paralyzed, staring at an unknown horror from which their mother was wildly fleeing. In an instant they too joined the mad rush. Peepy-Jenny ran a two hundred yards straightway, followed by all her children, then she turned and began to move in a big circle. Her progeny was lined up behind her, almost an equal distance apart. At the center of this circle stood the unhappy colt wearing its ghostly slip-over. On the ground a few yards away I lay choked with joy. I had got past laughing—I choked and gurgled. Meanwhile that flying ring went round and round about us. A scared mule will twist his head about forty-five degrees towards his rear and step very high as he runs; a horse makes a deep internal grunt that seems to come from away back under his loins. Each animal was either stepping high or grunting. And each one had his eyes fixed on that central horror. Once Peepy-Jenny neighed again. The colt moved forward a few, feeble steps. Again the bunch "quit the drive" and fled to the other side of the pasture. But fright and curiosity combined to drive them back, and the swiftly moving circle was resumed.

All happy moments must have an end. I heard my mother's shrill voice from the front porch: "What in the world is the

matter with the horses? I believe they have all gone crazy."
Then as if scenting the cause, for I was hidden in the tall grass,
she shouted: "You, John! You, John!" I snatched the sack
from the head of Princess and fled. The circus was over.

When the time came for my first year in college, both
drouths and floods in preceding years made it necessary for me
to sell my saddle horse, Selim, Peepy-Jenny's eldest son. It
nearly broke my heart. To Dallas from Meridian was a two
days' trip. For me it was a ninety-mile funeral procession. I
turned Selim into a lot in East Dallas. As I walked away, he
followed me as far as he could and then put his head over the
top plank and leaned against the fence. I didn't turn my head.
I couldn't have seen him if I had turned, for I was crying.
I never saw him again.

Years afterwards when I visited home, Peepy-Jenny walked
away from me when I stopped in the pasture to pat her. She
then turned and looked at me as if to say, "Where is Selim?"

A Boy's First Horse

By Arthur Babb

IN THE YEAR 1875, my family was living about two miles south of the little town of Wortham, Texas, on the old Manning farm, which lies along the side of the H. and T. C. railroad, now the Southern Pacific.

One day in early summer, my older brother—"Brother Willie," as we children called him—rode up to the house leading a dun mare, with a little bay colt following. When he dropped the rope, the mare flew back and snorted with a whistle, as none but a genuine mustang can do. My mother, who had come to the front, exclaimed, "Where in the world did you get that thing?"

"I traded for her," he replied. "Got her cheap. She's an outlaw."

"Well, who is going to take care of her, now that you are working away from home?"

"Arthur can stake her out every day on the prairie in front of the house and water her at the little pond," my brother answered. "I'll give him twenty-five cents every week."

"What! My child handle that wild thing? Why, she might kill him."

I was not yet ten years old and quite small for my age. I was afraid of the old reprobate mare, too, but I knew the job had to be done; so I set about it. In the days that fol-

lowed, I also did my best to tame the little colt, but it had
a cunning way of getting behind that old mother.

Before long, old Dolly Varden, the mare, had quit snorting
at me. Having learned the routine, she gave me little trouble.
But one day when I went for her, she had broken the lariat
and was feeding around loose on the prairie. I hurried back
to the house with the news. I knew there was a big tussle
ahead, for Dolly could run faster and longer than any horse
in the country and she was sure to go back to her old range,
Blue Ridge.

Brother Willie chanced to be at home. I hurried for our
neighbors, Mr. Townsend and Mr. Sanders, and the three on
their horses surrounded the mare while I opened the big gate.
The crops being pretty well gathered, they let Dolly Varden
run loose in the field. They headed her for the big gate, all
right, but she never stopped. She made straight for the back
fence, cleared it without touching a rail, paused to look back,
and then with that mustang whistle she raised her tail, waved
them a farewell, and was off for Blue Ridge.

Mr. Townsend roped the colt and I rejoiced when I saw
him come leading it back, with the rope on it. Now I could
have better success taming it; I was glad to be rid of the old
mare.

Mother gave me a name for the colt: Lucy. This pleased
me very much, for it was one of her own names. My task of
caring for Lucy soon was my chief pleasure. She would neigh
when she saw me coming and meet me at the full length of
her rope.

One day after caring for Lucy I dropped on a pallet for a
little siesta. Brother Willie had come home, and he sat talking
to Mother as she did some mending. I waked just in time to
hear Mother say, "You should give Arthur that colt. He took

care of that old outlaw of a mare for nearly a year, and he's cared for the colt since she got away."

I did not catch my brother's reply; maybe he did not answer. I thought sure they would hear my heart pounding against my ribs. Brother Willie did not always comply with Mother's wishes, but sometimes he did. Now it seemed to me that my entire future depended on how he took her suggestion. Mother soon left the room to attend to some duties, and my brother walked out into the front yard. I got up quietly and sneaked to the back door, making a bee-line for where I had Lucy staked.

She met me as usual and laid her chin on my shoulder. I knew that she had always thought she was mine, and I resolved never to tell her different, even if Fate was against me. Then I saw Brother Willie coming toward me. I thought that my heart would jump out of my mouth or stop still. I fancy I felt something like a girl when she is expecting a man to propose to her.

Brother Willie just walked up, made a few remarks as to how the colt was growing, and then he turned and walked away. He was going back to Jot Longbotham's to work and would be gone a whole week. How could I stand it? I felt faint, and had to lean against Lucy for support. Then I got mad. I guess that helped me to stand it.

The next week-end he came home and walked out to where I was holding the colt to take a few nibbles of choice grass. As he approached, he abruptly asked, "Howja like to have that colt for your own?"

"Oh, fine!" I stammered.

"Well," he told me, "you can have her."

"Sure enough?" I cried. "No fooling?"

"Yes," he said. "If you don't believe it, ask Mother."

If Mother verified a thing, there was no retracting. I dropped the rope and made a dash for the house, where Mother assured me that the colt was mine for keeps. I next made a rush for Lucy, and threw my arms around her neck. She doubtless wondered what it was all about.

Well, one evening some time later my Father came home somewhat earlier than usual. He worked in town in a wheel-wright shop and walked down the railroad track, ordinarily reaching home about an hour by sun (if you chance to know what that is—an hour before the sun would set). I was graz-ing Lucy along the right-of-way. Father stopped to comment on how fast the colt was growing. She was almost as large as the average pony, and he thought I might begin riding her. This I had put off doing for fear I might make her sway-backed. Now I looked for my younger brother, Guy, and drove a bargain with him that if he would lead the colt while I took a ride, I in turn would give him a ride. We spent the next day or so swapping rides until Lucy must have grown pretty tired of it. I had even ridden her down to the big gate all alone, and when I sat upon her back I felt like Croesus as he sat on his throne at the battle of Hell's Pond.

My happiness did not last long. A few days later several meteors fell in rapid succession. Then a very large one dropped. We learned later that it struck in Palo Pinto County. And by the way, years later I saw this missile exhib-ited in Fair Park, at Dallas, where it was brought, I am told, in an ox-wagon. The excitement caused by the meteor set people talking about the world's coming to an end. To cap the climax, the sun eclipsed. Our neighbors for the most part were uneducated people, and Mother could not make them understand what an eclipse meant. Indeed, her consoling counsel failed to have its usual effect even on my mind.

The neighbor women all gathered in, Mrs. Townsend and Mrs. Sanders, Mrs. Shirley, and Mrs. Baker from across the railroad. Mrs. Townsend said everything pointed to the end of time, that the sky was not nearly so bright as when she was a girl. Mrs. Shirley said her garden seed was all running out. Then, too, all the ladies noted the sinfulness and bad behavior of people—young folks especially—turning their back on the church, and dancing, too. They dressed so outrageously, the ladies went on. There was Molly Crumes, for example, a gay young thing wearing her dress skirts up to her shoe-tops! Mother did not look up. She was wondering if they knew that Brother Willie sometimes went with Miss Molly.

I retired to the peach orchard to think the matter over. I always went there to do my thinking. I decided to take the matter up with the Almighty Himself, though I must admit that I was a little skeptical. I remembered that in the early summer when the peaches seemed too slow ripening I had thought it fitting to ask the Lord to speed them up. Under one of the most advanced trees I had taken a position to send up my petition. Going back in about a week, I decided that I had gotten some results. But in order to make a more thorough check, I thought I would make a test on a tree at the back of the orchard. We called it the October peach. But with all my most earnest petitions, it still remained an October peach.

I took my past experience into account, but something had to be done. So out there in the peach orchard all alone, I assumed a position I felt would be pleasing in His sight and asked the Lord seriously to reconsider what I had heard He was contemplating at this most inopportune time. He well knew, I pointed out, that I had worked patiently the past two years to get my pony to where I could ride her, and now to be robbed of this expected pleasure was just too much.

And the Lord listened. Even as when speaking with Moses, He "repented of the evil that he had intended to do," and as the Children of Israel were spared by the request of Moses, so was the destruction of the earth abandoned by reason of my petition. I therefore lived to have many rides on Lucy's back, the longest of which was from Mexia to Denison, where we had bought a little farm northwest of town. There on this farm Lucy lived to the ripe old age of twenty-two.

—CHARLES M. RUSSELL

The Mescal-Drinking Horse

By JOVITA GONZÁLEZ DE MIRELES

THE thick brush country of the Rio Grande saw his birth.
His mother, a scrub mare, famous for her ability to smell
and dodge the law, had saved Juan José, her smuggler master,
from a prison fate. *El Viento,* she had been called, for she
raced with the fleetness of the Gulf winds as they blow over
the prairie, defying the thick mesquite thorns, and the screw-
like spikes of the *granjeno* and the flexible but tough cactus
needles. His father was a powerful stallion of Arabian blood
that had wandered away from the stables of his rich master.

And so it was that El Conejo came into existence. An awkward creature since birth, he had been a contradiction of
everything a horse should be. "He looks like a rabbit," his
master had said, laughing uproariously, seeing the trembling
creature with his mother's short, stubby hind legs and the
powerful front legs of his Arabian father. So he was called
El Conejo (the rabbit). He grew, a gentle, good-natured pony.
Juan José's children made him their pet, spoiled him, and he
in turn bore them from their home hidden in the thick *chaparral* to the *camino real,* where he and the children peeped
with curiosity at the outside world.

One never-to-be-forgotten day, his placid life of easy-going
contentment came to an abrupt end. Juan José, doubly drunk
—drunk both with success of his latest exploit and with a
quart of *Pajaro Azul mescal*—opened a new and vicious world
to him.

"Come here, Conejo," Juan José called to him, waving a newly opened bottle of *mescal*. "I don't like your looks," he laughed. "A horse like a rabbit is neither a horse nor a rabbit. I know you don't like your appearance, either. Come here to me; this will make you forget." And, saying this, he poured the quart of *mescal* into a tin wash basin.

Conejo approached the basin and, without even the faintest sniff, took a deep draught. He looked up, surprised at the fire that burned him, gave a snort and a kick, circled the pan gingerly, sniffed at the contents this time, and without hesitation quaffed the *mescal* to the last drop. He looked up. If ponies can smile, Conejo did so now, and foolishly too, rolled his eyes and wiggled his ears at the same time. Then, as if stung by a wasp, he bolted, kicked the air and ran away to the

nearest brush. All day long he was heard running and snorting. At dusk he returned slowly, a sober horse, his colthood days behind him.

Next day, Juan José, seeing the sadness in his eyes, and knowing how it felt to have a *cruda* (hangover), offered him the bottle he always carried in his hip pocket.

"You need it, Conejo," he told the horse, "but just a little this time—two drinks—three drinks—and plenty of cold water." The horse, seeming to understand what his master was telling him, drank two swigs—three swigs—and then swallowed enough water to float his own body.

From that day on Conejo took his daily drink of *mescal,* and he was none the worse for it. In fact, it made him a horse of reputation. Other smugglers came to see him drink, and all admired him. "He should be called *El Pájaro Azul,*" suggested one of the smugglers, noticing his fondness for that particular brand of *mescal.* And so *El Pájaro* he became now, little knowing that the name so glibly given would become a by-word among the people of the borderland.

A new relationship developed between El Pájaro and Juan José, one of respect and mutual admiration. But there was something he missed, the close contact with man, which only comes to a horse when he is ridden by his master. The children were no longer allowed to ride him; Juan José still laughed at his queer shape and thought him unworthy of riding. Every day, after his customary drink, he ran off like a flash of lightning to the brush, where he remained—unmolested—until the effects of the *mescal* left him.

Time passed for master and horse in this manner, and then on the feast day of Santiago, the patron saint of horses, Juan José, feeling unusually gay after their daily drink, said to El Pájaro, "Pájaro, I am going to ride you; you are to be my horse." And without more ado, he jumped on the unsuspecting horse. The struggle that followed was one of endurance— Pájaro trying to throw his master down, Juan José to hold on. At last, each recognizing the stubbornness and tenacity of the other, both stopped from sheer exhaustion.

The following day word came that a load of tobacco leaf and *mescal* was ready to be brought across the river. Calling his men together, Juan José planned the expedition for the first night after the last quarter of the moon, which would be four days hence.

El Pájaro was made ready for the expedition. He did not mind the saddle at all; and the bridle merely gave him a ticklish sensuous sensation in his mouth. Under cover of darkness Juan José and his men met at the river.

"*Vamos, Pájaro! Adentro,*" the rider whispered in his ear. Horse and rider plunged into the stream and swam to the other side. The hidden load of smuggled goods was found; the mules were packed, and the smugglers again plunged into the river. Land was reached in safety. Juan José was whispering commands into his horse's ear, but Pájaro was sniffing the air.

"*Ya, ya, Pájaro,*" whispered Juan José. "Keep quiet, steady."

Unheeding his master's words and caresses, Párajo reared on his powerful, short hind legs and without warning fled to the chaparral. Hardly had he brought his master to the safety of the brush when the Rangers fell upon the smugglers, wounding some and taking the rest under their custody.

Because of this incident, Párajo's fame as a "Ranger sniffler" spread over the borderland. Fleet as a rabbit, with the intelligence of his Arabian father and the endurance of his plebeian mother, he was the envy of all the *rancheros*. Fabulous sums of money were offered for this mescal-drinking horse, but Juan José would not sell him. He was too valuable to the smuggler; with his aid, Juan José and his men became unconquerable.

However, with the development of the lower Rio Grande Valley, swift changes came to the border. Smuggling became unprofitable. No longer did it pay the smugglers to bring in fresh supplies of tobacco leaf. Bull Durham and brown paper was taking the place of the corn shuck *cigarrillos*. No longer was it spectacular to swim the river under the very nose of the Texas Rangers. For these officers, seeing the demand for tobacco diminish, directed their activities to more active sources. And without the thrill of persecution smuggling lost all zest and glamor. Juan José, who always liked to occupy the center of the stage, did a dramatic thing then. Repenting of his sinful life, he acquired religion and decided to lead the life of a saint. It was then that he sold El Pájaro, the wonder horse. A rich ranchero, Don Manuel de Guevara, became his new master. Juan José wept over his horse at parting, begging Don Manuel not to give him any more *mescal*.

"He is part of my very soul," Juan José explained. "With my repentance came his too. He is as much of a Christian as I am."

But with the new master and the new life, El Pájaro lost spirit. His eyes lost luster, he refused to eat, and when saddled merely stood still. His new master cursed and swore, saying he had been cheated in the bargain. Then like a flash a thought came into his mind. The horse needed *mescal*. And he was right. A quart of the fiery liquid restored the horse to his former manner. El Pájaro pitched and snorted as of old. He became so spirited that no one, except the ranchero, could ride him. A man in his early forties, Don Manuel was the typical ranchero of his time. A good *jinete*, he bragged that no horse could throw him and no rider could outride him. And to a certain extent the boast was true. Except when he was "in the grape," the polite border way of saying he was drunk, he could ride any horse. He used to boast that if Pegasus himself, the fabulous winged horse, were placed before him, he could ride him—wings and all. El Pájaro had met his match.

In those days, at the turn of the nineteenth century, there was no better known figure than Father José María. A native of France, he had come to the border country as a young man of twenty-five, forty years before. Because of his excellent horsemanship, he was lovingly known as the "Cowboy Priest." Now as an aging man of sixty-five, he still rode all over the lower border administering the sacraments and preaching the gospel. Loved and respected by all, his word was law among a people who had very little liking and less respect for American law.

One evening, just at sunset, Father José María, riding his white mule, arrived at Don Manuel's ranch. Hearing the cries of a woman, the hoarse swearing of a man, and the weeping of children, he entered the yard of the ranch house without announcing himself. The sight that met his eyes did not surprise him at all, for he knew Don Manuel only too well.

The ranchero was much "in grape" and so was El Pájaro. Don Manuel could hardly stand on his feet; yet he was trying to ride the snorting and pitching horse. His wife stood on the porch wringing her hands and weeping. The children were adding their wails and tears to hers, and the two peons standing against the house were paralyzed with fear. Don Manuel would surely be killed if he succeeded in getting on El Pájaro.

Father José María took in the scene at a glance. Dismounting from his mule, he came to where Manuel struggled with El Pájaro. "*Hola, Padre,*" the ranchero called out, "watch me ride this devil of a horse."

"Stop a moment, Manuelito," answered the priest. "I'll make a bet with you."

Manuel stopped, for if there was a thing he loved more than *mescal* and horses, it was to make and win an honest bet.

"A bet, Padre, did you say?"

"Yes, I bet I can ride El Pájaro."

"All right, Padre. I take your bet. If you ride this demon of a horse, he is yours. Agreed?"

"Agreed," the priest answered.

With slow steps the priest approached the horse—caressed him gently, patting his mane and rubbing his nose. In less time than any one realized, Father José María was riding El Pájaro. The *mescal*-drinking horse and the *mescal*-drinking ranchero had been defeated.

From that time on El Pájaro was the priest's property. Years passed. The black-robed, white haired priest, learned in Latin, and the gentle, queer-shaped horse, Stella Matutina now, *alias* El Conejo, *alias* El Pájaro, traversed the borderland, bringing consolation to the sick and afflicted. Whenever the good priest talked to some impenitent sinner, he would often comment, "My horse, Morning Star, is a good example of what religion can do for a man. Imitate him. He has left his evil ways."

As Smart as a Cutting Horse

By J. Frank Dobie

In the language of the range, to say that somebody is "as smart as a cutting horse" is to say that he is smarter than a Philadelphia lawyer, smarter than a steel trap, smarter than a coyote, smarter than a Harvard graduate—all combined. There just can't be anything smarter than a smart cutting horse. He can do everything but talk Meskin—and he understands that. The man who trains a cutting horse that becomes outstanding may pardonably become as foolish over him as a two-year-old heifer over her first calf. The owner may understandably be as proud of him as a mother over the first gurgle of her clearly inspired son.

Cutting chutes, small pastures as compared with large pastures and the open range, the inactivity of heavy modern cat-

FRANK ANTHONY STANUSH IN *Epic-Century*

tle as compared with the agility and running powers of the old-time Longhorn breed, and the easy way in which cattle are now generally worked in contrast to the old cut-and-slash chousing have all combined to diminish the work of cutting horses and make them scarcer. But cutting horses are still used, are still the objects of pride and of talk. Sometimes, to show his horse's ability, a rider, after selecting an animal in a herd to be cut out, will remove his horse's bridle and allow the horse to exercise his own judgment. Wonderful tales that grew up about cutting horses are still a part of the living lore of the range.

Perhaps the business of cutting should be explained for the benefit of some people not familiar with it. There is a round-up of, say, two thousand cattle. Among them are several strays. The herd is composed of cows with calves, dry (calfless) cows, steer yearlings, heifer yearlings, and a sprinkling of two-year-old steers and also of older steers and of bulls. Perhaps the owner wants to ship all the big steers. They must be cut out, or parted, from the herd. A man rides in on his cutting horse, spots one of the steers, and works him to the edge of the herd. Then he scoots this steer out to one side—often with a few other animals to give him company. This animal, or handful of animals, becomes the nucleus for the herd to be cut into. It is called the "cut." It, as well as the big herd, must be guarded by cowboys while the cutting is going on.

Cattle held in a herd are restless and want to be released, but an individual animal does not as a rule want to be cut off from its fellows. It will often dodge and resist being taken away. The cutter and the cutting horse must not run in the herd and thus make it uncontrollable and also cause the cattle to lose weight. Man and horse must be very alert, quiet and skillful in anticipating cow dodges. If a hard-headed cow and her calf are to be cut out, they must be kept together. If a big herd is being trimmed extensively, there may be various cuts from it—a cut for strays, perhaps a cut for steer yearlings, and so on.

A cutting horse, like any other good cow horse, has cow sense—"saveys the cow." Like any other master artist, he knows his business and delights in doing it. You'll see him working his ears as he starts following an animal out of the herd, eager to whirl if the critter makes a false turn. Often a good cutting horse will take the starch out of some stubborn cow brute by biting it on the back or elsewhere. No lusty, dressed-up cowboy ever "swung his pardner" with more zest and pride than a cutting horse feels and exhibits towards his work. He's so "rearing to go" that sometimes, according to the stories, he will invent a little work for himself.

One morning right after a good rain a Mexican vaquero reported to Jack Maltsberger that he had found where some cow thief had roped an animal out in the pasture. He'd seen the fresh tracks. Jack went with him to make examination. Plainly a horse had followed a cow and the cow had been thrown. But no track of a dismounted man was visible. Jack rode on. Soon the cow tracks and the horse tracks separated. Following those of the horse, Jack found an extra good roping and cutting horse that had been turned out to get over lameness. The horse was well. Wanting some exercise, he had evidently run the cow and knocked her down.

O. Z. Fenley had a cutting horse named Cole. One time O. Z. was driving a bunch of horses, including Cole, from one pasture into another. At the gap a Mexican *potro* cut off and made back at full speed. Fenley took after him, but the *ladino* was gaining when a noise like the clattering wheels of creation began to pound from the rear. Looking around, O. Z. saw

Cole coming. Cole had gone through the gap with the other horses but had turned back, eager to join the chase. He circled the *potro,* headed him for the gap, and put him through it. These are true stories.

"The best cutting horse I ever see," Al Jackson likes to tell, "was Bosley Blue. He belonged to the Ogallala Land and Cattle Company of Nebraska back in the eighties. There was nothing in the way of cow work he could not do; in fact, it looked like he could do everything but read and cipher.

"Well, along in the late fall of '87 the round-ups ended, the saddle horses were turned loose on the range, and the hands paid off. Sam Blair, Bud Chambers and me decided we would test out the monte games at Scottsbluff, and so with the checks for our summer wages in our pockets and slickers behind our saddles we lit a shuck for town.

"About six or eight miles from the ranch, we noticed a terrible dust over to our right. The wind wasn't blowing; no cow work was supposed to be going on; the dust held too long for a whirlwind; and we got mighty curious. Of course we were in a hurry to get rid of our money, but we decided that we could take time out to investigate, even if we did have to turn out of our course. There was a chance that a bunch of cow-thieves were at work. We rode up a draw to the edge of some timber, concealed our horses, and then crawled up to a high, grassed ridge to peep over.

"Well, sir, you never saw anything like it. There rounded up in a basin over on the other side of the ridge was a herd of maybe fifteen hundred head of cattle. We could not see a single rider though. Then through the dust we made out a riderless horse trotting around among the cattle. It was Bosley Blue. D'reckly he cut out a big brindle steer that we recognized as belonging to the Fiddleback outfit. Then we seen that Blue had a cut off to one side of the herd and that, besides cutting out strays, he was holding both the main herd and the cut. That brindle, though, was hell-bent on keeping with the main herd. Three times Bosley Blue had to cut him out. The last time he brought him out he had his ears back and was chawing on his rump. Still the steer persisted in coming back as soon as Blue had turned him. Blue seen him out of the corner of his eye, wheeled after him, got him on a straight run, grabbed his tail in his teeth, and with as purty a twist as you ever saw turned the steer a somersault. Then he deliberately set down on the steer and held him there for ten minutes, I guess."

Any time Doc Burris, a character from Karnes County, got a chance he'd talk about his dun cutting horse. "All I had to do," said Doc, "was to show Dun Man what brands I wanted cut out of a herd. Then I'd pull off saddle, briddle, everything and dismount myself, and that dun horse would start in and cut out every critter wanted."

"Purty good horse," agreed Buck Gravis. "I had two cutting horses—one a dun and the other a bay. I generally put Dun to working in the herd and Bay on the outside. Dun wasn't much on brands. The only brand he could pick out was my own, but when it came to classifying cattle he was as smart as the top buyer for the packers in Kansas City. Say I wanted all the heifer yearlings out of a herd. I'd set Dun loose on them and while he worked I'd often mount another horse and cut out the strays, fat steers, or any other class of cattle. Bay meantime was working between the main herd and the cut, and whenever Dun brought out something, Bay would take it over and put it where it belonged."

In addition to being smarter than most folks and being always on his toes, the cutting horse is so well reined and is so agile that he can be brought to a stop on a quarter of a dollar and give you back fifteen cents in change. "This little grey pony was named Toro," Frank M. King remembers in *Wranglin' the Past.* "He was a neck-reined wonder, a flash as a cut horse, a corral and prairie rope-hoss, a demon of determination in his work, but lovely as a baby when at ease. It was often said by the cowboys that Toro could cut the baking powder out of a biscuit without breaking the crust."

Cutting horses have not had a corner on smartness, however, either in fact or fabrication. In *A Vaquero of the Brush Country* I told about the night horse named Sid—his brand being C I D—that Asa Jones used to ride. When the time came to change guard, according to Asa, Old Sid might, by main strength and awkwardness, be persuaded to make two or three more circles around the herd. Then, in spite of hell and high water, he would head for the chuck wagon. Something inside of him told him—as accurately as the boss's watch ticking, for general consultation, in the hopper of the cook's coffee grinder—as correctly as the swing of the Great Dipper around the North Star—when his time was up and the next relief would come on. If, after he reached the chuck wagon, his rider would dismount, throw the reins over his head, and wait a minute before remounting, he could persuade Sid to go back to the herd. Maybe the smart old night horse did not know about waking up the next guard, but he had been ridden to camp many a time with the result that a few minutes later he would be relieved from duty. Every range man has his story of a smart horse.

(1)

"Not caring to be left out in the cold for want of something to ride, I bought for forty dollars a very nice little black horse of about fourteen and one-half hands. He was handsome, quick, and clever, but full of tricks and as knowing as a monkey. One day when I was riding him over a flat piece of ground, he got a cactus thorn in his foot, and began to go very lame. I extracted the thorn, brought him back very gently and turned him out for a week's run, using meanwhile another of my horses, of which by that time I owned five or six. At the end of the week he was quite well. On my taking him up again he came in for a couple of days' pretty hard work. This he did not like as well as running free on range, so the third morning on starting out he pretended to be dead lame. Of course I turned him loose and got up another horse, whereupon he ran away without showing the slightest lameness. The same thing happened on two or three occasions, but I noticed that it was not always the same foot which he favored. I decided then to try whether he was scheming or not, and after examining his foot carefully and finding nothing wrong, I continued my ride. He went very lame, first on one foot and then on another, but finally, seeing it was useless, gave it up, although with a very bad grace, and went quite well the rest of the day. He tried the same dodge several times, till he found it had no effect, and then gave it up for good and all."[1]

(2)

"I staked my horse near that night and he was as smart as a man," Frank Mitchell praised. "Every little bit he'd come in and smell of me, where I lay under my slicker, to see if everything was all right, and then go back and graze. A horse doesn't lie down till near morning. About four o'clock he lay down and slept an hour—I could hear him snore. We

[1]Pollock, J. M., *The Unvarnished West*, London, n.d., 61-62.

thought as much of our horses as of the best friends on earth, because they were the best friends we had."[2]

(3)

"In the late sixties Uel Livingston of Hamilton County, Texas, went up the trail with a herd of cattle. One night while he was on guard he became so overpowered by sleepiness and the cattle were so quiet that he decided to risk a nap. He was dead asleep, and then the shaking of the whole earth brought him to life. The cattle had stampeded. He was in no danger of being run over, however. There his horse was standing over him, two feet on one side of his body and two on the other."[3]

(4)

"In the spring I went to Ellsworth, Kansas, and got a job helping trail a herd of cattle to the Dodge City country. We got along fine until we made camp near Hayes City. I had been on night guard and had been in my bed only a short time when suddenly a freight engine let out a blast that sounded like the crack of doom, and the cattle jumped and stampeded. I had staked old Trusty, my night horse, to a sagebrush close to my bed. Now on hearing the cattle start to run, he came as close to my bed as his picket rope would allow him. I could see the cattle coming my way. Without putting the bridle on Trusty, I jumped into the saddle and started in the lead of the running cattle. I had never been in a stampede; so I let my horse have his way. By running even with the leaders for a ways, he came in close to them and got them running in a

[2]Haley, J. Evetts, *Charles Goodnight, Cowman and Plainsman*, Boston, 1936, 340-341.
[3]Everett, Malissa C., "A Pioneer Woman," *West Texas Historical Association Year Book*, 1927, 68.

circle and they finally stopped, heaved a long breath, and began grazing. Old Trusty knew his job was done."[4]

(5)

Along in the early eighties W. H. Kilgore was trading for sheep down in Duval County and driving them through the prickly pear flats and chaparral thickets to the San Antonio market.

"We had," he said, "a pack pony we called Old Pack. He would follow us just like a colt, and he soon learned to work behind the sheep and nose them along. When he would get into the prickly pear, the sheep would become almost impossible to drive. They would get to eating that pear and you couldn't budge them. Old Pack caught on that they wouldn't go unless they got scared. He would stop and give his pack a genuine good shaking. Those tin cans and skillets and the coffee pot and the butcher knife and long-handled spoon and tin cups would rattle worse'n a kerosene can loaded with flint rocks tied to a mustang's tail. The rattling would stampede the sheep every time and they'd pull out. Then, if a horse ever laughed, Old Pack shore would. He would stand there and watch the crazy sheep trying to run over each other to get ahead, and it looked like he got downright pleasure out of the little stampede he had caused. He'd pull this trick every time we got stalled."[5]

(6)

"This pack horse, which had been purchased from Indians, was gentle, and a pitiful-looking, decrepit beast. The outfit did not use pack saddles, and the horses' backs would some-

---

[4]*Hoofs and Horns,* Tucson, Arizona, May, 1940, 4.

[5]Angermiller, Florence Fenley, in the *Leader-News,* Uvalde, Texas, March 18, 1938.

times have small galled sores on them. If this old horse had a galled place on his back no longer than a finger nail, he would when being packed, squirm and twist as if he were being killed, and when the pack was once on his back, he would come up to some of the outfit, and twist and squirm, and look at him with as sanctified and pity-soliciting look as was ever put out by the most consummate hypocrite. His eyes would actually fill with tears, and he would close them as if in agony, and tremble as with a chill. No human could have begged with more eloquence to have the pack loosened. This old reprobate knew just how loose that pack had to be for him to be able to turn it. If loosened, but not enough to be turned, he would start off, and as soon as he would discover that fact he would return with the same pitiful plea to have the ropes on his pack loosened. If it was again loosened, the instant he discovered that the pack was sufficiently loose to turn, he would give a vicious lunge, jump, kick, and twist until the pack was on his side, when he would tear like a demon through the bunch of horses, and invariably stampede the entire herd.

"We soon learned this trick of this old villain, but before we did, we had several stampedes, were compelled to gather up our horses, and retrieve pots, pans, blankets, and other camp equipment."[6]

(7)

"If we were cutting yearlings out of a herd, I had only to show Old Harvey the first one. He'd work that herd until not a yearling was left in it. He did not like for me to pull on the bridle reins. If I did, he'd shake his head as if to tell me that he knew his business. I don't remember ever getting

---

[6]Ridings, Sam P., *The Chisholm Trail*, Guthrie, Oklahoma, 1937, 388-389.

down off him that he did not turn his head and nudge me on the shoulder with his nose. Perhaps he was trying to tell me we had done a good job. . . .

"Red Bird always counted his cattle as he cut them by giving a little nicker when the animal was out of the herd and we started to turn back for another. One day I bet a man that he would cut out a jackrabbit that was dodging around some bushes in the middle of a loose herd. I rode Red Bird in, showed him the rabbit, and then pulled the bridle off. He brought that rabbit out."[7]

[7]Arthur Howard and Joe Merrick in *Yesterday in Hall County, Texas*, by Inez Hall, Memphis, Texas, 1940, 205-206, 218.

Skeerce Tail

By D. C. Earnest

"HAIR on that bay pony's tail is kinder skeerce," Lump Mooney, boss of the Deep Creek outfit in Mitchell County, remarked. And so Skeerce Tail became his name. He had been well broken, but from the start there was no love lost between us. When I tightened the saddle girth too much to suit him one morning, he reached around and nipped me on my left arm. When I mounted him, I roweled him with my sharp Petmecky spurs to pay him back.

A few days later while I was galloping after a bunch of cattle, I noticed that the girth was loose and got down to tighten it This time Skeerce Tail did not take time to bite. He kicked me so hard that I thought my leg was broken, but it wasn't. After I got up, he kept out of my way until he stepped in the reins. When I got on him, my leg was hurting me so much that I let him go unpunished. We kept up the feud all that year, but I was extremely careful about tightening the girth.

In November we turned Skeerce Tail out with other saddle horses, keeping up only a few to feed for the winter's riding. I was watching the mudholes, occasionally pulling some cow out of the bog. Every once in a while I'd see Skeerce Tail with three other ponies over on Morgan Creek, near Flat Top Mountain, where he had given me such a kick. No doubt he liked the grass in that vicinity, but I had a suspicion that pleasant memories had something to do with his choice.

That winter was cold—like all the winters. One morning

before daylight I heard a horse walking around the house. This was unusual. The horse was so persistent that I finally stepped out on the gallery in my sock feet. Although it was still dark, I recognized Skeerce Tail and saw that he was limping. He stood while I slipped a rope around his neck. Tying him to a gallery post, I said, "Just wait till there is plenty of light, and I'll examine your foot."

It was mighty queer, I thought, that the one horse of my string that I did not like and that did not like me should come to my house to call me before daylight. He had never been to the house voluntarily before. Now he was alone.

After the sun was up, I went out to make the examination. Skeerce Tail could hardly put his foot to the ground. His ankle just above the hoof was swollen and festered. I finally located the butt-end of a big mesquite thorn buried deep in the flesh. "Old boy," I said, "if you bite and kick at having a girth tightened, what will you do when I pull that thorn out? I'll keep away from your heels and put a feed bag on your head so you can't bite." About this time the four horses I was feeding regularly became so impatient for their breakfast that I couldn't be easy until they were quieted. When I returned from the corral, Skeerce Tail was patiently waiting.

I lifted up the sore foot, got a good hold on the thorn, and jerked it out. Skeerce Tail hardly flinched. After washing the wound with some hot water, I turned him loose. When I came out of the house the next morning, he was waiting for me. I washed his foot again. The third morning, he was there, the swelling nearly all gone down. "Skeerce Tail," I said "I'll wash your foot one more time, but that's all."

About a week later I saw him over on Flat Top Mountain, and when I came near he trotted away. I know what the professors of psychology say about a horse not being able to think, but I figure that something like this went through Skeerce Tail's head: "Instead of getting better, this hurt in my foot keeps getting worse. As much as I hate to do it, I've got to hunt up a human being. Even if he don't like me, maybe he'll do something." And then on three legs Skeerce Tail made it over the six miles between his range and the man's house. From then on we were the best of friends.

He became one of the best cutting horses in the outfit, but nobody rode him but me. He always ran with his head very close to the ground, watching an animal's every movement. One time in cutting out a frisky yearling he became careless —or maybe he was tired. Anyway, at the edge of the herd the yearling dodged back. Before I realized what was happening, Skeerce Tail was back in the herd on the yearling's tail. He didn't have to be shown that particular yearling. He brought him out in a fury, biting him on the back. Skeerce Tail had lots of horse sense and lots of humanity in him.

JOHN W. THOMASON IN *Gone to Texas*

Horseback Men

By Badger Clark

The horseback men were the freest men
  From the days of the big ice pack,
When they first crawled out of their musty den
  And followed a horse's track.
The cave man crouched in the dark and died,
But his son found out that the world is wide
  When he climbed on a horse's back.

  Horseback men, O horseback men,
    Bowlegged, brave old crew!
  Here's to your kin where the free stars spin—
  Cowpuncher, Cossack and Bedouin,
  Gaucho, Mongol and Sioux!

The bold Goth spurred into lazy Rome;
  Great Genghis loped with his force;
Our Westerner fought for his wide new home—
  Bestriding a bronc, of course.
New land, new freedom, or just the deuce—
Whenever the spirit of man broke loose
  He went and straddled a horse.

Horseback men, O horseback men,
   The weak hide under their roofs,
But only the strong to your tribe belong;
So history's mostly a horseback song,
   And set to the thud of the hoofs.

But the sword bows down to the monkey-wrench
   And the saddle fades from the scene,
For the warrior squats in a miry trench
   Or charges by gasoline—
And grim Time, quitting his old horse jog,
Whirs us forward into the fog
   On the wings of a swift machine.

Horseback men, O horseback men,
   Your long day dims at last,
But your fame will climb to a myth sublime
From the horse tracks thick on the trail of Time
   And the echo of hoofs from the past.

—WILL JAMES

Contributors

Riley Aiken's "Pack Load of Mexican Tales," in *Puro Mexicano*, is one of the outstanding contributions published by the Texas Folk Lore Society. Aiken, a border Tejano, has spent much time in Mexico. He teaches Spanish in the Kansas State Teachers College at Emporia.

Arthur Babb, now nearing the three-quarters of a century mark, has spent many of his years in Dallas. He is professionally interested in bookbinding, but neither time nor business has taken much from his interest in early Texas life. His drawing of the log home around which the incidents in "A Boy's First Horse" took place is now in the Texas archives.

Frank Bryan, oil scout, with headquarters in Dallas, belongs to the Piney Woods and to the breed of men whom Canebrake served. He has written articles for newspapers, and more from him is promised.

In the realm of frontier chronicles the writing of educated Englishmen like George F. Ruxton and R. B. Townshend, men with the perspective of civilization, with imagination and with a lust for primitive nature, stand out. To this class of men belongs **Frank Collinson of El Paso**, who came to Texas going on seventy years ago, heard the elephant and saw the owl in all sorts of places, and often now contributes reminiscences to the magazine *Ranch Romances*. He is an individual.

Letters and Notes of the Manners, Customs and Condition of the North American Indians, by **George Catlin** (1769-1862), has since its publication in 1841 been one of the best basic works on early America. Any good biographical dictionary gives the outline facts of Catlin's remarkable life.

Badger Clark is a popular writer of Western verse.

The full and authoritative history of the Spanish horse in America is being written by **Robert Denhardt**, a native son of California, who in 1938 came from the University of California to teach in the Agricultural and Mechanical College of Texas. His articles on horses in *The Hispanic American Historical Review, The Cattleman*, and other publications have already made him well known. He is secretary of the American Quarter Horse Association, recently organized in Texas.

Ruth Dodson, Mathis, Texas, is out of the old Texas rock and, by virtue of inheritance and experience, is *puro ranchero*. She wrote a small book in Spanish on the life of a Mexican medicine man named Pedro Jaramillo and has contributed articles to the Publications of the Texas Folk-Lore Society.

419

According to his own report, **Thomas A. Dwyer,** educated in Dublin and London for the law, arrived in Texas in 1847, and went straightway to the liveliest part of the spacious frontier, where—in the extraordinary manner of educated Englishmen—he made a harmonious mixture of Latin, Comanche yells, coyote howls, horseback work and memories of culture and leisure.

D. C. Earnest, located at Edinburg now and dealing in pink grapefruit, can't keep from living back in the eighties, when he, no more than the horses he rode, had ever been curried below the knees. He has written numerous sketches of longhorns, horses and range men, and a book of reminiscences is to be expected from him.

Old-Timers, published in Uvalde, Texas, by **Florence Fenley** in 1939, is an outstanding example of reporting, not only rich in fact but richly flavored with the speech of the old-timers of Southwest Texas that she interviewed. Mrs. Fenley lives in Uvalde.

For fifteen years **Jovita González de Mireles** has been writing essays and tales of her own people, who were living on the Texas border long before English-speaking colonists came to Texas. Her refreshing sketches are to be found in *Texas and Southwestern Lore* and other books issued by the Texas Folk-Lore Society and in the *Southwest Review.* Her present home is Corpus Christi, where her husband has charge of Spanish-teaching in the public schools.

Frank Goodwyn, Kingsville, Texas, was reared on the great King Ranch. Besides publishing Mexican ballads and tales, he has to his credit *The Devil in Texas* and two small books of verse.

Among the score or so of excellent books by **R. B. Cunninghame Graham** is *The Horses of the Conquest.* Born in Scotland in 1852 and dying near Buenos Aires in 1936, he had not only roamed the world but sucked into himself its strongest life-juices. Intimate on one hand with W. H. Hudson and Joseph Conrad, he was *compadre* on the other with the wild-riding *gauchos* of the pampas. He helped establish the South American *Crillo* Association for preserving the Spanish horse. He wrote tales and sketches of Texas and Mexico, as well as of South America. *Rodeo,* a collection of his shorter pieces, was made up, soon after his death, by his friend, A. F. Tschiffley, who rode—as celebrated in *Tschiffley's Ride*—the horses Gato and Mancha from Buenos Aires to Washington.

Bois d'Arc to Barbed Wire, by **James K. Greer,** is rich in horse lore. Greer, a native Texan, is at present teaching history in the University of Texas. He is the author of *Buck Barry, Texas Ranger* and of *Grand Prairie.*

General L. A. (Don Alberto) Guajardo, although he reads English, Latin and French in addition to his own language, was really educated by the vaqueros and Lipan Indians of the Mexican frontier a long life-time ago. He has made an extraordinary collection of documents pertaining to the history of Coahuila and Texas; he ships native herbs to Europe for medical uses, employs old-style Indians to weave blankets, ranches, makes his home in Piedras Negras, and is one of the most interesting conversationalists on either side of the Rio Grande. His horse sketches in this book are extracted from an unpublished manuscript entitled *Around the Camp Fire*, a copy of which is in the Archives of the Library of the University of Texas.

As a boy in Kansas around 1870, **Frank Hastings** saw herds of Texas Longhorns coming off the trail. After much experience with packing companies, he became manager of the great S M S Ranch in West Texas. While in this position he used to contribute essays and simple narratives to the *Breeder's Gazette*, Chicago, published principally for stock people. He wrote for the love of capturing into words what he knew of and felt for the range and range people. In 1921 a collection of his writings was issued under title of *A Ranchman's Recollections*, and it is a pity that this wholesome and delightful book is no longer in print. Hastings died in 1922.

Homer Hoyt, an old-timer, was living in Greeley, Colorado, in 1934.

Merely to remind the reader that there is but one **W. H. Hudson**—the Hudson of *Tales of the Pampas, The Naturalist in La Plata, Birds of La Plata*, that lovely autobiography *Far Away and Long Ago*—the Hudson who wrote of the wild life of South America and of the wild gauchos as no other man has written of them and as few men have written of anything—is sufficient.

Born in Ireland in 1867, **Lincoln A. Lang** came to America at the age of sixteen and settled with his family on the Little Missouri River in Dakota Territory. Later on, Theodore Roosevelt came to ranch in the vicinity. To Roosevelt's own record of ranch life and Hermann Hagedorn's beautiful *Roosevelt in the Bad Lands*, Lang's *Ranching with Roosevelt* is a fit complement—another of the good books on the West by a British gentleman.

Frank M. Lockard (Francis Marion Lockard, 1855-1928), of Norton, Kansas, was an authority on both the topography and early history of Kansas. Besides *Black Kettle*, he wrote *The Early Settlement of Nelson County* and *The History of the Early Settlement of Norton County*. He took part in both legislative and public welfare activities, having been a member of the State Board of Charities in 1896-1897. A description of his capture of Black Kettle was published in *The Topeka Daily Capital*, December 31, 1933.

Cowboy Songs and Other Frontier Ballads, American Ballads and Folk Songs, and other related books, together with lecturing and the placing of hundreds of records in the Song Division of the Library of Congress, have made the name of **John A. Lomax** synonymous with

American song and balladry. His son, Alan Lomax, has in recent years been associated with him in his work. His "Will Hogg, Texan," in the May, 1940, *Atlantic Monthly* is perhaps the finest character sketch of any Southwestern figure that has yet been published by any man of the Southwest.

Chief Buffalo Child Long Lance, Blackfoot Indian, graduated from Carlisle University, served with the Canadian forces during the first World War. He killed himself in California in 1932. Evetts Haley once remarked, "It is doubtful whether any white man of a sensitive nature could read *Long Lance* and ever again regard the Plains Indians as he regarded them before reading this book."

Helen Hall Michaelis was reared on a horse ranch in Concho County, Texas, earned part of the money for her education in the University of Texas by bringing in ranch horses and conducting a riding stable, married a man with whom she ranches in the Mexican state of Coahuila and in the Big Bend of Texas, is raising a son as well as good horses, and is writing a book on quarter horses.

Nearly every Sunday during the year 1888—and perhaps at times both before and after that year—the *San Antonio Express* published a column or more of reminiscences, dated from San Diego, Texas, and signed "Sesom," the pen name of **J. W. Moses**—his family name spelled backwards. Moses came to Texas from the Carolinas in the forties, mustanged and fought Indians, was living at Banquette, Nueces County, during the Civil War, read law in Rockport later, and was elected county judge of Duval County, of which San Diego is the seat, where he died many years ago. A reprinting of his articles in book or pamphlet form would make an interesting contribution to pioneer history.

O. W. Nolen, a frequent contributor of feature articles to country newspapers, lives at Odem, Texas, and is a minister of the gospel.

George Pattullo, born in Canada in 1879, has published many stories in the *Saturday Evening Post* and elsewhere dealing with horses and ranch people, which he knows at first hand. *The Untamed,* unfortunately out of print, is a collection of nine stories about a mule, a coyote, a roping horse, an outlaw steer, a wolfhound, a range cow, a man-eating mountain lion, a jack, and a mountain cow horse. Another collection of short stories, under the title of *A Good Rooster Crows Everywhere,* appeared in 1939. *The Sheriff of Badger* is a novel. While not fishing or otherwise engaged, Mr. Pattullo lives in Dallas.

Beyond the curious contents that he put into his pamphlet and the learned title, *Tachyhippodamia,* that he chose for it, nothing else is known about **Willis J. Powell.**

Alfred (better known as Alf) Robinson was a Texas veteran of the Civil War. He had a memory like a vise that he transmitted to numerous children. Consequently, his son, **G. Clabe Robinson,** remem-

bered not only everything he had seen and read and heard but everything his father had experienced and told about. Born in Live Oak
County while it was still a part of the open range, he rode and read.
About the opening of the present century he became a surveyor and then
a lawyer, self-made, specializing in land titles. Without having to consult records he had once examined, he could give, off-hand, minute data
on the titles of most of the ranches of his part of Texas. He was a remarkable man in many ways and a fine friend, and it is a great pity that
poverty and other causes prevented him from drawing out of his wonderful storehouse of knowledge and putting down much else than the
essays he wrote on Mustangs, here reproduced, and on Longhorns, published in *The Cattleman*, August, 1929. He sent the manuscript of
"His Master's Voice" to the son of his friend, R. J. Dobie, about fifteen
years ago.

   Hortense Landauer Sanger is a poet in Dallas. **Thomas James**
(1782-1847) was a Santa Fé trader and lived among the Indians in the
1820's. His personal narrative, *Three Years Among the Indians and
Mexicans*, published in all too limited an edition by the Missouri Historical Society in 1916, was edited by Walter B. Douglas. **W. A. Whatley,**
owner of a printing plant in Austin, was reared on a ranch in northern
Mexico.

Index

"Cow Horse Names, Colors, and Cures,"
by J. Frank Dobie, 234-249
"Creasing." See "Mustangs"
"Cristiano, A Sentinel Horse," by W. H.
Hudson, 316-319
Cruz, Santa Ana, 175-176
Craig, C. W. T., on pitching horses,
293-294
Custer, John, trail-driver, his story,
295-296
Cutting horses, 403 ff.

D

"Death Comes at a Trot," by Riley Aiken,
351-355
"Deathless Pacing White Stallion, The," by
J. Frank Dobie, 171-183
Deep Creek, 414
Deep Point Creek, 81
Deer hunting, 50
Denhardt, Robert M., "Horse Lore of the
Conquest," 197-226, 419
De Soto, 221 ff.
Dickens County, 89
Diesmero Ranch, 54
Dix, Captain John J., surveyor, 26
Dobie, J. Frank, "As Smart as a Cutting
Horse," 403-413; "Cow Horse Names,
Colors, and cures," 234-249; "The Death-
less Pacing White Stallion," 171-183;
"Pitching Horses and Panthers," 291-
303; *Tales of the Mustangs*, 171; *Tongues
of the Monte*, 248; *A Vaquero of the
Brush Country*, 408
Dobie, Neville, 19-20, 275
Dockum Flats, 89
Dodge, Theodore A., on horses, Intro.,
246-247
Dodson, Ruth, "Texas-Mexican Horse
Breaking," 269-290, 419
Dogfight Crossing on Tanyard Creek, 359
"Dog Soldier," 104-105
Domador, horse-breaker, 194, 269-283
Double Circle Ranch, Remuda Book of,
234 ff.
Double Mountain, 81; Fork of the Brazos,
81
Duck Creek, 89, 90
Duval County, 411
Dwyer, Thomas A., "From Mustangs to
Mules," 47-60, 420

E

Earnest, D. C., "Skeerce Tail," 414-416,
420
East Texas, horses in, 367 ff.

Ellis, S. H., mustanger, 44
English, John and Levi, ranchers, 62-63
Everett, Malessa C., 410

F

Falcón, General Esteban, account of Canelo,
339 ff.
Fant Pasture, 19-20
Fenley, Florence, "The Mustanger Who
Turned Mustang," 61-66, 420
Fenley, O. Z., 405
"Fifty Thousand Mustangs," by Frank
Collinson, 69-95
Flat Top Mountain, 414, 415
Fort Griffin, 80, 81
French, William, *Recollections*, 296
Frio County, 44, 61, 62
"From Mustangs to Mules," by Thomas a
Dwyer, 47-60
Frothingham, Robert, *Songs of Horses*,
Intro.

G

Ghost Horse. See "Pacing White Stallion"
and "Steel Dust Stallion"
"Ghost Horse, The," by Chief Buffalo
Child Long Lance, 155-170
Godmother Death, 353-355
Goodwyn, Frank, "Ballad of Manuel
Rodriguez," 304-306, 420
Graham, R. B. Cunninghame, "The Horse
of the Pampas," 187-196, 198, 203, 247-
248, 420
Grant, mustanger, 109-111
Gravis, Buck, 407
Gray, Charles Wright, *Hosses*, Intro.
Greatorex, James, sketch, 229
Greer, James K., "Anti-Indian Horse,"
325-335, 420
Guajardo, Alberto, "Horse Sense," 343-350,
420

H

"Hackamore," origin of word, 272
Haley, Evetts, anecdote told by, 241, 409-
410
Hall, Inez, 412-413
Hamilton County, 410
Hampton, General Wade, 367
Hastings, Frank, *A Ranchman's Recollec-
tions*, 240; "Old Gran'pa," 373-383, 421
Havie, buffalo hunter, 79
Hediondo, El, 25-26
"He Knew His Master's Voice," by G. C.
Robinson, 309-315

Roosevelt, Theodore, *Ranch Life and The Hunting Trail*, 237
Roque brothers, mustangers, 49-50
Running Water, 84, 92
Russell, Charles M., sketches, 237, 250, 268, 313, 330, 385, 395
Rountree, J. L., mustanger, 172

S

Sanger, Hortense Landauer, "Adam and Eve of the Mustangs," 153-154, 423
San Juan Celebration *(Dia San Juan)*, 288-290
San Patricio, 22, 312
Santee, Ross, Intro.; sketches, 56, 351; on cow horses, 242-243
Saunders, George W., 238-239
Simpson, William, 111 ff.
Sheffy, L. F., on horse names, 240
Shipman, W. K., rancher, 181
Siringo, Charles A., *A Texas Cowboy*, 240
Six Up and Down, anecdote, 239-240
"Skeerce Tail," by D. C. Earnest, 414-416
Smith, Beaver, 90
"SMS Kid." See "Old Gran-pa"
SMS Ranch, in story, 373-383, *passim.*
"Sorrel Top, Booger-Hunter," by Lincoln A Lang, 319-322
Spanish horses, in Mexico, 197 ff.
Spring Lake, 85
Staked Plains. See "Llano Estacado"
Stallion, Blood-Bay, 181-183; Pacing White, 11-12, 171-183, 245; Legendary Black, 179 ff.
Stallions, man-fighting, 79 ff., 164
Stamford, 373
Stampede, 17, 25-26, 38, 47, 129-132
Stanush, Frank A., sketches, 45, 63, 403
Steedman, Charles J., story of Blanco, 301-302
Steel-Dust Stallion, becomes a Legend, 170
"Strawberry Roan," 295
Street, W. D., account of Black Kettle, 103, 140-141

T

Tales of the Mustangs, by J. Frank Dobie, 171
Tanyard Creek, 359
Tankersley, Mrs. F. V., anecdote told by, 336-337
Tascosa, 96

Taylor, W. T., pioneer, 337
"Teaching a Horse Trust and Distrust," by Willis J. Powell, 322-324
Tecumseh Peaks, 182
Terrazas, Don Luis, rancher, 95
"Texas-Mexican Horse-Breaking," by Ruth Dodson, 269-290
Thistlethwaite, E. W., sketch, 316
Thomason, John W., sketch, 416
Thorp, Jack, "Sky-High," a ballad, 301
Throckmorton Ranch, 373
Tierra Blanco Creek, 96
Tongue River, 84, 88, 89
Tonkawa Indians, 325-328
Trujillo, Pedro and Soledad, mustangers, 77 ff., 88 ff.
Tulia Draw, 92
Tyng, Griswold, sketch, 357

V

Van Ryder, Jack, sketch, 397
Villa, Pancho, 339-340

W

Wakeeny, Kansas, naming of, 112
Walnut Spring, 327
Waud, A. R., sketch, 15
West, George W., cowman, 19
Weston, Atlee, Negro cowhand, 20
Whatley, W. A., "Mexican Color Terms for Horses," 227-233, 423
Wheeler, Captain Homer W., mustanger, 105-106
Wild Cattle, 36-37, 48
Wild Horse Draw, naming of, 114
Wild Horses. See "Mustangs"
Wilkerson (or Wilkinson), 74, 19
Wilson County, 342
Wolves, 155-156
Woodhull, Frost, 248
Wortham, 390
Wynn, Afton, anecdote told by, 337-338

Y

Yellow Horse Lake, 93-94
Young, John W., cattleman, 173, 174

Z

Zapata, Don Clemente, mustanger, 27 ff.
"Zebra Dun," 295-296
Zuluago, Don Carlos, rancher, 95